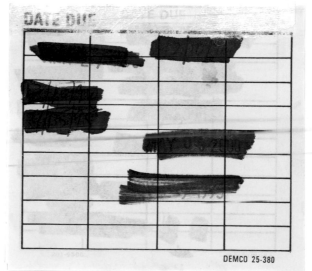

The Language of Children Reared in Poverty

Implications for
Evaluation and Intervention

EDUCATIONAL PSYCHOLOGY

Allen J. Edwards, Series Editor
*Department of Psychology
Southwest Missouri State University
Springfield, Missouri*

In preparation
Judith Worell (ed.). Psychological Development in the Elementary Years

Published
John B. Biggs and Kevin F. Collis. Evaluating the Quality of Learning: The Solo Taxonomy (Structure of the Observed Learning Outcome)

Gilbert R. Austin and Herbert Garber (eds.). The Rise and Fall of National Test Scores

Lynne Feagans and Dale C. Farran (eds.). The Language of Children Reared in Poverty: Implications for Evaluation and Intervention

Patricia A. Schmuck, W. W. Charters, Jr., and Richard O. Carlson (eds.). Educational Policy and Management: Sex Differentials

Phillip S. Strain and Mary Margaret Kerr. Mainstreaming of Children in Schools: Research and Programmatic Issues

Maureen L-Pope and Terence R. Keen. Personal Construct Psychology and Education

Ronald W. Henderson (ed.). Parent–Child Interaction: Theory, Research, and Prospects

W. Ray Rhine (ed.). Making Schools More Effective: New Directions from Follow Through

Herbert J. Klausmeier and Thomas S. Sipple. Learning and Teaching Concepts: A Strategy for Testing Applications of Theory

James H. McMillan (ed.). The Social Psychology of School Learning

M. C. Wittrock (ed.). The Brain and Psychology

Marvin J. Fine (ed.). Handbook on Parent Education

Dale G. Range, James R. Layton, and Darrell L. Roubinek (eds.). Aspects of Early Childhood Education: Theory to Research to Practice

Jean Stockard, Patricia A. Schmuck, Ken Kempner, Peg Williams, Sakre K. Edson, and Mary Ann Smith. Sex Equity in Education

James R. Layton. The Psychology of Learning to Read

Thomas E. Jordan. Development in the Preschool Years: Birth to Age Five

Gary D. Phye and Daniel J. Reschly (eds.). School Psychology: Perspectives and Issues

The list of titles in this series continues on the last page of this volume.

The Language of Children Reared in Poverty

*Implications for
Evaluation and Intervention*

EDITED BY

Lynne Feagans
Dale Clark Farran

Frank Porter Graham Child Development Center
University of North Carolina
Chapel Hill, North Carolina

1982

ACADEMIC PRESS

A Subsidiary of Harcourt Brace Jovanovich, Publishers

New York   London   Toronto   Sydney   San Francisco

ACADEMIC PRESS, INC.
111 Fifth Avenue, New York, New York 10003

United Kingdom Edition published by
ACADEMIC PRESS, INC. (LONDON) LTD.
24/28 Oval Road, London NW1 7DX

Library of Congress Cataloging in Publication Data
Main entry under title:

The Language of children reared in poverty.

(Educational psychology)
Includes bibliographies and index.
1. Socially handicapped children--Language.
2. Socially handicapped children--Education.
I. Feagans, Lynne. II. Farran, Dale C. III. Series.
P40.5.S57L3   401'.9   81-14939
ISBN 0-12-249980-8   AACR2

PRINTED IN THE UNITED STATES OF AMERICA

82 83 84 85   9 8 7 6 5 4 3 2 1

*To all the children at
the Frank Porter Graham
Child Development Center*

Contents

I

Environmental Effects on Language Learning

1
Language, Poverty, and Disadvantage in School   3
JOAN TOUGH

2
Mother–Child Interaction, Language Development, and the School Performance of Poverty Children
DALE C. FARRAN

3
Routines in Mother–Child Interaction
CATHERINE E. SNOW, CLARA DUBBER, AND AKKE DE BLAUW

II
Language Use and Schooling

4
Language and School Failure: Some Speculations about the Relationship between Oral and Written Language
MARION BLANK

III
Language Evaluation

8
Test-Taking Behaviors of Black Toddlers: An Interactive Analysis   163
GRACE C. MASSEY, ASA G. HILLIARD, AND JEAN CAREW

9
Assessing Oral Language Ability in Children   181
ROGER W. SHUY AND JANA STATON

IV
Language Interventions

10
Process in the Teaching of Pragmatics   199
BETTY HART

11
The Language of the Poverty Child: Implications from Center-Based Intervention and Evaluation Programs   219
GAEL D. MCGINNESS

V

From Theory to Practice—Some Implications

12
Moving Beyond the
Difference–Deficit Debate 245
MARION BLANK

13
Contingencies in Communication 251
BETTY HART

14
Group versus Individual Differences:
Avoiding the Deficit Model 253
ELSIE G. J. MOORE

15
Knowledge and the Use of Language 257
CATHERINE E. SNOW

16
The Importance of Understanding Function from a
Sociolinguist's Perspective 261
ROGER W. SHUY

17
Teachers Can Create Enabling Environments for
Children and Then Children Will Learn

JOAN TOUGH

18
Intervention for Poverty Children:
Alternative Approaches

DALE C. FARRAN

List of Contributors

Numbers in parentheses indicate the pages on which the authors' contributions begin.

MARION BLANK (75, 245), Department of Psychiatry, Rutgers Medical School, College of Medicine and Dentistry of New Jersey, Piscataway, New Jersey 08854

AKKE DE BLAUW (53), Institute for General Linguistics, University of Amsterdam, Amsterdam, The Netherlands

JEAN CAREW (163), Research for Children, Menlo Park, California 94025

CLARA DUBBER (53), Institute for General Linguistics, University of Amsterdam, Amsterdam, The Netherlands

DALE C. FARRAN (19, 269), Frank Porter Graham Child Development Center, University of North Carolina, Chapel Hill, North Carolina 27514

LYNNE FEAGANS (95), Frank Porter Graham Child Development Center, University of North Carolina, Chapel Hill, North Carolina 27514

ALICE M. GORDON (241), Frank Porter Graham Child Development Center, University of North Carolina, Chapel Hill, North Carolina 27514

BETTY HART (199, 251), Juniper Gardens Children's Project, Kansas City, Kansas 66101

ASA G. HILLIARD (163), Department of Educational Foundations, Department of Counseling and Psychological Services, Georgia State University, Atlanta, Georgia 30303

GRACE C. MASSEY (163), Toddler and Infant Experiences, Oakland, California 94612

GAEL D. McGINNESS (219), Frank Porter Graham Child Development Center, University of North Carolina, Chapel Hill, North Carolina 27514

ELSIE G. J. MOORE[1] (141, 253), Boys Town Center for the Study of Youth Development, Boys Town, Nebraska 68010

JOHN U. OGBU[2] (117), Department of Educational Studies, University of Delaware, Newark, Delaware 19711

ROGER W. SHUY (181, 261), Department of Linguistics, Georgetown University, Washington, D.C. 20057

CATHERINE E. SNOW (53, 257), Graduate School of Education, Harvard University, Cambridge, Massachusetts 02138

JANA STATON (181), The Center for Applied Linguistics, Arlington, Virginia 22209

JOAN TOUGH (3, 265), School of Education, The University of Leeds, LS2 9JT England

---

[1] PRESENT ADDRESS: Counselor Education, Arizona State University, Tempe, Arizona 85287.

[2] PRESENT ADDRESS: Department of Anthropology, University of California at Berkeley, Berkeley, California 94720.

Preface

Children reared in poverty have been the subject of concern by a variety of professionals. These children have been seen as at-risk for problems in school adaptation and developmental processes. In the 1960s, the reasons given for these problems were dominated by an emphasis on a "deficit" model in which language development played an important role. In the 1970s it was clear that such a model was untenable, not only because of new perspectives but because intervention strategies based on the deficit model were not particularly effective. As is the case with any complex issue, the controversial nature of this topic is still with us, but with a new sense of sophistication and knowledge.

Whether such factors as ethnicity, environment, the dominant culture, or the schools themselves contribute to the poverty child's language difficulties is not in question. It is agreed by all at this point that each plays a role. Professionals differ on the emphasis or importance placed on each factor.

It seemed timely, then, that a conference be convened to discuss the present issues of language and poverty in order to understand better the current theoretical perspectives as well as to discuss their practical and applied implications. In May 1980, such a conference was held at the Frank Porter Graham Child Development Center in Chapel Hill, North Carolina. Professionals from many disciplines were brought together to discuss similarities and differences in their views of the poverty child. Those discussions provided the impetus for preparing the chapters presented here and, as can be seen through their diversity, a number of different perspectives are presented.

This book is derived from the conference and, like it, is divided into sections that reflect both theoretical and applied aspects. The hope was to link specific views of language and poverty at various age levels with specific intervention strategies and then to discuss the effectiveness of such strategies for poverty children.

The book is directed to a wide audience of professionals interested in poverty children and their language. Academics interested in the broad issues of language and poverty will find state-of-the-art perspectives from psychologists, sociolinguists, anthropologists, and educators. Educators are also provided with specific implications for prevention and intervention. Other professionals interested in such issues as preschool programs, cross-cultural perspectives, and policy implications will find the book a useful summary.

Acknowledgments

Initial versions of the chapters in this book came from the conference sponsored by the Frank Porter Graham Child Development Center under the auspices of James Gallagher and Craig Ramey. We wish to thank all those people who helped extensively with the conference itself, including Mary Ann Kimball, Katherine Polk, and John Bernard. A special debt of gratitude goes to those people who were extensively involved with every aspect of the manuscript and its preparation. They are Susan East, Ella Akin, Agnes Mallard, Jennifer Mastrofski, Gina Walker, Marie Butts, Pam Mann, Julia Stockton, and Debbie Jeffreys.

1

Environmental Effects on
Language Learning

Concern for the language development of poverty children is long standing among educators and those social scientists involved in intervention. In fact, problems with language were considered by some to be at the heart of the difficulty poor children experienced in school. The following three chapters are all focused on the effects of the verbal and behavioral interactions of mothers with their children on language development. The chapters are all based on longitudinal research in the United States and in other countries. Joan Tough's research and curriculum development work took place in England. Here she reports the major findings from her longitudinal study of 3- to 7½-year-old children from different social-class groups. Those findings culminated in a curriculum that now involves 1500 British teachers. Reporting on a longitudinal study in the United States, Dale Farran describes mother–child interaction patterns during the preschool years and language differences of kindergarten children from different socioeconomic backgrounds. She places these patterns in the context of the broader effects of poverty and suggests that there is a cumulative interaction of many forces affecting poor children's school performance. Catherine Snow suggests that specific mother–child interaction patterns are facilitative of language development in young children. Her work is based on studies conducted longitudinally in the Netherlands and in the United States.

1

Language, Poverty, and Disadvantage in School
JOAN TOUGH

POVERTY AND EDUCATIONAL DISADVANTAGE

During the last 10 years there has been a growing disillusionment with the view developed during the 1960s that intervention during the preschool period could prevent the early failure of children in school and thus help solve the problems of disadvantage and inequality. Bloom's (1964) research into the stability of several human characteristics, in which he estimated that about 50% of the development of intelligence takes place between conception and age 4 and a further 30% between ages 4 and 8, encouraged an optimism about the possibilities of changing the face of disadvantage by early recognition of disadvantage and intervention through early education. Since then many programs have been used in an attempt to offset the disadvantage of social origins.

In Britain a considerable amount of research explored the possibilities of intervention in much the same way as the Head Start program in the United States. Provisions for nursery education have been increased and other forms of preschool provision have been encouraged, and, in particular, the play-group movement has flourished. In addition, social policies were adopted that directed greater resources into areas of disadvantage, as was recommended by the Plowden Report (DES, 1965).

During the 1970s, however, it became clear that the steps taken

3

THE LANGUAGE OF CHILDREN
REARED IN POVERTY

were not radically altering the association between school failure and social origins. The inability to offset the disadvantage of social origins led to a growing belief that the roots of educational failure lay in the conditions of disadvantage and that only the eradication of those general conditions could bring about changes in educational achievement.

Recently, with further research into the problem, it has been shown that although poverty is the biggest single factor contributing to disadvantage, education can make a difference. Longitudinal evaluation studies of early childhood intervention policies, as in the case of Head Start programs, have shown that there were some long-term advantageous effects (Lazar & Darlington, 1978). In a study of parents and children in an inner city area, Wilson and Herbert (1978) reached the conclusion that, although school and nursery could not counteract the effects of poverty, they could repair the damage to some extent and prevent alienation from society and school and the onset of delinquency.

A study of disadvantage by Rutter and Madge (1976) rejected the idea that poverty alone breeds alienation and lack of educational achievement. They claim, rather, that it is the structure of society that transmits disadvantage, not family factors. However, an examination of the patterns of variation in the educational attainment of children from different social class and regional backgrounds shows that variation in policies and resources in the regions contributes to the variation in educational attainment (Byrne, Williamson, & Fletcher, 1975). The view is supported by Jencks (1972), who examined the achievement of children who had stayed at school beyond the statutory limit and related the attainment of education to educational provision in the community. Jencks found that the level of educational provision had a direct bearing on the educational life chances of children. This conclusion runs contrary to the findings of Coleman's (1965) investigation into equality of opportunity in the United States, which found that, when other things were equal, the amount of money spent per pupil made little difference in the amount of education attained. Byrne's findings suggest that, when education and environment are equal, the influence of class background on the attainment of children in different local authority areas is markedly reduced (Byrne *et al.*, 1975). An examination of the influence of schools on children's performance (Rutter & Madge, 1976) also concludes that the quality of schools and the length of schooling can make a difference in educational achievement.

Clearly, the conditions of poverty are the major factors influencing educational achievement, and special policies to eradicate poverty are crucial in the pursuit of greater equality of opportunity. The danger is that we shall come to regard schools as impotent in this battle until poverty has been eradicated. The recent finding that schools can make a difference indicates that we must identify the means by which schools can confer greater benefit on poverty children so that the benefits can be maximized.

It is clear that children's physical conditions may prevent an adequate response to school experiences. If children are hungry, ill, uncomfortable, or feeling threatened and insecure, they probably cannot focus on educational experiences, and learning will be impeded. Although in the United Kingdom the welfare state intervenes to prevent extreme poverty, teachers must be vigilant in recognizing, and taking steps to alleviate, problems of learning that originate in lack of basic requirements. Poverty at this level, however, is not the cause of educational failure in the majority of socially disadvantaged children. We must look to other causes.

During the last 10 years, claims were made that so-called "progressive" methods of teaching were the cause of falling standards. However, a survey of primary schools found little evidence to support the claim (DES, 1978). This investigation found that teachers generally focus time and attention on establishing skills of literacy and that, far from deserting traditional methods of teaching, generally use these methods in the teaching of basic skills. The most effective teachers combine traditional methods with a "discovery" approach.

Although this survey and other research indicate that standards are not falling, there is little to suggest that the education of children from the poorer section of the community, with whom lower achievement is associated, is improving. Why should this association still hold when the effects of extreme poverty have largely been removed? Why should children from this section of the community continue to be disadvantaged within school?

DISADVANTAGE AND THE USE OF LANGUAGE

There is now a considerable amount of evidence to support the view that the development of language makes an important contribution to the course of cognitive development. The work of Vygotsky (1962) shows how using words helps stimulate the development of those concepts that cannot be abstracted directly from concrete experiences and so are dependent on the use of language with adults. The work of Luria (1961) is also important in showing the part language plays in helping children gain control over their own actions. Further, his study of grossly deprived twins illustrates the dramatic effects language has on the development of an individual's understanding of the world because language makes possible the communication of ideas (Luria & Yudovitch, 1959).

All these views indicate the basic importance of language to the learning process and the possibility that disadvantage in school is at least partly transmitted through children's development and the use of language.

Some evidence of differences that might be important in education emerged from a longitudinal study of the development of language between the ages of 3 and $7\frac{1}{2}$ years (Tough, 1977c). In this study the language of two groups of children from different social environments was recorded in a variety of situations at the ages of 3, $5\frac{1}{2}$ and $7\frac{1}{2}$. The parents of one group had had the minimum period of education and were unskilled or semiskilled manual workers. One or both parents of a second group of children had received higher education and worked in a profession or occupation of comparable status. At the time of selection, all the children were 3 years of age, friendly, talking clearly, well cared for, and of average intelligence or above. The mean IQ of the two groups was about the same at the age of $3\frac{1}{2}$. From an analysis of the language records the following facts emerged.

On all measures of complexity of linguistic structure—including utterance length, the use of clauses, and the complexity of the noun phrase and the verb phrase—the children of educationally advantaged parents scored significantly higher than the children of educationally disadvantaged parents. However, when the range of complexity of these same measures was examined, the differences between the groups were found to be less. All children used complex structures, but the children of educationally disadvantaged parents used them less frequently than did the other group.

When the purposes for which the children used language were examined, it was found that the children of parents with educational advantage more frequently used language to analyze and reflect on present and past experiences, to reason and justify, to predict and consider alternative possibilities, to talk about events in the future, to project into the lives and feelings of others, and to build up scenes, events, and stories in the imagination.

Such differences in the purposes for which language was used explain the differences in the complexity of the structures of language used by the two groups. It is clear that in referring to past experience the use of nouns, the extension of verbs, and the use of descriptive words necessarily increases. And similarly, in talking about the future extensions of the verb are needed. In imaginative play children must rename the objects and materials they use so that others know what they represent. The quality of imaginative play depends on children being explicit in their talk so that their companions are made aware of their intentions. It seems that it is also essential for children themselves, since they frequently talk to themselves when they play alone or alongside other children.

Children also frequently make associations with their present activity and refer to past experiences. For example, a child playing with a car may say, *I've seen a big tractor like this. It was on the road. It was pushing the rocks out of the way. They were making a road.* The association of the past with present play leads the child to make an idea explicit, and language is the only means with which the child can represent the idea in play. Adults often react to the ideas children express in imaginative play and reinforce the use of language to express more complex thinking.

Children also expand their use of language when they try to talk about other people's feelings, a function that can be termed *projecting into the feelings of others.* A child may comment: *He's crying because someone pushed him down in the playground. He hurt himself and he didn't like it.*

Another difference between the two groups was in language used for "self-maintaining." The disadvantaged group in protecting their rights and needs might say: *I want that.* or *It's mine. Give me it.* Children in the advantaged group were more likely to elaborate and justify when making similar requests: *Can I have my car, because I brought it from home this morning and I want to play with it now?*

The conclusions from this study were that all participating children had language experiences from which they had established similar knowledge about the language system but they had different orientations toward the use of language. These orientations accounted for the different purposes for which they chose to use language and for the differences in mean scores on measures of linguistic complexity. The purposes for which the advantaged group used their language involved the use of more complex language. For significant differences of this kind to emerge, it seemed that children must have had experiences that differed widely, and attempts were made to discover something of the nature of those experiences.

Research into differences in mother–child verbal interactions has not been extensive. Hess and Shipman's (1965) study is almost unique in examining talk of mothers from different social backgrounds as they taught their children how to carry out a simple task. The results suggested that children were being socialized into different cognitive modes.

Studies of parent–child interaction by Halliday (1975) show how early holophrases gradually emerge into differentiated grammatical elements. Studies by Snow have shown that, on the whole, parents provide a well-formed model from which children learn language, but they tend to reduce the complexity of their utterances when talking with young children (Snow, 1979; Snow, Arlman-Rupp, Hassing, Jobse, Jooster, & Vorster, 1976; Snow & Ferguson, 1977).

A major project by Gordon Wells (1979) at the University of Bristol has attempted to follow over several years the informal conversations of mothers and children at home. This study relies on the random recording of 90-sec samples of the child's talk throughout a day. Recording in this way has provided a unique collection of data from which the sequence of language development in relation to a child's experience of talk with parents can be plotted. However, 90-sec samples cannot provide evidence of the buildup of discussion and the elaboration of ideas that develop through a number of exchanges, and it seems unlikely that the data will be entirely representative of either children's experiences or children's skills. Wells's study shows that even families of similar social background differ considerably in what he refers to as "the reciprocal negotiations of meaning."

Among studies of language in the home there are a few related to reading books. For example, Bakher-Renes and Hoefnaghe-Hohle (1974) showed that mothers' speech was more complex in free situations, which include playing, chatting after a meal, and reading a book. It was found that the most complex use of language occurred when reading books. Snow and associates (Snow *et al.,* 1976) also found that reading books stimulated the most complex speech. Several studies have examined the effects of reading stories on children's growth of vocabulary or on producing more complex adult–child interaction (Ackerman, 1976; Irwin, 1960; Mitner, 1951). Although children are clearly becoming familiar with books during such activities, it may be that the predominant benefit is due to the stimulation given to language development by their attempts to deal with complex ideas presented in books through talk with the adult.

As part of the longitudinal study of children's use of language, an attempt was made to discover something of the nature of children's experiences at home. Although some recordings were made of talk between mother and child, this was not feasible for all. Elizabeth Sestini (1975) carried out a structured interview with each mother when the children were $7\frac{1}{2}$ years of age. The interview was devised to produce evidence of the mothers' views of their children and the kind of talk and activity the mothers had with them, including methods of control, views of education and of the children's progress in school, and of their hopes for their children's future. The mothers' responses in the interviews also provided evidence of their way of thinking and of expressing ideas in talk.

Analysis of these data produced interesting insights about differences in the ways mothers viewed their children, saw the relationships between themselves and their children, and in the expectations that were conveyed to the children. The analysis also provided a view of the different characteristics of the mothers' thinking and use of language, characteristics that must influence interaction between members of the family, and the purposes for which talk is used. From this study it seemed that mothers with educational advantage tended to see children as individuals to be helped toward realization of their potential, and they tried to understand the child's perspective. They might say, for example, *I know he's got problems in school, but it's difficult for him because his sister's so good.* Those with minimum education, on the other hand, tended to see their children as stereotypes cast in a mold that was the same or different from that of others in the family. They might say, *He's just like his uncle. He never got far in school.* or *He's just like his father.*

Mothers with educational advantage tended to believe that children could be changed and difficulties, both of learning and personality, could be overcome. They might say, *Just now he's going through a difficult period. But we're doing all we can to help him and we hope that in time he'll be more tractable.* Mothers who had minimum education tended to believe that children were already set in their personalities and that changes were not possible. For example, they might say: *I quarrel with her all the time. She's a little so-and-so.* or *We're just different people; we don't get on well.* All of the mothers interviewed were fond of their children, yet they approached problems differently.

Mothers with educational advantage more often saw themselves as playing a part in the children's education, and they approached teachers to gain help for their children's learning difficulties. Mothers with minimum education tended to feel that children's achievement in school was the business of the teachers, and they accepted teachers' judgments about their children.

From the information given by the mothers, it seemed that those with educational advantage tended to use negotiating strategies to influence children's behavior, whereas those with minimum education tended to use discipline to make their children conform. The educationally advantaged mothers saw talk with their children as important and quoted examples of involving their children in family decision making when it was deemed appropriate. To gain a view of the strategies used, the interviewer proposed a hypothetical situation to the mother: If it is bedtime and the child is watching a television program to which he is very attached, but you are going out and need to get him off to bed, how do you do it? Some of the mothers of disadvantaged children responded to the effect that they would not deal with it at all but would leave such problems to the child's father. One exceptional answer in the advantaged group was given by one mother who said, *Well, you'll laugh at this, but we have a system. We decided one day with the children at a round table discussion how we were going to deal with this because they were getting older and wanting to stay up. So we decided they all could have an hour and a half extra staying-up time, but they would have to choose how and when they spent it.* She said, *It's remarkable. It works. My son will sit and discuss with me whether he should have a game of chess with his father, or whether it would be better to watch whatever program is on television, or whether he should go to bed tonight at 7 o'clock because tomorrow there's something better on.* So the parents settled at an hour and a half. They placed their limits but through a negotiating strategy and their children were put in the position of considering possibilities and making choices.

Mothers with minimum education tended to report conversation with the children in which there were disputes over control or in which they were asked for information that they felt ill-equipped to give. *She asked me about the difference between Methodists and Protestants the other day,* one mother said, *and I couldn't tell her.* Most parents would have difficulty responding to such a question, but this mother felt defeated by it.

The groups were not so clearly differentiated as the above summary may suggest. On all issues there was a continuum along which mothers' views were distributed, but the two groups tended to bunch at opposite ends. Any spread remained close to the position taken up by the majority of the group, so that overlap between the groups was quite small.

The mothers' talk in the interview was examined and classified by its predominant characteristics. These characteristics ranged from categorical statements, to the expression of associated ideas with some awareness of other people's viewpoints, to, finally, a position judged as "reflexive." The reflecting characteristic is best illustrated when the mothers examined what they said and then made further qualifications as they reflected on their own ideas and considered what might be alternative ways of viewing the situation being discussed. Some mothers had hardly begun talking when they started to reflect on what they were saying and modified their points: *But I expect people see it other ways* or *What I'm saying is this, but my husband sees it rather differently . . . and in school they see it differently.* The talk of the majority of mothers with educational advantage fell into the reflexive classification, a few into the associative, and none fell into the categorical classification.

The talk of mothers with educational disadvantage fell mainly into the categorical classification, a few came into the associative, and none fell into the reflexive classification.

When the data were examined for evidence of the relationship between mothers' and children's talk, it was clear that children with the lowest range of uses of language were those whose mothers' talk was characterized by categorical statements. The children with the widest range of uses and the greatest complexity all had mothers whose talk was characterized by reflexiveness.

TALK AND LEARNING IN THE HOME

Children's language experiences of talk at home are likely to be very different from one another, and the differences, it seems, are associated with educational disadvantage. How important to achievement in school are the differences in children's experiences of talk with adults in the home?

First, experiences of talk are crucial for the child's development of language. All normal children have a potential for acquiring language during their first 5 years. They learn not by direct teaching but by exposure to the use of language. As parents talk with children, they are intuitively offering a model from which children gradually identify basic structures and rules of the grammar. As a result, all normal children, by 5 years of age, are using a form of language near to that of the adults with whom they live. All normal children learn to use their mother tongue competently, but they learn a version made available by parents and other members of the family and neighborhood.

Second, the children learn to use language for the same purposes as do the adults with whom they live. Piaget's (1929) work has demonstrated that all children have difficulty in developing concepts and learning how to think, and that children have difficulty in taking several dimensions of experiences into account. Additionally, Piaget has shown that young children have difficulty in taking the other's point of view, and this is reflected in their use of language. At first the children's language and their thinking are egocentric, and they fail to take account of the information their listener does not share with them. Gradually, the children's positions change as they begin to recognize the other's need for clear information. But several studies that have investigated differences in the development of language skills, including the longitudinal study described earlier, suggest that this is due to the differences in children's experiences of the purposes for which language is used.

Parents who are disposed to reason with the children about their behavior, who share their interests with them—expressing ideas about particular activities and encouraging the children to think about their experiences, who are responding to the children's interest in various aspects of the world around—helping them to observe, to compare, and to understand are offering the children experiences of the ways in which the parents think. Children who are drawn into the experiences of thinking through the talk in which they are involved with their parents gradually come to use language in these ways spontaneously. But parents' talk may actively discourage children from thinking, may seek to make them obedient without understanding the reasons for required behavior. Talk may hinder the development of curiosity and interest in the world around, and it may be used to prevent children fron sharing in decision making or in reflecting on past experience. Talk may inhibit children from expressing ideas, or it may offer very limited ways of thinking about experiences. A mother may be willing to play with her child, but if the child says to her, *Dolly's arm's broken,* and mother responds, *No, it's not,* and the conversation goes on, *Yes it is, No, it's not,* then the child is likely to come to accept these categorical statements and to use them in the same way.

Clearly, young children can only learn from their experiences, and these include both concrete experiences as well as experiences of talk. As experiences are repeated, attitudes are reinforced, and habitual responses are established, thereby developing an orientation to meet all experiences in the familiar way. This is the conclusion drawn from the longitudinal study of children's and mothers' use of language and of mothers' attitudes toward their children's upbringing and education referred to previously. Once particular orientations toward the use of language have been established, children can only approach their experiences in school in ways familiar to them.

Such conclusions raise questions about the environment provided for children's learning during their first years in school. Since children have a capacity for learning language, and learning to think through the use of language, might they not be expected to establish new uses of language in the new environment of school? In order for this to happen, experiences in school must involve children in new ways of thinking so that their use of language and their thinking is extended. Research in this area tends to give a very different picture of experiences in school.

Research carried out in British nursery schools and classes indicates that teachers and nursery assistants spend little time talking with individual children; when they do, it is likely to be with children who already have the most extensive use of language (Tizard, Philps, & Plewis, 1976). In a longitudinal study of children in their homes and in school, Wells

(1978) has indicated that children have less opportunity to extend ideas through the use of talk in school than they do at home. A recent survey of primary school classes has shown that much of the teachers' talk is concerned with instruction and management, and there is little that challenges cognitive development (Galton, Simon, & Croll, 1980). Other research has shown that teachers' talk dominates in the classroom and that there is little engagement of children in dialogue or discussion. Indeed, it would seem that the kind of talk children are likely to encounter in school reinforces the view that children are not expected to think or express ideas. Learning in many schools is seen as a passive activity in which talk serves mainly to check children's memory for facts by way of one- or two-word answers to the teacher's questions. Studies of classroom interaction endorse this view (Boydell, 1974; Garner, 1972; Garner & Bing, 1973; Hilsum & Cane, 1971).

EARLY EDUCATION AND CHILDREN REARED IN POVERTY

What then should be the characteristics of early school experiences for children who are educationally disadvantaged because they are born into the culture of poverty? Some educators have seen the problem as one of children's lack of knowledge of language and have constructed programs that are devoted to language teaching. Several programs concentrate on building vocabulary, the practice of syntactic structures, and the use of locational prepositions. In our view, this approach misrepresents not only the problem but also the purpose of education. The main problem in educating children from disadvantaged sections of the community is not that they generally lack language but that their expectations about using language do not support learning. Furthermore, education for young children is concerned with more than learning language. The importance of language is that it is central to learning throughout the curriculum. Education in the early years should not only be concerned with helping children to become literate and to numerate but must be concerned with developing personal qualities, general skills of communicating, and the ability to think and reflect on experiences. The promotion of children's skills in using language should create the impetus for the child to seek further understanding and to acquire new skills and knowledge; that is, to develop self-motivated learning. The development and use of language should not therefore be seen as one curriculum objective to be realized but as the major means through which most other objectives for the child's education will be reached.

The important fact that must be recognized is that the skills of thinking and using language are developed through talk with others. Children's experiences of talk may extend or limit their thinking: This is as true for the school as it is for the home. Many children have not met the kind of interaction through which the skills of thinking are extended. This does not mean that school should provide a "middle-class" environment. The failure of many disadvantaged children in school is often explained by referring to their unfamiliarity with the middle-class ethos of school. But many schools operate in a way that is similar to the disadvantaged home in terms of using language and developing thinking skills. School does not usually regard children as becoming involved in their own learning. Advantaged children may succeed in school because their parents are helping them to understand why they should go to school and why they should conform to teachers' expectations. They are being helped to look forward and to anticipate rewards that come from success in school. At home their parents talk with them, sharing the children's experiences, and so continue to extend their thinking skills.

The necessary environment is one in which relationships between teachers and children support the development of ways of thinking that are essential for a wide range of learning. A crucial characteristic of such an environment is that the activities and expectations are seen by the children as relevant and worthwhile. Thus activities will vary from school to school, building on what is relevant for children in such a way that through the process of dialogue, learning is supported by the development of essential skills of thinking and using language. The relationships between teachers and children must be those that encourage children to become responsible, creative learners who are motivated by the increasing meaningfulness that comes from their participation in learning. Children must not only have an involvement in adult ways of thinking but in ways of thinking about things that are interesting to children. It is of little use to expose children to ideas if the ideas are not meaningful and relevant.

Some programs will go to extraordinary lengths to teach concepts such as *backward*. Yet children readily learn the meaning of the term *backward* when they experience its use in an appropriate context. For example, if a child is pushing his car backward, it is an opportune time for an adult to say, *You're pushing it backward, aren't you?* or to talk with him about pushing it backward and forward. With such experience children readily come to understand and use such terms.

There is no ready-made, "attainable-from-the-publisher" solution to the education of children disadvantaged by poverty. No "teacher-proof" program based on a package of materials can achieve interaction of the kind that facilitates thinking and understanding. The approach demands particular skills in the teacher and a method of working that makes the quality of teacher–child interaction the most crucial element. The only way to bring about an environment with these characteristics for learning is through the teachers' recognition of the role of talk in learning and by their critical awareness of their own part in the process. Research referred to earlier has indicated that this means that teachers need a new understanding of the part they can play in children's education. They need insight into the role that language plays in learning and of the way in which children learn to use language through interaction with adults. They need to be aware of the kinds of skills each child has developed in using language in order to have the ability to diagnose particular needs and provide beneficial dialogue experiences. Teachers need to recognize that many children will not have experiences through which their thinking might be extended unless these are provided in school and to recognize the critical importance of the experiences they themselves provide through their own talk with children. Teachers must have a critical awareness of the need to plan both concrete experiences and experiences of talk if learning is to be effective for all children throughout the curriculum.

A CURRICULUM DEVELOPMENT APPROACH TO LANGUAGE IN SCHOOL

In 1973 a project was set up by the Schools Council in the United Kingdom—a government-funded body responsible for stimulating and supporting curriculum development—to undertake work with teachers that would explore the implications of this approach to language for the education of young children, particularly of those brought up in poverty.

The full scale project was set up following a feasibility study that had investigated the practicability of using a framework of language uses as a means of monitoring and appraising children's talk. This framework was based on the classification developed from the previously reported longitudinal study (Tough, 1977c). During the feasibility study, the classification system was modified so that it became a tool that teachers could use to aid their observations as they listened to children's talk.

When the full scale project began work, some 1500 teachers in 93 groups throughout the United Kingdom took part in the further development of materials to help teachers improve the use of dialogue in the classroom. It was agreed from the start that materials for children to use were not required. The normal activities of nursery and infant schools were seen as providing appropriate concrete experiences as a basis for children's learning. The purpose was to explore the possibilities for dialogue during these activities and to help teachers develop abilities first, in appraising children's skills in using language; then, in developing effective dialogue with children by the deliberate choice of dialogue strategies; and, finally, in recognizing opportunities for using dialogue to assist learning in all areas of the curriculum.

Videotape recordings of children talking to adults and to one another were used to illustrate children's skills and difficulties in using language and to give teachers the opportunities to practice appraising children's use of language. The groups of teachers received draft introductions to a number of topics and worked with videotaped examples illustrating these topics. They tried out activities in the classroom and brought their own recordings for discussion to the groups' meetings. At regular intervals the groups evaluated the materials, criticized them, and suggested modifications and new ideas. In this way the project team was helped to revise and reshape the materials for publication.

As a result of this development work with teachers, two books, *Listening to Children Talking* and *Talking and Learning,* were completed and published, together with two sets of videotapes under the same titles (Tough, 1976a,b, 1977a,b). The books and videotapes form materials to be used in a series of workshop meetings for groups of teachers or student teachers. The essence of a workshop is to enable a group of teachers to develop insight and skills together as a result of discussion and analysis of their own practice. The materials offer no easy prescription for meeting the needs of children. To bring about change, they rely on increasing teachers' understanding and skills of listening to and talking with children. As teachers come to recognize children's skills and difficulties, so they are able to modify their practice to help children more appropriately. The approach is one that takes into account the skills and needs of all children, but it focuses attention particularly on children whose needs are greatest. A method of educating young children is advocated in which the extension of children's skills of thinking and use of language during normal activities is central.

In these workshops a sampling of interaction is taken from the classroom, the teachers are exposed to the workshop course, and they transcribe part of each recording and build up a record of their work. They analyze their dialogues and the changes that take place. At the end of the course the teachers in the groups discuss the changes in their own classrooms and examine the process of developing an enabling environment in which teachers change and children benefit.

One goal is for the teachers to examine the aims of education for young children and realize that they include more than establishing the early skills of reading, writing, and number. Teachers generally agree that self-discipline, social responsibility, creativity, and problem-solving attitudes are also important. The workshop course also directs teachers to examine the way in which skills such as reading and writing are learned, and how, in mediating the learning of any learning activity, children are helped to become involved in self-control through reflection on their own behavior. Learning is a multifunctional process, and language is the means through which the process is mediated.

This approach is not seen as an intervention program to offset the disadvantage of some children but as a way of educating all children, where the needs of individual children are appraised, and dialogue experiences are used to foster and extend children's language and thinking skills. The materials are now being widely used in the United Kingdom and several areas overseas, and a program of evaluation is under way.

Can this way of educating children offer children brought up in poverty a better chance? It is too early to give firm evidence, but the indications are that many teachers are finding that children make greater progress not only in using language and thinking and understanding but in all areas of the curriculum including reading and writing. As a result of this approach, teachers are beginning to take more account of the skills and potential for the learning of disadvantaged children. Such a changing view may bring about changes in the school environment that will promote greater success for these children, at least during their primary school years.

REFERENCES

Ackerman, P. D. Final report for story repetition and early language development. Department of Psychology, Wichita State University, 1976.

Bakher-Renes, H., & Hoefnaghe-Hohle, M. Situatie verschillen in Toolgebruck. Masters Thesis, University of Amsterdam, 1974.

Bloom, B. S. *Stability and change in human characteristics.* New York: Wiley, 1964.

Boydell, D. Teacher–pupil contact in junior classrooms. *British Journal of Education and Psychology,* 1974, *11,* 313–318.

Byrne, D., Williamson, B., & Fletcher, B. *The poverty of education.* London: Martin Robertson, 1975.

Coleman, J. S. *Equality of educational opportunity.* Washington, D.C.: U.S. Office of Education, 1965.

Department of Education and Sciences. *Children and their primary schools.* London: Her Majesty's Stationery Office, 1965.

Department of Education and Sciences. *Primary education in England.* London: Her Majesty's Stationery Office, 1978.

Galton, M., Simon, B., & Croll, P. *Inside the primary classroom.* London: Routledge & Kegan Paul, 1980.

Garner, J. Some aspects of behavior in infant school classrooms. *Research in Education,* 1972, *7,* 28–47.

Garner, J., & Bing, M. Inequalities of teacher–pupil contacts. *British Journal of Educational Psychology,* 1973, *43,* 234–243.

Halliday, M. A. K. *Learning how to mean.* London: Arnold, 1975.

Hess, R. O., & Shipman, V. Early experience and the socialization of cognitive modes in children. *Child Development,* 1965, *36,* 867–886.

Hilsum, S., & Cane, B. S. *The teacher's day.* Slough: National Foundation for Educational Research, 1971.

Irwin, O. C. Infant speech: Effects of systematic reading of stories. *Journal of Speech and Hearing Disorders,* 1960, *3,* 187–190.

Jencks, C. *Inequality.* London: Basic Books, 1972.

Lazar, I., & Darlington, R. B. *Lasting effects after preschool.* U.S. Dept. of Health, Education, and Welfare, Pub. No. (OHDS) 79-30178, 1978.

Luria, A. R. *The role of speech in the regulation of normal and abnormal behavior.* London: Staples Press, 1961.

Luria, A. R., & Yudovitch, F. I. *Speech development and mental processes in the child.* London: Staples Press, 1959.

Mitner, E. A study of the relationship between reading readiness in grade one and patterns of parent–child interaction. *Child Development,* 1951, *22,* 95–112.

Piaget, J. *The language and thought of the child.* London: Routledge & Kegan Paul, 1929.

Rutter, J., & Madge, N. *Cycles of disadvantage.* London: Heinemann, 1976.

Sestini, E. *Maternal values and modes of communication.* Unpublished masters thesis, University of Leeds, 1975.

Snow, C. E. Conversations with children. In P. Fletcher & M. Gorman (Eds.), *Studies in language acquisition.* London: Cambridge University Press, 1979.

Snow, C. E., Arlman-Rupp, A., Hassing, Y., Jobse, J., Jooster, J., & Vorster, J. Mothers' speech in three social classes. *Journal of Psycholinguistic Research,* 1976, *5,* 1–20.

Snow, C. E., & Ferguson, C. A. (Eds.). *Talking to children: Language input and acquisition.* London: Cambridge University Press, 1977.

Tizard, B., Philps, J., & Plewis, I. Staff behavior in pre school centres. *Journal of Child Psychology and Psychiatry,* 1976, *17,* 21–23.

Tough, J. *Listening to children talking: A guide to the appraisal of children's use of language.* London: Ward Lock Educational Ltd., 1976.(a)

Tough, J. Videotapes: *Listening to children talking: A guide to the appraisal of children's use of language.* A series of six videotapes, Cardiff, England: Drake Educational Associates, 1976.(b)

Tough, J. *Talking and learning: A guide to fostering communication skills in nursery and infant schools.* London: Ward Lock Educational Ltd., 1977.(a)

Tough, J. Videotapes: *Talking and learning: A guide to fostering communication skills in nursery and infant schools.* A series of 10 videotapes, Cardiff, England: Drake Educational Associates, 1977.(b)

Tough, J. *The development of meaning.* London: Allen & Unwin, 1977.(c)

Wells, G. *Language development in pre-school children.* Final Report to Social Science Research Council, 1978.

Wells, G. Variations in child language. In V. Lee (Ed.), *Language Development.* London: Croom Helm, 1979.

Wilson, H., & Herbert, G. W. *Parents and children in the inner city.* London: Routledge & Kegan Paul, 1978.

Vygotsky, L. S. *Thought and language.* Cambridge, Massachusetts: MIT Press, 1962.

2

Mother–Child Interaction, Language Development, and the School Performance of Poverty Children

DALE C. FARRAN

Studying the language of poverty children is of interest for two primary reasons. First, it is important as a basic research question: How is language altered or modified given different environmental conditions? Second, it is of educational interest because language deficits are presumed to be at the heart of poor children's problems on standardized tests and in school (Bereiter, 1972). Standardized tests tell one little about the nature of the difficulty in language. Yet, according to Baldwin and Baldwin (1973), specification of the difficulty is essential to any well-planned intervention program:

> As a result of the lack of solid knowledge about the psychological ecology of impoverished children, intervention projects have cost millions and produced little: either the intervention was wrongly directed, the methods were ineffective, or the measures used to measure the effects of intervention were inadequate. Again, it is a sad commentary on the field of psychology, so sophisticated in the study of so many problems, that we have shed so little solid knowledge on these problems of great social significance. [p. 714]

Intervention is not the goal for studying poor children's language; knowledge is. However, intervention is already underway, and if knowl-

19

THE LANGUAGE OF CHILDREN
REARED IN POVERTY

edge would serve to make the intervention efforts better focused and more successful, that alone would justify the investment of much more research and thought.

This chapter is concerned with family patterns during the preschool years and their effect on language development and the later school performance of children reared in poverty. In order to investigate this three-way interaction—family, language, and school performance—the chapter is organized in the following manner. First, attention is given to the broader question of environmental effects on any developmental process and the means by which environmental effects have been demonstrated. Given the probability of environmental effects on some language skills (with family interaction as a likely carrier of those effects), patterns of interaction within families are described: their course over the preschool years and the different patterns followed by different social-class subgroups. A finer focus is then given to the linguistic interactions between mothers and children in different social-class groups. Next, the language skills of children from different groups are described as the children enter kindergarten. The subsequent section attempts to determine which factors associated with social class are the ones most likely related to differences in parent–child interaction styles and school-entry language skills. The final section of the chapter is devoted to the dual effects of family interaction patterns and school-entry language skills in determining school performance initially and later.

Detailed information is presented from research projects conducted at the Frank Porter Graham Child Development Center's longitudinal study of high-risk black children. These children are called high risk because their families are poor, relatively uneducated, and have unstable occupations. Emphasis is placed on the results of this project for illustrative purposes; the data are most familiar to the author and serve to highlight many findings from other research in the area.

Finally, a word ought to be said about the groups of children who are being compared in the studies that are reviewed. Children included in these studies are frequently reared in extreme poverty; their families are characterized by low income, dependence on public assistance, low occupational prestige, family instability, and low educational attainment. The group to which they are compared frequently is composed of children from families with moderate to high incomes, prestigious occupations, and high levels of education—often both parents have at least a college degree. Clearly these are extreme groups, and where these groups differ by race as well, it is even more difficult to disentangle the factors involved. As the studies are reviewed in this chapter, an effort will be made to describe the samples on which conclusions are being based, but the reader should keep in mind the professional nature of most of these middle-class families.

THE RELATIONSHIP BETWEEN ENVIRONMENTS AND DEVELOPMENT

Importance of the Early Social Environment

The more one studies the growth of sociability in infants during the first year of life, the more it seems that infants are "preadapted for social interchange [Schaffer, 1979, p. 283]." For example, Fagan (1979) has demonstrated the infant's ability to recognize and have a preference for facial patterns in the early months of life; Condon and Sander (1974) have shown that infants move in synchrony with adult speech on the first day of life. It is also clear that most infants adapt readily to whatever specific environments they inhabit. In a longitudinal study of infant temperament, Thomas, Chess, and Birch (1968) found that most infants were "easy" children. They adapted readily to a variety of environmental demands. Only a small percentage of children were difficult and non-adaptive. Infants adapt to all sorts of environmental demands including such elementary ones as feeding on a schedule—they even adapt to 3- or 4-hr schedules, depending on the decisions made by their parents (Schaffer, 1979).

Thus one's picture of the newborn is of a being eager for social interchange and willing to adapt to whatever situation surrounds it. Consequently, many child development theorists and researchers have argued that the early cognitive and social environment is crucial to the child's early and later development (Ainsworth, 1973; Hess & Shipman, 1967). The statement, "The role of early social interaction in influencing later cognitive and social development is well attested . . . [de Blauw, Dubber, van Roosmalen, & Snow, 1979, p. 53]," is presented as such an accepted fact that no references need be cited to support it.

There can be no doubt that later development is dependent upon early experience if one assumes that development is an orderly process and that the environments that infants successively encounter are not radically different from one another. However, one must take care to avoid assuming that one pattern of development is the correct or desired pattern and all others are less desirable. For example, the next sentence in the de Blauw et al. (1979) chapter makes clear that what is meant by the idea of the influence of early experience on later development is that certain maternal behaviors toward infants lead to "normal development [p. 53]." The natural corollary to this statement is that where these behaviors are absent, abnormal development occurs. Yet no controlled studies imposing the presence of certain rearing conditions on some and depriving them from others are possible with human infants.

The tendency among researchers is to focus on the population at hand, too frequently a middle-class group from within a university community, and to assume that whatever factors are present in that group of mothers are those that result in the good, or normal, development of their children.

To determine the effects of the early environment on later development, one would need to look for the relationship between the presence of certain conditions and specific effects and not the absence of certain conditions. The implicit, often unrecognized, assumption is that the standard for normal functioning is middle-class behavior, a position that ignores the adaptive capacity of infants as well as the variety of environments they encounter.

The position taken by Hess and Shipman (1968) illustrates this assumption. They argue that children obtain information-processing strategies through their experiences with their early environment and that these strategies may "set limits on the potential mental growth of the child [p. 103]." It is not a position that assumes a different outcome for a child in a different environment; rather it assumes that environments that differ from the modal one for the middle class will restrict or limit the child. In any investigation of environmental effects, it is important to determine what the children are being socialized to do in *that* environment. Moore's chapter in this volume illustrates the kind of descriptive approach needed to compare children from different subcultures. Moore describes divergent behaviors exhibited by children from different subcultures in a testing situation. One gets a clear sense of their differing styles. By contrast, behaviors that are described in terms of their absence do not provide anything useful for understanding children.

Another issue related to the importance of the early social environment is the reversibility of its effects by subsequent experiences. Clarke and Clarke (1976) argue persuasively that the idea of long-term effects from early experience is a myth, unsupported by most available evidence. In a review of parental effects on children's development, Clarke-Stewart and Apfel (1978) state that the issue of whether early mother–child interactions result in irreversible developmental outcomes for the child is still an open question.

It appears that in order to investigate the importance of the early environment, one would have to be aware of two factors: First, what particular behaviors are emerging as related to specific environments; and second, how stable the behaviors are.

Determining Environmental Influence

Determining environmental influence on any behavior is difficult; it is particularly difficult to determine the influence of a broad array of environmental variables such as those subsumed under the terms *social class* or *subcultural group*. The most common strategy is to compare subcultural groups. Therefore, there are behaviors and outcomes in one group and different behaviors and different outcomes in another group. Given that situation, how does one determine a causal connection between any factor and any outcome? There is no direct test; one cannot isolate which factors, if any, in either subgroup are related to the outcomes. Given the large number of potential causal factors, the likelihood is great, in fact, that one has not even measured the appropriate ones.

One possible strategy for making the comparisons between groups is to identify factors within one group that theoretically appear to be causal and to look for their presence in the other group. Presumably their presence in the other group will be linked to the same outcome as in the first. This strategy, however, ignores the complexity of environmental interactions because the meaningfulness of certain behaviors may be altered radically by the other circumstances surrounding it. For example, a warm, loving, verbal mother who reasons with her children may be the ideal in economically stable families but may be looked on as weak and ineffective in families coping with the exigencies of poverty. Ramey and Farran (in press) investigated the behaviors of poverty mothers and the developmental outcomes of their children. Poor mothers who exhibited the same behaviors as middle-class mothers had children whose Binet test scores at age 4 differed by only one point from those children of poor mothers not showing middle-class behaviors.

Studies of Environmental Influence

There are few studies that are adequate to show the effects of environments on developmental outcomes. The ones that are adequate involve the study of children who have been removed from one environment to be reared in another, in effect allowing the imposition of certain environmental conditions. For example, Tizard, Cooperman, Joseph, and Tizard (1972) investigated children reared in 13 residential nurseries in England. The nurseries differed in the ways in which they were organized as well as on the amount of "informative" staff talk addressed to children. Informative talk is contrasted by Tizard *et al.* to administrative talk where the latter primarily involved simple directives to the children. The relationship that emerged was significantly positive between language comprehension (assessed by the Reynell Developmental Language Scales) and the amount of informative talk teachers used with the children.

This result is intriguing in that it concerns groups of children reared differently by chance and seems to demonstrate an environmental influence. The finding would be strong evidence for environmental influence if there were certainty, as Tizard *et al.* assert, that the children were not selectively placed in the institutions. One would also want to determine if this difference is important for later language growth or if it is possible that these early effects can be compensated for by the children's subsequent experiences.

Other studies have focused on children who were adopted and thus are being reared in families genetically unrelated to them. Scarr and Weinberg (1976) reported that black children adopted into white homes scored 15 points higher on IQ tests than other black children reared in the same state. This finding suggests that intelligence test results are malleable and open to environmental influence. However, it does not address the process by which this IQ difference took place.

Robert Plomin's Colorado adoption project assessed children's linguistic competence at 12 months and related it to environmental and genetic factors (Brown, 1980). Brown found that wide individual differences in communicative competence appeared early. Some of the differences were related to a genetic factor—the tested memory level of the biological mother. Two environmental factors did emerge as important for communicative competence, both of which were mother language behaviors: (*a*) vocal responsivity to the infant; and (*b*) imitativeness of the mother to infant vocalizations. These factors appear to relate to a conversational style some mothers adopt with their infants. These factors were not related to the biological mother and thus may truly show an environmental influence.

This is exciting work, and one would hope that it continues, assessing the children and the environment at older ages. There is great variability among infants at the younger age, but no one really knows how meaningful that variation is at 12 months. Only a portion of the variation was accounted for either by genetic or environmental factors in the Brown sample. We now recognize that there are individual differences in patterns of language acquisition (Nelson, 1979), but the long-term effect on language of these early acquisition strategies has yet to be shown.

Poverty as an Environmental Influence on Language

Children learn language in all sorts of rearing situations; they learn to talk with only a minimal input from the environment. As Nelson (1979) says, "Development of language by the human infant is as nearly universal as walking [p. 307]." The crucial question is not whether children in different environments will learn to talk but rather what they know to talk about and how they use language to express their understandings about the world (see Tough, Chapter 1).

The focus of much psycholinguistic research has been on the early acquisition of language and not as much on qualitative differences in the language learned. It is, of course, a fascinating thing to study children mastering such a complex system as language, but that focus has tended to overshadow efforts to understand the environmental effects on the nature of language itself. This is particularly the case with children who are past the early acquisition stage and who are using language to manipulate their environments. The ways in which language is used and the manner in which children learn these ways are not well understood but are very much at the heart of work represented in this book.

One effort to understand the ways language is used in different environments was that of Bernstein (1960; 1972). Bernstein developed a theory about the effects of working-class and middle-class environments on language in England. His work has been the basis for other work in the United States, notably that of Hess and Shipman (1965, 1967, 1968). His theory concerns the means and language patterns parents use to socialize the child. He argues that working-class English parents use a "restricted code" with their children, whereas middle-class parents use an "elaborated code." The different codes are coupled with differences in socialization styles; the restricted code is linked to authoritarianism and the elaborated code to democratic values. In combination, the language and socialization styles serve to determine the type of language mastered by the child and to perpetuate certain information-processing strategies that affect later learning.

Initially Bernstein's work was a theory of the acquisition of language given different environmental inputs. Other work following his (Cook-Gumperz, 1973) involved the responses of mothers to interviews about various problems they might encounter with their children. These interviews were coded both for their socialization and linguistic style content. There has been little direct study of the language of children from working- and middle-class backgrounds to verify Bernstein's theory and to determine the importance of linguistic style differences for learning or behavior in school.

The environmental effects on the development of language demonstrated in these studies justifies looking more closely at the factors that differentiate environments and might be related to language. One of the most frequently studied aspects of the environment is mother–child interaction. Mothers are often presumed to be the carriers for environmental effects, and their behaviors are compared across groups. The next section summarizes those comparisons.

MOTHER–CHILD INTERACTION DURING PRESCHOOL YEARS

Focus on Mothers

The interactions between parents and children have been rated (Jay & Farran, in press; Schaefer, 1959; Sears, Maccoby, & Levin, 1957), observed (Farran & Haskins, 1980; Kamii & Radin, 1967; Thoman, 1978), and induced in laboratory settings (Baumrind, 1967; Hess & Shipman, 1967; Mulhern & Passman, 1979). The citations listed are but a few of the number of studies that exist in those areas. What has led to so much effort? In general, one could argue that for the past 30 years psychologists have been trying to find out how parents affect their children, and lately, how children affect their parents (Lewis & Rosenblum, 1974). More generally, though, psychologists have been interested in how parent–child interactions differ across cultures and subgroups, with the notion that these differences might hold the key for understanding developmental differences in children of those subgroups.

In studies of parent–child interaction, the mother has been the primary focus rather than both parents or the family as a whole. Though the actual reasons for this may be logistical or philosophical ones, there are two possible justifications for the matriarchal focus. The first is that the mother is considered to be the prime agent of socialization (Schlossman, 1978; Willerman, 1973). It is presumed that she has the primary responsibility for childrearing and that cultural norms are transmitted through her to the child. The second justification is that the mothers are representative of the type of adult–child interactions children encounter during the preschool years. By observing mothers' actions, one can generalize from their behaviors to those of other persons with whom children have contact in their cultural group.

Unfortunately, there are problems with both of these justifications. The first position is often explicitly or implicitly taken by those who want to intervene in the mother–child behavioral pattern. Schlossman (1978) has written a particularly good review of this rationale and the problems it engenders. The belief that the mother is the prime socialization agent is especially inappropriate in homes with extended kin networks where socialization and child-care responsibilities are likely to be shared by a number of adults and older siblings (Haskins, 1980; LeVine, 1970; Stack, 1974; Ward, 1971; Whiting & Whiting, 1975).

In our longitudinal study at the Frank Porter Graham Center, we have observed more than 100 mother–child pairs four times during the preschool years (Farran & Ramey, 1980; Ramey, Farran, & Campbell, 1979). There are a few notable examples in which the assumption that the mother is the prime socialization agent is definitely unwarranted. In one case, a mother—whose behavioral style was warm, loving, intelligent, and directly in tune with her child's behaviors—had never lived with the child. She lived next door to him. She was a "street" person engaging in petty crime, and she thought it better for her child to be raised by his aunt.

There are other cases where mothers have relinquished their children to temporary foster care situations for months at a time. In a study of attachment, Farran and Ramey (1977) cited evidence that 14 of 23 children included in the study did not go home from the daycare center to their mothers in the afternoons. They went to aunts, grandmothers, or other family members because their mothers were in school, working, or were otherwise not available in the afternoons.

The second justification for focusing on the mother may not be appropriate either. It is difficult to determine whether any particular mother is representative of adults with whom the preschool child interacts. There is evidence that where the mother is not similar to the prevailing culture, her behavior with the child does not buffer the child from the influences of the surrounding society. Ramey and Farran (in press) indicated that poverty mothers whose behaviors were typical of middle-class mothers had children whose development did not differ from other children growing up in poverty. A large study in England in the early 1960s yielded the same general finding with respect to respiratory illness (Douglas, 1964). Mothers who were judged as providing good quality care for their infants had children whose number of illnesses was equivalent to that among children with poor mothering—if they were in poor quality housing. In good quality housing, good mothering did have the effect of lowering the number of respiratory illnesses.

This kind of interactive effect has also been demonstrated by Rutter and Quinton (1977) in an ecological study of behavioral disturbance in children. Families whose behavioral disturbance was low produced children whose incidence of behavioral deviance was high if they attended poor quality schools. The worst situation was one in which family deviance and school dysfunction were both high, but the second worst interactive situation was one in which school dysfunction was high and family deviance low. This study indicates dramatically the importance of the cultural milieu in determining how children will function.

Despite the problems associated with the focus on mother–child interactions, a summary of work in that area may be justified, depending on how one treats the findings. First, it is important to realize that comparative studies of groups of mothers who differ by economic and educational status provide information about the groups and not about individual mothers. The variances for different maternal behaviors within any one group are great (Ramey, *et al.*, 1979).

A second important perspective to keep in mind when reviewing this line of research is the nondeficit approach, or put more positively, an approach that attempts to determine what behaviors are occurring in groups of mothers being compared. It is an important truism that all patterns are adaptive—or else people would not engage in them. Maladaptive patterns for groups of people do not persist for long. However, patterns that are adaptive for current circumstances may not be adaptive for future circumstances or for changing current conditions. Patterns that enable poverty families to cope with the situation in which they exist may not facilitate change, but one cannot assume that patterns derived from middle-class status would be suitable for effecting change either.

Patterns of Mother–Child Interaction

First Year of Life

In early infancy very few differences have been observed in mother–infant interactions among groups who differ by education, income, or race (Cohen & Beckwith, 1975; de Blauw *et al.*, 1979; Farran & Ramey, 1980; Kilbride, Johnson, & Streissguth, 1977; Ramey *et al.*, 1979). In some studies, vocalization rates of mothers to their infants have been found to be different; some show middle-class mothers vocalizing more (Kilbride *et al.*, 1977; Ramey *et al.*, 1979; Tulkin, 1977); one shows no difference between the groups (de Blauw *et al.*, 1979); and one shows poverty mothers vocalizing more (Lewis & Wilson, 1972). There have been virtually no differences found in caretaking behaviors or in the amount and type of stimulation provided. Farran and Ramey (1980) have argued that interacting with their infants may be a matter of individual preference for mothers; some mothers like the early infancy period and some do not. The baby requires a minimum level of involvement, but the demands it makes on its mother are relatively uniform across infants and also somewhat difficult to ignore. A minimum amount of involvement is demanded by the infant; doing more than the minimum may be a matter of individual maternal preference.

Second Year of Life

The second year of life, however, is a very important year for the infant, and one to which mothers of varying backgrounds appear to react differently. In an extensive review of this period of development, Nelson (1979) suggests that the infant is in the process of synthesizing the object world and the social world. The first year of life has marked the differentiation between the object and social world. A higher level of coordination is required to bring them back together in the second year. According to Nelson, this process of active synthesis accounts for the relative plateau in language attainment one observes for 6 to 8 months between the 12-month-old speaking one word and the 20-month-old combining two words. If Nelson is correct, then the second year of life, when the synthesis is being achieved, is a prime time for input to the child's language development.

The relative importance of the 12–24-month period compared to the first 12 months has been confirmed in a number of studies. The videotaped interaction patterns of 50 poverty mothers and their 6-month-old babies were subjected to many of the currently suggested analytic strategies by Farran and Burchinal (1980). Neither summary measures nor factor scores nor scores based on behavioral contingencies were related to any current or subsequent measures of infant development. Ramey and Farran (in press) found that ratings of mothers' behaviors at home when infants were 6-months-old were unrelated to the children's later IQ scores at 48 months. However, those mothers engaging in minimal maternal involvement when their babies were 18-months-old had children who scored 10 points lower on an IQ test at 48 months.

Evidence for the importance of the second year was presented in another longitudinal study of poverty families conducted by McGlaughlin, Empson, Morrissey, and Sever (1980) in England. They observed mothers and infants at 12, 18, 24, and 30 months—a portion of the group was observed twice, 1 week apart. Observations at 12 months were marked by great instability, which was not present in the observations at the older ages. The changes that occurred in the interactions between 12 and 18 months involved many of the mothers beginning to follow their children's lead and engaging in more of what McGlaughlin *et al.* called *intellectual interactions*. Although the definitions are not clear, these presumably involve more verbal and instructional activities, which showed a sharp increase from 12 to 18 months and then stabilized. Within this group of poverty mothers (estimated to be from the bottom 20% of the population), variations in the amount of time mothers engaged in these kinds of interactions were related to the children's performance on the Reynell Developmental Language Scales at 30 months.

The amount of adult interaction provided infants between 12 and 24 months varies greatly with mothers from different backgrounds. Farran and Ramey (1980) demonstrated that middle-class mothers increased their involvement with their infants from 6 to 20 months, whereas poverty mothers decreased theirs. There were no group differences when the infants were 6 months; about half of each group of mothers was actively involved with their infants. When the infants were 6 months old, 88% of the middle-class mothers versus 30% of the poverty mothers were actively involved.

Farran and Ramey argue that this finding may derive from different maternal expectations of children's competence. When children can walk and have begun to talk, mothers from well-educated backgrounds may view them as budding conversational partners; mothers from poor educational and economic backgrounds may view the children as being competent enough to play alone. Ward (1971) writes powerfully of the differences in the amount of adult interaction with babies as compared to toddlers in a poor, black, isolated region of Louisiana. Babies were loved, cuddled, and held constantly; when children began to walk and talk, they were looked upon as trouble and seldom interacted with, except to be told to go outdoors.

Third Year of Life

Differences in the amount of interaction between mothers and children of different educational and economic backgrounds were demonstrated in a sample of 36-month-old children in the Frank Porter Graham Center's longitudinal study (Farran & Haskins, 1980). Middle-class, well-educated mothers played with their 3-year-olds twice as much as poverty mothers. Moreover, each interactive episode was twice as long, and the pattern for initiating and terminating mutual play episodes was different. Poverty mothers tended to join their children's play for a little while and then to pull back and watch while the children completed the activity. Middle-class mothers, however, joined the play and then continued until the activity was completed. This pattern suggests that poverty mothers were providing as little structuring help as needed and were basically following a Piagetian model of development—letting the children make the discoveries on their own. The other mothers were providing a great deal of input to the children, well beyond what was needed merely to keep the activity going.

Once again speculation about the reasons for these differences has more to do with modal patterns of behavior in different subcultures than with deficient parenting styles. For example, Farran and Haskins (1980) also conducted a series of contingency analyses with these same dyads. They asked whether or not the pattern of the mothers' responses to the children's behavior was different in the two groups—one poor and black, the other relatively wealthy, educated, and predominantly white (83%). There were no differences in the profiles of interactive style. Poor mothers were just as likely as middle-class mothers to direct their children's behaviors when the children were unfocused or doing nothing. They were also equally unlikely to interfere when their children were playing independently. The major differences between the groups related to the amount of time mothers played with their children and not to the nature of their interactive styles.

The value of adults playing with children may be a relatively new concept in childrearing. Those from educated and economically secure backgrounds certainly hold that value, and they assume others must hold it as well—but are just not acting on it. In fact, other groups of people may not believe in the importance of adult play or may not have the economic or social resources necessary to pursue it through even if they did hold the value. This is a case where one must be very careful not to confuse the cause with the effect—many would presume that the greater amount of adult–child play time observed in these middle-class dyads was responsible for the dyads' middle-class status. It is much more likely that adult–child play was sanctioned and encouraged once middle-class status was achieved; it derived from economic and educational security. Many other factors contribute to attaining middle-class status, factors beyond the scope of this chapter.

Patterns from 6 to 60 Months

The preliminary data presented by Ramey and Farran (1980) indicated that the interactive patterns of the groups observed longitudinally became similar at 60 months. Thus, the pattern in mother–child interactions comparing poverty mothers to middle-class mothers appears to be similarity at 6 months, divergence at 20 months to 36 months, and similarity at 60 months. At 60 months, the groups were equal in the amount of time mothers and children played together as well as in such behaviors as issuing directives and complying with directives.

Implications of Differences in Interactive Styles

If the mother–child interactive pattern described is an accurate de-
piction of what takes place over the preschool years, explanations for
it are necessary, even if they are tentative. It may be that mothers from
middle-class backgrounds view the preschool years as crucial ones for
preparing their children to function in academic, technological environments. Economists term this *time invested in children,* count it as a cost
of childrearing, and see variations in the investment as a sign of cultural
values. Middle-class mothers invest about twice as much time in their
children as do mothers who are poor (Leibowitz, 1977). This does not
mean that the groups value their children any differently; rather, they
place different values on both the importance and the long-term significance of adult input during the preschool years.

One assumes that a part of childrearing must be preparation of the
young for the roles they will assume in adulthood. Over time, that preparation must change because the roles are changing—which is not to say
that adults are preparing children for roles the adults themselves have
not experienced. Adults simply prepare children in ways they themselves
have learned are important. One could even argue that the limited number
of children middle-class families allow themselves is part of the same
process; fewer children means more time to prepare each of them for
the roles they are to assume later.

If one wanted to use the middle-class mother–child interaction patterns described here as the modal or desired way to raise preschool
children, one would have to make the qualification that this is a pattern
to prepare children to be competitive in an academic environment. It
may well carry with it other outcomes that are less desirable (e.g.,
neuroses, unhappiness, insecurity, hedonism). Preparing children to function in a farming community or a nontechnical society may involve a
different pattern of parent–child interactions over the preschool years.

LINGUISTIC INTERACTIONS BETWEEN
MOTHERS AND PRESCHOOL CHILDREN

The interactions of mothers and children have a large verbal component, especially once the children begin to talk. Clearly there is less
adult–child talk in low-income dyads—there is less interaction altogether.
There have also been investigations into whether the quality of the verbal
interactions differs across cultural and economic groups. This portion
of the chapter summarizes these studies.

Participation in Dialogues with Adults:
The Importance of Responsivity

Tough (1977) and Blank (1975) have argued that participation in dialogues with an adult where several turns are taken on the same topic is crucial to the development of both cognitive and linguistic abilities. The *form* of mothers' speech is not related either to social status (Snow, Arlman-Rupp, Hassing, Jobse, Joosten, & Vorster, 1976) or to the child's language or tested development (Nelson, 1973). The frequency of mothers' *spontaneous* speech also does not appear to be related to cultural or economic conditions, or later child development (Schachter, 1979; Tough, 1977). However, there do appear to be extensive social-class differences in the responsivity of maternal speech to the child's speech, and some have argued that this difference accounts for certain language skills being more evident in middle-class children (Blank, 1975; Tough, 1977).

The most extensive study focusing on the functions of maternal speech across different groups of mothers was done by Schachter (1979). She studied three groups of mothers and their toddlers: (*a*) a group of black disadvantaged mothers whose average education was less than high school; (*b*) a group of black advantaged mothers; and (*c*) a group of white advantaged mothers. Education of the mothers in the last two groups averaged more than a college degree. Schachter observed mother–child interaction in the dyads' homes. There are a number of important findings from her comprehensive study.

The first is that the differences she found among the groups of mothers were between the advantaged and the disadvantaged groups and not between the two advantaged but racially different groups. Thus there were many differences between mothers whose socioeducational status differed but not between mothers who differed merely by race. This finding is in agreement with the cross-cultural similarity in rates of mental retardation associated with socioeconomic status (Farran, Haskins, & Gallagher, 1980) and with studies comparing mother–child interaction across socioeconomic groups in other countries (Snow *et al.*, 1976) or in this country but with an all-white population (Tulkin, 1977; Tulkin & Kagan, 1972).

The major differences between the disadvantaged and advantaged mothers can be clustered into a factor of responsivity. As Schachter (1979) wrote, "Whether advantaged mothers are responding to the child's communications, minimizing or modulating prohibitions, or repeating the child's speech, they seem to persistently adapt and adjust their communications to support the child's own actions [p. 156]." These educated mothers appeared to be talking with their toddlers, not to their toddlers—

exactly the sort of situation Tough (1977) has argued is most conducive for the young child to learn the higher functions of language: synthesizing, predicting, reasoning, and abstracting.

Blank (1975) has also argued that participation in dialogues with adults is crucial to mastering the intangibles of language (referring to the use of language to think about language or to think about thinking). Her work on the development of understanding the term *why* in a single child was corroborated by Hood and Bloom (1979) with eight other children. The sequence of the acquisition of *why* appeared to be related to the mother's responsivity to the child's initial immature efforts to express causality. In Hood and Bloom's study, it was not until children began making causal statements in their own speech that mothers began asking *why* questions. A 2-month lag followed between these adult *why* questions and any causally interpretable responses on the part of the children. In effect, mothers were responsive to readiness clues provided by their children and then engaged them in dialogue necessary to allow the children to master a tricky linguistic form.

Maternal Repetitions

The importance of responsivity can also be seen in the different types of repetitions provided by low- and middle-income mothers with their children. Both Schachter (1979) and Snow *et al.* (1976), working in different countries, found that low-income, uneducated mothers engage in more exact repetitions of their own speech, whereas middle-income, educated mothers engage in more repetitions of their children's speech. "It seems that educated mothers tend to repeat and expand what their children say, whereas less educated mothers tend to repeat exactly what they themselves say [Schachter, 1979, p. 102]." Gleason (1977) described mothers' use of repetition of the child's speech as a tool to guide and direct the behavior of the child from the outside—as a substitute for inner speech, which the child will develop later.

Some of the self-repetitions of low-income mothers can be serving the function of directing the child's behavior. Often they are used to emphasize a command that the child is to carry out (Schachter, 1979). Ward (1971) describes a litany of commands routinely engaged in by poor, isolated mothers and children: A command was not taken seriously by a child until it had been repeated three times, each time in a louder voice. The presence of more imperatives in the speech of low-income mothers to their children has been noted frequently (Schachter, 1979; Snow *et al.*, 1976; Tulkin, 1977). Nelson (1973) contrasted directive behavior with responsive behavior in the long-term impact of each on the child's language behavior: "The most salient relationships between mother and child speech are those involving the mother's active role in directing the child's behavior, which has a negative impact [on later language development], and of responding to his verbal behavior, which has a positive impact [p. 93]."

Teaching Interactions

One of the questions raised in investigating the verbal interactions of mothers and children in different social class groups is whether mothers in one group are directly teaching their children certain skills. Certainly the presumption behind some preschool programs is that children have not been taught skills at home that are necessary to good performance in school (Bereiter, 1972). Schachter (1979) found no difference in the total amount of time advantaged and disadvantaged mothers engaged in teaching their children. They did differ, however, in what they were teaching. Poverty mothers taught their children more letters and numbers, that is, more specific content, than did the educated mothers. This finding is similar to that of Tough (1977), who found low-income English mothers engaging in more didactic teaching than middle-income mothers.

Didactic teaching is particularly inappropriate for the fleeting and nondirected attentional capabilities of the 2- to 4-year-old. John (1963) argued that what small children need is experience in talking with adults in ways that serve to integrate the children's knowledge of the world. Opportunities for such integrative talk are rare for all children, John argued, but would be especially difficult to capitalize on in crowded, low-income homes. Burton White and his colleague made a similar observation 10 years later (White & Watts, 1973), when they described the best mothers as teaching "on the run," seizing the moment of the child's interest to provide the input to facilitate learning when the child was most receptive.

The Importance of the Period between 36 and 60 Months

Pilot work on two poverty children at the Frank Porter Graham Child Development Center supports the importance of responsivity in conversation in mother–child interaction episodes. This author has applied Dorval's (1979) system for categorizing the topic-relatedness of each conversational turn in mother–child interactions at 36 and 60 months. The Dorval System assesses each turn by a speaker in terms of its topic-relatedness to the preceding turn by the other speaker. A turn can be unrelated, which means the topic has shifted; it can be tangentially related, that is, related to the topic but introducing a new topic as well. A turn can be topic-related but only of a marginal contribution, which means the turn maintains the topic but does not expand it. A turn can also expand the topic; that is, it can maintain it and provide further information about the topic. Applying this system to two poverty mother–child dyads when the children were 36 and 60 months has yielded some interesting findings worthy of more effort in this direction.

The data are presented in Table 2.1 for the two dyads. The table displays the percentage of conversational turns by both mother and child across the categories at 36 and 60 months. One can see that the majority of the speech of the mother of MC was topic related but not expansive; only 20% of her turns expanded the topic at 36 months. The majority of the child's conversational turns were marginally topic-related. When MC was 60 months, his mother's speech had shifted somewhat; more of it was topic expanding. The child's conversational style, however, remained roughly the same as it had been when he was 36 months.

TABLE 2.1

The Topic-Relatedness of Conversational Terms for Two Mothers and Children at 36 and 60 Months: Pilot Analyses

| | Summary of MC | | | |
| | 36 months | | 60 months | |
Codes	Mother	Child	Mother	Child
Uncodable	.02	.06	.03	.08
Unrelated	.007	.09	.02	.04
Tangentially related	.09	.04	.03	.04
Topic related	.68	.66	.56	.61
Topic expanding	.22	.15	.36	.22
Total turns	151	151	209	213

| | Summary of KA | | | |
| | 36 months | | 60 months | |
Codes	Mother	Child	Mother	Child
Uncodable	.008	.16	.03	.06
Unrelated	.06	.03	.03	.11
Tangentially related	.02	.08	.006	.07
Topic related	.27	.63	.33	.40
Topic expanding	.62	.11	.60	.34
Total turns	120	109	175	174

The second mother and child, also from a poverty background, demonstrated a different pattern of interaction. The mother's talk when the child was 36-months-old was predominantly topic expanding. The child at 36 months was similar to the other child; much of her talk was marginally topic related, and little of it added to the topic. However, at 60 months the child's speech began to seem more like her mother's. When KA was 60 months her mother continued the same style: engaging in conversations with KA that involved dialogue turns in which the topic was expanded and developed. At 60 months KA was becoming more of a conversational partner, introducing new topics and expanding on topics under discussion.

The differences between these two mothers in their conversations with their children at different ages are of more than academic interest. MC and KA both showed normal development (as tested by the Bayley Scales) through infancy. At 18 months the two began to diverge, with MC beginning to score lower. Some have argued that a critical period for assessing development is 18–24 months, when the tests become more verbal (Golden, Birns, Bridger, & Moss, 1971). By 5 years of age, MC scored in the 70s on a Stanford Binet; KA's scores remained in the high 90s, or normal. Their performance in kindergarten was also quite different. MC was retained in kindergarten and was considered by his teacher to have well-below-average language skills. KA was promoted and rated as average.

How much did the linguistic interactions of these two mothers affect their children's development? There is no way to say with certainty, of course. Both mothers were equally interactive if the total number of turns taken in a conversation is an indication of participation. But it is also probable that KA's mother talked to her more; expanding a topic involves longer utterances than merely maintaining it.

Both these children attended an intervention daycare program at the Frank Porter Graham Child Development Center. This program was not sufficiently powerful to help MC maintain his normal development from infancy. It may have been the program, in conjunction with the expanding conversational style of KA's mother, that promoted her development over the preschool years. We can investigate this interactive effect by doing the same kinds of analyses on the conversational interactions of mothers and children who were not in the program. If conversational expansion is determined as being related to tested abilities in the children, the next step would be to determine why some poverty mothers view this as an appropriate way to interact and others do not. Many reasons are possible. For example, mothers who themselves are upwardly mobile, and working in more verbally oriented environments, may be modeling characteristics of that linguistic environment in their interactions with their children. In other words, it would not be sufficient to demonstrate a relationship between mother–child conversations and the child's school performance without determining why the relationship exists.

LANGUAGE SKILLS OF POVERTY CHILDREN AT SCHOOL ENTRY

Differences and Deficits

Children from poverty environments learn all the uses of language; as a group they do not have a deficit in language skills. What distinguishes poverty children from middle-class children is the frequency with which they use certain language functions. Tough (1977), in her interviews with children from varying backgrounds, has described the presence, at a low frequency level, of all the higher functions of language among poverty children. Shuy and Staton (see Chapter 9) distinguish between teaching children forms they do not know and teaching them to say something more frequently that they do know. They, too, assert that poor children know all the functions of language but lack practice in using them very often.

Individual children, however, may well enter school with language deficits. Blank and her associates (Blank, 1975; Blank, Rose, & Berlin, 1978) have provided evidence that some 5-year-old poor children have not mastered certain *wh* forms correctly (notably, *why* and *when*). They do not encode or decode these forms correctly because they have not mastered the cognitive skills the words reference (i.e., causal relations and time). These children are at a severe disadvantage when entering school, a situation that the initial school experience does not appear to remediate. The children in Blank's study who lacked those skills did not develop them until they were 10- to 11-years-old. Development of the cognitive and linguistic skills involved in causality and time requires extensive interactions with adults. Blank argues that in contrast to most language forms, children must practice these *wh* forms before they can begin to understand them; less practice means a longer time before understanding. Practice in extended dialogues with adults is unlikely to occur in most kindergarten classrooms.

Thus, generally, it appears that the language of poverty children entering school is different from that of children from middle-class families. Many of the forms of language usage that are frequently found in the language of middle-class children are found much less frequently in the language of poor children. Moreover, a few children are entering school with some specific gaps in their linguistic and cognitive development, and these gaps are slow to be remediated in school. Both of these circumstances require the kind of educational treatment Tough (Chapter 1) and Shuy and Staton (Chapter 9) are calling for—helping teachers learn to recognize and extend the incidence of certain forms of language.

Skills with Connected Discourse

The research conducted by Feagans and Farran (in press) over the past several years offers some specific information about the language skills of poor children in connected discourse as they enter kindergarten. By *connected discourse* Feagans and Farran mean comprehending and producing verbal sequences, that is, language beyond the sentence level. Feagans and Farran have developed tasks to assess comprehension, production, and rephrasing skills with two types of connected discourse. One task involves narrative material in the form of short stories; the other involves a set of instructions for opening a puzzle box with an invariant sequence of steps. The performance of children on the latter task seems to illustrate many of the language problems of poor children as they enter school.

Four groups of children were tested with the puzzle boxes in the fall of their kindergarten year. Two of the groups were from the longitudinal sample of poverty children the Frank Porter Graham Child Development Center has been following since birth: One had been randomly assigned to the daycare program, the other, to the control group. When these two groups entered kindergarten, a match was randomly selected for each child from the same classroom. From that matched group, Feagans and Farran selected all those children who were not from poverty backgrounds; the criterion was that the mothers had to have at least a high school education. The fourth group was drawn from a neighboring county in an attempt to locate a white sample living in poverty. These children were found through their birth records, the criterion was that their mothers had to have less than a high school diploma at the time of their children's births. Thus, the groups were (*a*) a black poverty sample from Frank Porter Graham (FPG), (*b*) a black poverty sample attending day care at FPG, (*c*) a white low-income sample, and (*d*) a white middle-income sample.

The puzzle box task has three parts. First, children learn to open a puzzle box with three invariantly sequential steps, and comprehension is assured before going to the next part of the task. Second, children must teach a blindfolded adult how to open the box. Finally, the adult probes the flexibility of the children's language by asking them to provide more information on each step. There are two sessions in this experiment, each with a different box. In one, children are shown how to open the box without verbal instructions; in the other, children are told how to open the box without an accompanying nonverbal presentation.

The performance of all four groups will be described for the three parts of the task: comprehension, production, and rephrasing. In the comprehension part, all children required more trials to learn to open the box if the instructions were verbal. Children from middle-class backgrounds learned faster; they required one fewer trial for both the verbal and nonverbal instructions.

Major differences were found among the groups in the production section of the task. The two poor black groups used many fewer words in teaching the adult and provided fewer specific information units to the adult than the other two groups. (An information unit is defined in a way similar to that used by Pratt, Scribner, & Cole, 1977: any piece of information that would be useful to a nonsighted adult.) There were no differences among the groups in the use of nonreferential words; that is, words that are nonspecific but could refer to specific information ("Push it"; "Do it").

Other work supports a description of the language of poverty children as lacking specific school-related vocabulary (Johnston & Singleton, 1977; Tough, 1977). Such words as *front, side, back, push,* and *pull* were not used by the poverty children in teaching adults. These words were certainly known to them. The children were asked to demonstrate knowledge of these words initially before the experiment continued. The poverty children did not include many of these words spontaneously in their instructions to the adult.

The lack of difference between the groups on nonreferential words suggests that children were not substituting nonreferential terms for vocabulary that they could not quite remember. Middle-class children used just as many such references. Johnston and Singleton (1977) found the same result and concluded that few 5-year-olds are very adept at communicating to a listener. It may also be the case that nonreferential talk is perfectly permissible for any speaker as long as it is accompanied by a sufficient amount of specific information.

The other important aspect of the production part of the task is a comparison across the two instructional methods for the four groups. When middle-class children heard the instructions, their performance in telling the adult was much better than when they had just seen the demonstration. They used half again as many information units; they used fewer nonreferential terms, and they used more words. The difference between the two instructional conditions was not as evident in the performance of the poor black groups; it was evident for the low-income white group. The two Frank Porter Graham Center groups improved slightly in the verbal presentation condition. The control group actually used more nonreferential terms in the verbal condition (suggesting perhaps that they were searching for the vocabulary words they had just heard someone produce).

There is evidence that poverty children have difficulty in attending to—or more importantly, making use of—verbal material when it is provided. Golden, Wagner, and Montare (1974), in a study of 2-year-old white children from different socioeconomic groups, found that high SES children significantly improved their performance when there were verbal cues. The low SES group did not.

In the rephrase part of the Feagans and Farran task, children were asked to repeat the directions "step-by-step." As each step was communicated, the adult feigned noncomprehension twice with phrases such as, *I don't understand, could you tell me more?* Thus there were six such rephrase requests for each box. The four groups did not differ in the number of rephrase requests they responded to with more information; about 50% of the time children responded appropriately to lack of comprehension by the listener. It was not the case that children from poverty backgrounds misunderstood such cues and were unable to respond appropriately. Yet there were group differences on this aspect of the task. Middle-class children provided much more information on each step and each rephrase request than did the Frank Porter Graham Center groups. Although these children had already communicated about twice as much information as the other groups on the production part, they were still able to communicate new information to the rephrase requests.

The conclusion suggested by these data is that the children followed by the Frank Porter Graham Center are entering kindergarten at a slight disadvantage for learning new material, particularly if it is presented verbally, and are much less able than other children to put what they know into words. When children are less capable at encoding their understandings about the world, there are two major consequences:

1. One does not have ready access to children's knowledge and capabilities. In problem-solving situations, for example, one cannot be sure if children cannot do the problem or merely lack the developed ability to explain or describe their actions;

2. The children themselves may suffer from not having the skills to learn more. As Lois Bloom (1974) said, "The major achievement in

language development is the ability to use a linguistic code independently of the situational context in which utterances occur [p. 307]."

Of note here is the fact that the white children who were selected as a comparison poverty group performed better than the black poverty children on some aspect of the tasks. This relatively better performance occurred although their tested intelligence was equal to that of the Frank Porter Graham experimental group. Thus these children are entering kindergarten better able to take advantage of verbal material when it is offered and more able to communicate knowledge they possess. The explanation for their better performance may be that they are not a poverty group; they are a low-income group. The group was selected with maternal education as the criterion, and low maternal education is not sufficient to create a poverty environment.

THE RELATIVE IMPORTANCE OF FACTORS ASSOCIATED WITH SOCIAL CLASS IN SCHOOL-ENTRY LANGUAGE SKILLS

Race

Consistently in studies of language development where race and social class have been included so that one could begin to isolate the effects of one from the other, the socioeconomic status of the family has proven to be the more critical of the two factors. Higgins (1976), in assessing communicative accuracy in children, found neither race nor sex to be as related to performance as social class. Rosch (1977) compared two lower-class groups of children, one white and one black (defined as lower-class because they lived in government housing projects); she also included a middle-class (professional occupations) white group. She found no race or sex differences but large social class differences in the performance of the three groups on encoding abstract stimuli and facial stimuli. Both lower-class groups of children said less; they also used a different encoding style when communicating to a listener. Middle-class children tended to describe the parts of the stimulus, whereas both lower-class groups gave descriptions of the whole.

Rosch and Higgins compared children's behavior; Schachter compared maternal behaviors across different groups. Schachter (1979) also included groups that differed by race and social class. Her three groups consisted of two middle-class/professional groups of mothers who differed by race but not by maternal education and a poor black group. She found that the mothers' talk to their toddlers differed by social class but not by race. The two educated groups of mothers talked more to their children and were more responsive in their speech to the children's talk. The less educated group of mothers issued more directives and used language more to control the children.

Maternal Education

The Schachter study suggests that the critical factor associated with social class and related to children's language may be maternal education. Other evidence also indicates the importance of maternal education in influencing the language directed to children. Educated middle-class mothers used a larger vocabulary and a greater number of abstractions in their speech to children when looking at books (Ninio, 1980) and when teaching a task (Olim, Hess, & Shipman, 1967). Even within a relatively homogeneous group of mothers, where the average maternal education was 14.8 years, Brown (1980) found greater education to be associated with more declaratives and questions, fewer imperatives, and more time spent reading books with the children.

Given the reported importance of maternal education, it is possible to believe that maternal education is the critical factor in studies comparing social class groups. Hence Farran and Feagans recruited a sample of children who were white and who had mothers with an education equivalent (9.66) to that of the poor black groups (10.02) followed longitudinally at the Frank Porter Graham Center. The performance of these children on the puzzle box task was better than the poor black group's though not as good as the middle-class group's. Although maternal education was similar, the most notable difference between the poor black and the low-income white groups involved the number of two-parent families; all white families except one were two-parent families. Of those families, all fathers except one were working. In contrast, the black groups had fewer two-parent homes; clearly, in single-parent homes income is half or less than what it is in two-parent homes with both parents working. Haskins (1980) has reported that 84% of the Frank Porter Graham Center's groups received some sort of public assistance. None of the white families was receiving public assistance.

Maternal education does not appear to be the critical factor for the children's language performance; rather, it may act in combination with a factor of *family stability* to affect development. Children who were developing in stable families where both parents were present, and often both working, had language skills at school entry nearly commensurate with children from middle-class backgrounds. The families of these children did not fit the definition of poverty provided earlier; they constituted

a working-class group of families. In order to test adequately the interaction between race and social class on the kinds of language skills
assessed by Feagans and Farran, investigators will need to recruit another
population, one composed of white families who have the same degree
of marital, economic, and occupational instability as the black families
being studied. Such an attempt is now underway.

Living Conditions

This chapter has concentrated on mother–child interaction patterns
and their association with language development in the child. It has been
noted that those patterns cannot be understood separately from the context in which they occur. Raising children in impoverished circumstances
involves many more factors that affect the development of the children
than the particular parent–child relationship of an individual child. Clark
(1965) wrote eloquently of the difficulty middle-class blacks had in trans-
ferring their achieved status to their children because segregated housing
patterns forced them to live in poor and crime-ridden residential areas.
Those areas are characterized as well by greater unemployment, poorer
health, and increased marital and social instability (Hochstein, Athanasopoulos, & Larkins, 1968). Summarizing a number of ethnographic
studies of the poor, Gallagher, Haskins, and Farran (1979) concluded
that "the common elements across all groups in poverty were the exclusion from the mainstream culture, the lack of autonomy, and the
consequent sense of alienation from middle-class society [p. 252]."

Other studies have identified factors associated with living in poverty. Poor families tend to be larger than middle-class families, and the
siblings are more closely spaced (Birch & Gussow, 1970; Broman,
Nichols, & Kennedy, 1975). Moreover, the families occupy smaller living
quarters, so there is more crowding in the homes (Haskins, 1980). Associated with the greater number of people is a diffusion of education
and socialization responsibility for the child to a larger number of adults
(Tough, 1977; Tulkin, 1977) and a larger number of peers (Tough, 1977;
Ward, 1971).

Whiting and Whiting (1975) summarized the effects of early peer
socialization in various cultures. Their work illustrates dramatically the
different conclusions one can reach about whether a factor has positive
or negative effects on a child, depending on which outcome behaviors
one assesses. Early child care by peers was associated with greater
nurturance and cooperation in the children of the cultures Whiting and
Whiting assessed. Socialization almost exclusively by adults, as in middle-class homes in this country, was associated with greater competi-

tiveness in children. Once again, we are reminded that children are being socialized to behave appropriately for their cultural groups.

Ward's (1971) description provides a picture of life in a poor black community in Louisiana. The organization of the day for a child in this community was quite different from that of a middle-class child. There were no regular mealtimes—though food was always available—no nap-times for younger children, no blocks of times for different kinds of activities during the day. The television was always on, children were constantly in groups together, and adults and children were often back and forth among each other's houses.

This kind of living situation is not restricted to isolated subgroups; some variation of it can be found among any group isolated by poverty and therefore forced into greater interdependence. Haskins (1980), interviewing the Frank Porter Graham Center families, found that the children were in contact with an average of 24 different relatives every month. Haskins (1979) also found, as did Ward, that there was very little aggression among the children; the children played in multiaged groups in an organized and highly cooperative fashion.

The picture of poverty families that emerges from ethnographic descriptions and data-based studies is of a rearing situation characterized by a tremendous amount of stimulation but with little individual attention to children after they are babies. There are many people nearby of varying ages, many of whom are relatives. Unemployment and dependence on public assistance are both quite high, so that many of the role models for the children are not participants in the larger, technological society. The day is more loosely structured and, because resources are tight, there is less privacy and more group dependence. (For example, both Haskins, 1980, and Ward, 1971, report that children frequently slept in beds other than their own and that hardly anyone slept alone.) Groups of children are organized along an age hierarchy, with older children responsible for younger children. Spending much of the day together without adult supervision means that group cohesion develops to a high degree.

THE RELATIVE IMPORTANCE OF SCHOOL-ENTRY LANGUAGE SKILLS TO SCHOOL ADAPTATION

Initial Adaptation to School

The well-established disproportionate percentage of school failures (Farran, *et al.*, 1980) among poor children may not be a result of poorer language skills at school entry. The language skills of poor children are not as well developed in some areas, but that fact may be only a small part of the explanation for poorer school performance. If Ward (1971), Haskins (1980), Stack (1974), and Whiting and Whiting (1975) have provided accurate descriptions of poor and extended kin environments, poorer school performance may result from the fact that the structure of the day is unlike any the child has experienced before. Education is accomplished in blocks of time; there is so much time allotted for reading, so much for arithmetic, so much for recess, and so much for lunch. There are other differentiating factors; in most classes all peers are same-aged, and authority stems from an adult. Often the adult does not directly command but issues orders in long verbal chains.

Early adaptation to school may depend on a number of equally plausible factors for the child:

1. Self-confidence
2. Normal cognitive development
3. Familiarity with the routines of a structured day
4. Knowledge of certain vocabulary
5. Responsivity to the verbal demands of the classroom
6. Compliant responses to adult authority

If these factors are related to initial school adaptation, they may be affected by the overall stability of the family and its participation in the mainstream work culture. For example, in England, Douglas (1964) attempted to determine why some poor children do well in school while many others do not. The factor he isolated as important for the child's success was whether or not the parents visited the school. But visiting the school was related to a number of other factors about the family, factors that imply stability: Those parents who visited the school were those likely to have had their children immunized during preschool years. This association suggests a set of parental activities that means that the parents were involved with and spent time with their children during the preschool years.

Later School Achievement

The differences between children reared in poverty and those who are not grow greater during the school years (Jensen, 1977; John, 1963; Whiteman & Deutsch, 1968). A related finding is the "wash-out" of gains from preschool programs that occurs some time after the second grade (Lazar, Hubbell, Murray, Rosche, & Royce, 1977). Both the cumulative deficit and the wash-out effect may be due to a difference in skills required to do well in school after the first few years. The factors related to initial school adaptation may not be the same as those related to later school adaptation.

Normally, in the second grade children begin to read, and the entire educational process becomes much more dependent on written language than on oral language. The conventions and prosodic rhythms of written language are different from those of oral language. (See Blank, Chapter 4, for a description of the conventions of written language.) Once education becomes intertwined with written language, the early adaptive skills may not be enough to carry all children through. It is possible that maternal education is more related to later school performance than to early performance. Compliance and an average vocabulary may no longer be enough; children may need prior familiarity with written language in order to understand the material with which they are presented.

The Responsibility of the Educational System

How one makes education relevant to children from poor backgrounds is a complicated question. In a sense, it relates to the function of education in general. Silberman (1970) has argued that the educational system has never provided the means for any group to rise out of poverty. Other avenues to middle-class status—crime and small business—were followed by subgroups originally living in poverty. After middle-class status was achieved, then education was valued for the next generation.

Traditionally, one can argue, the function of education was to prepare children for the roles they were to assume in adulthood, and the family provided the preparation. Gradually, provision of education was turned over to the community but with the same goal—preparing children for adult roles.

Poor children are faced with a terrible dilemma. There are few occupational roles for them in their subculture. Their primary contacts are often with people who are out of work and who are dependent on the largesse of the wider community. The schools cannot prepare them for what the children see around them. The other part of the dilemma is that if the educational system does represent preparation for roles in the larger society, then poor children have had little experience with that larger society or those roles or many of the experiences that provide the requisite skills for handling the educational system. The distance between the world and the school and the world of the child is too great; the children may not have the skills to bridge the gap.

Preschool programs were initially established to bridge the distance between the child and the school by altering the child while leaving the educational system untouched. Tough is one of the few researcher practitioners who has assessed poor children and then attempted to alter the educational system so that the children's development would be facilitated. Other efforts in that direction—having teachers speak black dialect or the like—are only token efforts that do not address the fundamental nature of the distance between the poverty child and the schools.

SUMMARY

The evidence presented in this chapter suggests that there are language differences at school entry between children who are reared in poverty and children from middle-class homes. There are also parent–child interaction differences between these two groups across the preschool years. Differences are found both in the amount of interaction between mothers and children and in the kind of talk mothers of different groups address to their children. There are two important questions to be derived from this review: (a) Is there sufficient evidence now to indicate that the mother–child verbal and behavioral interaction patterns are causally related to language development?; (b) Whether they are or not, where should one intervene in order to help poor children perform better in school?

The answer to the first question is that there is not sufficient evidence to single out mother–child interactions as the causal factor for the development of language skills. If mother–child interactions and language learning are related, the interaction patterns act in conjunction with other environmental factors to affect the development of certain language skills. Even if mother–child interaction were the primary causal factor, the ecological validity of various patterns of mother–child interaction must be recognized. The place for intervention to facilitate school performance for poor children is not in the families but in the schools. "Altering the schools" is not merely a glib generalization with which to end this chapter. Professionals who are concerned with child development must begin to work seriously with the implications of our accumulated research findings. The futures of many children are involved; there is no excuse for delay.

REFERENCES

Ainsworth, M. D. S. The development of infant–mother attachment. In B. Caldwell & H. Riccuiti (Eds.), *Review of child development research* (Vol. 3). Chicago: University of Chicago Press, 1973.

Baldwin, A. L., & Baldwin, C. P. The study of mother–child interaction. *American Scientist*, 1973, *61*, 714–721.

Baumrind, D. Child care practices anteceding three patterns of preschool behavior. *Genetic Psychological Monographs*, 1967, *75*, 43–88.

Bereiter, C. An academic preschool for disadvantaged children: Conclusions from evaluation studies. In J. C. Stanley (Ed.), *Preschool programs for the disadvantaged: Five experimental approaches to early childhood education*. Baltimore, Maryland: Johns Hopkins University Press, 1972.

Bernstein, B. Language and social class. *British Journal of Sociology*, 1960, *11*, 271–276.

Bernstein, B. A critique of the concept of compensatory education. In C. B. Cazden, V. P. John, & D. Hymes (Eds.), *The functions of language in the classroom*. New York: Teachers College Press, 1972.

Birch, H. G., & Gussow, J. D. *Disadvantaged children: Health, nutrition and school failure*. New York: Grune & Stratton, 1970.

Blank, M. Mastering the intangible through language. In D. Aaronson & R. W. Rieker (Eds.), *Developmental psycholinguistics and communication disorders*. New York: The New York Academy of Sciences, 1975.

Blank, M., Rose, A., & Berlin, L. T. *The language of learning: The preschool years*. New York: Grune & Stratton, 1978.

Bloom, L. Talking, understanding, and thinking. In R. Schiefelbusch & L. Lloyd (Eds.), *Language perspectives—acquisition, retardation, and intervention*. Baltimore, Maryland: University Park Press, 1974.

Broman, S. H., Nichols, P., & Kennedy, W. *Preschool IQ: Prenatal and early developmental correlates*. Hillsdale, New Jersey: Erlbaum, 1975.

Brown, K. *An analysis of environmental and genetic influence on individual differences in the communicative development of fifty adopted one-year-old children*. Unpublished doctoral dissertation, University of Colorado, 1980.

Clark, K. *Dark ghetto*. New York: Harper & Row, 1965.

Clarke, A. M., & Clarke, A. D. B. (Eds.). *Early experience: Myth and evidence*. New York: Free Press, 1976.

Clarke-Stewart, A., & Apfel, N. Evaluating parental effects on child development. *Review of Research in Education*, 1978, *6*, 47–117.

Cohen, S. E., & Beckwith, L. *Maternal language input in infancy*. Paper presented at the annual meeting of the American Psychological Association, Chicago, September, 1975.

Condon, W. S., & Sander, L. W. Synchrony demonstrated between movement of the neonate and adult speech. *Child Development*, 1974, *45*, 456–462.

Cook-Gumperz, J. *Social control and socialization*. Boston: Routledge & Kegan Paul, 1973.

de Blauw, A., Dubber, C., van Roosmalen, G., & Snow, C. Sex and social class differences in early mother–child interaction. In O. K. Garnica & M. L. King (Eds.), *Language, children and society: The effect of social factors on children learning to communicate*. Oxford, England: Pergamon Press, 1979.

Dorval, B. *The development of conversation*. Unpublished doctoral dissertation. Duke University, 1979.

Douglas, J. *The home and the school: A study of ability and attainment in the primary school*. London: Macgibbon & Kee, 1964.

Fagan, J. The origins of facial pattern recognition. In M. Bornstein & W. Kessen (Eds.), *Psychological development from infancy: Image to intention*. Hillsdale, New Jersey: Erlbaum, 1979.

Farran, D. C., & Burchinal, P. How important is early mother-infant interaction during infancy? Paper presented at the International Conference on Infant Studies, New Haven, Connecticut, April, 1980.

Farran, D. C., & Haskins, R. Reciprocal influence in the social interactions of mothers and 3-year-old children from different socioeconomic backgrounds. *Child Development*, 1980, *51*, 780–791.

Farran, D. C., Haskins, R., & Gallagher, J. J. Poverty and mental retardation: A search for explanations. In J. J. Gallagher (Ed.), *New directions for exceptional children* (Vol. 1). San Francisco: Jossey-Bass, 1980.

Farran, D. C., & Ramey, C. T. Infant day care and attachment behaviors toward mothers and teachers. *Child Development*, 1977, *48*, 1112–1116.

Farran, D. C., & Ramey, C. T. Social class differences in dyadic involvement during infancy. *Child Development*, 1980, *51*, 254–257.

Feagans, L., & Farran, D. C. How demonstrated comprehension can get muddled in production. *Developmental Psychology*, in press.

Gallagher, J., Haskins, R., & Farran, D. C. Poverty and public policy. In T. B. Brazelton & V. C. Vaughan (Eds.), *The family: Setting priorities*. New York: Science and Medicine, 1979.

Gleason, J. B. Talking to children: Some notes on feedback. In C. E. Snow & C. A. Ferguson (Eds.), *Talking to children: Language input and acqusition*. London: Cambridge University Press, 1977.

Golden, M., Birns, B., Bridger, W., & Moss, A. Social class identification in cognitive development among black preschool children. *Child Development*, 1971, *42*, 37–45.

Golden, M., Wagner, H. B., & Montare, A. Social class differences in the ability of young children to use verbal information to facilitate learning. *American Journal of Orthopsychiatry*, 1974, *44*, 86–91.

Haskins, R. Children's play in their neighborhoods. In C. T. Ramey (Chair), *The social ecology of advantaged and disadvantaged children*. Symposium presented at the annual meeting of the National Association of Young Children, Atlanta, November, 1979.

Haskins, R. Personal communication, 1980.

Hess, R. D., & Shipman, V. C. Early experience and the socialization of cognitive modes in children. *Child Development*, 1965, *36*, 869–886.

Hess, R. D., & Shipman, V. C. Cognitive elements in maternal behavior. In J. P. Hill (Ed.), *Minnesota symposia on child psychology*. Minneapolis: University of Minnesota Press, 1967.

Hess, R. D., & Shipman, V. C. Maternal influences upon early learning: The cognitive environments of urban preschool children. In R. D. Hess & R. M. Bear (Eds.), *Early education: Current theory, research, and action*. Chicago: Aldine, 1968.

Higgins, E. Social class differences in verbal communicative accuracy: A question of "which question?" *Psychological Bulletin*, 1976, *83*, 695–714.

Hochstein, J. R., Athanasopoulos, D., & Larkins, J. Poverty area under the microscope. *American Journal of Public Health*, 1968, *58*, 1815–1827.

Hood, L., & Bloom, L. What, when and how about why: A longitudinal study of early expressions of causality. *Monographs of the Society for Research in Child Development*, 1979, *44*, (6, Serial No. 181).

Jay, S., & Farran, D. C. Predicting IQ from mother–child interactions using molecular versus molar codes. *Journal of Applied Developmental Psychology*, in press.

Jensen, A. R. Cumulative deficit in IQ of blacks in the rural south. *Developmental Psychology*, 1977, *13*, 184–191.

John, V. The intellectual development of slum children: Some preliminary findings. *American Journal of Orthopsychiatry*, 1963, *33*, 813–822.

Johnston, R. P., & Singleton, C. H. Social class and communication style: The ability of middle and working class five-year-olds to encode and decode abstract stimuli. *British Journal of Psychology*, 1977, *68*, 237–244.

Kamii, C., & Radin, N. Class differences in the socialization practices of Negro mothers. *Journal of Marriage and the Family*, 1967, *29*, 302–310.

Kilbride, H. W., Johnson, D. L., & Streissguth, A. P. Social class, birth order and newborn experience. *Child Development*, 1977, *48*, 1686–1688.

Lazar, I., Hubbell, V., Murray, H., Rosche, M., & Royce, J. *The persistence of preschool effects: A long-term follow-up of fourteen infant and preschool experiments.* (Final Report for grant # 18-76-07843). Ithaca, New York: Cornell University, Community Service Laboratory, 1977.

Leibowitz, A. Parental inputs and children's achievement. *Journal of Human Resources*, 1977, *12*, 242–251.

LeVine, R. Cross-cultural study in child psychology. In P. H. Mussen (Ed.), *Carmichael's Manual of Child Psychology*, (Vol. 2). New York: Wiley, 1970.

Lewis, M., & Rosenblum, L. A. *The effect of the infant on its caregiver.* New York: Wiley-Interscience, 1974.

Lewis, M., & Wilson, C. D. Infant development in lower-class American families. *Human Development*, 1972, *15*, 112–127.

✗ McGlaughlin, A., Empson, J., Morrissey, M., & Sever, J. Early child development and the home environment: Consistencies at and between four preschool stages. *International Journal of Behavioral Development*, 1980, *3*, 299–309.

Mulhern, R. K., & Passman, R. H. The child's behavioral pattern as a determinant of maternal punitiveness. *Child Development*, 1979, *50*, 815–820.

Nelson, K. Structure and strategy in learning to talk. *Monograph of the Society for Research in Child Development*, 1973, *38* (1-2, Serial No. 149).

Nelson, K. The role of language in infant development. In M. Bornstein & W. Kessen (Eds.), *Psychological development from infancy: Image to intention.* Hillsdale, New Jersey: Erlbaum, 1979.

Ninio, A. Picture book reading in mother–infant dyads belonging to two subgroups in Israel. *Child Development*, 1980, *51*, 587–590.

Olim, E., Hess, R., & Shipman, V. Role of mothers' language styles in mediating their preschool children's cognitive development. *The School Review*, 1967, *75*, 414–424.

Pratt, M. W., Scribner, S., & Cole, M. Children as teachers: Developmental studies of instructional communication. *Child Development*, 1977, *48*, 1475–1481.

Ramey, C. T., & Farran, D. C. *Patterns of dyadic involvement: Infancy to public school.* Paper presented at the International Conference on Infant Studies, New Haven, Connecticut, April, 1980.

Ramey, C. T., & Farran, D. C. The functional maternal concern of mothers for their infants. *Infant Mental Health Journal*, in press.

Ramey, C. T., Farran, D. C., & Campbell, F. A. Predicting IQ from mother–infant interactions. *Child Development*, 1979, *50*, 804–814.

Rosch, R. Style variables in referential language: A study of social class difference and its effect on dyadic communication. In R. Freedle (Ed.), *Discourse production and comprehension* (Vol. I). Norwood, New Jersey: Ablex, 1977.

Rutter, M., & Quinton, D. Psychiatric disorder—ecological factors and concepts of causation. In H. McGurk (Ed.), *Ecological factors in human development.* Amsterdam: North-Holland, 1977.

Scarr, S., & Weinberg, R. IQ test performance of black children adopted by white families. *American Psychologist,* 1976, *31,* 726–739.

Schachter, F. F. *Everyday mother talk to toddlers: Early intervention.* New York: Academic Press, 1979.

Schaefer, E. S. A circumplex model for maternal behavior. *Journal of Abnormal and Social Psychology,* 1959, *59,* 226–235.

Schaffer, H. R. Acquiring the concept of the dialogue. In M. Bornstein & W. Kessen (Eds.), *Psychological development from infancy: Image to intention.* Hillsdale, New Jersey: Erlbaum, 1979.

Schlossman, S. The parent-education game: The politics of child psychology in the 1970s. *Teacher College Record,* 1978, *79,* 788–808.

Sears, R. R., Maccoby, E. E., & Levin, H. *Patterns of child rearing.* New York: Harper & Row, 1957.

Silberman, C. E. *Crisis in the classroom: The remaking of American education.* New York: Random House, 1970.

Snow, C. E., Arlman-Rupp, A., Hassing, Y., Jobse, J., Joosten, J., & Vorster, J. Mother's speech in three social classes. *Journal of Psycholinguistic Research,* 1976, *5,* 1–20.

Stack, C. B. *All our kin.* New York: Harper & Row, 1974.

Thoman, E. B. Infant development viewed within the mother–infant relationship. In E. Quilligan & N. Kretchmer (Eds.), *Perinatal medicine.* New York: Wiley, 1978.

Thomas, A., Chess, S., & Birch, H. *Temperament and behavior disorders in children.* New York: New York University Press, 1968.

Tizard, B., Cooperman, O., Joseph, A., & Tizard, J. Environmental effects on language development: A study of young children in long-stay residential nurseries. *Child Development,* 1972, *43,* 337–358.

Tough, J. *Focus on meaning: Talking to some purpose with young children.* London: Allen & Unwin, 1973.

Tough, J. Children and programmes: How shall we educate the young child? In A. Davies (Ed.), *Language and learning in early childhood.* London: Heinemann, 1977.

Tulkin, S. R. Social class differences in maternal and infant behaviors. In P. H. Leiderman, S. R. Tulkin, & A. Rosenfeld (Eds.), *Culture and infancy: Variations in the human experience.* New York: Academic Press, 1977.

Tulkin, S. R., & Kagan, J. Mother–child interaction in the first year of life. *Child Development,* 1972, *43,* 31–41.

Ward, M. C. *Them children.* New York: Holt, Rinehart, and Winston, 1971.

White, B. L., & Watts, J. C. *Experience and environment.* Englewood Cliffs, New Jersey: Prentice-Hall, 1973.

Whiteman, M., & Deutsch, M. Social disadvantage as related to intellective and language development. In M. Deutsch, I. Katz, & A. Jensen (Eds.), *Social class, race, and psychological development.* New York: Holt, Rinehart, and Winston, 1968.

Whiting, B., & Whiting, J. *Children of six cultures: A psychocultural analysis.* Cambridge, Massachusetts: Harvard University Press, 1975.

Willerman, L. Social aspects of minimal brain dysfunction. In F. F. De Le Cruz, B. H. Fox, R. H. Roberts, & G. Tarjan (Eds.), *Minimal brain dysfunction. Annals of the New York Academy of Science,* 1973, *205,* 164–172.

3

Routines in Mother–Child Interaction[1]

CATHERINE E. SNOW
CLARA DUBBER
AKKE DE BLAUW

There are many reasons to expect that social class would affect a parent's ability to provide a child with the linguistic environment optimal for supporting language acquisition. Social-class groups differ, for example, in their ideologies of childrearing—their notions about such things as what behavior traits are desirable in the child, how much effect the adult can have on the child's course of development, and what teaching or training methods are effective (Ninio, 1979). The social-class group that believes that certain kinds of verbal facility are highly desirable in children, and that verbal facility can be trained, is more likely to provide a linguistic environment that supports that kind of development than a group that values quiet and obedient children (Schaefer, in press; Tulkin & Kagan, 1972). The failure of the second group to provide an optimal language-teaching environment does not result from inability but from a positive choice to optimize other behavior traits; it cannot really be seen as a failure at all since the members of this group in fact succeed in achieving what they desire—children who do what they are told without protest. The failure, if any, occurs when the children from this group

[1] The data presented in the first part of this chapter were collected with financial support from the Faculty of Letters, University of Amsterdam. The transcription and some analysis of the book-reading data were carried out by Beverly Goldfield. An early version of this chapter was presented by Catherine Snow to the American Educational Research Association, April 1980, Boston, Massachusetts.

53

THE LANGUAGE OF CHILDREN
REARED IN POVERTY

are put in situations where they have to live up to expectations more appropriate to children from the other group. At school, for instance, their parents' norms for the ideal child are suddenly superseded by the teachers' norms, which may place higher value on verbal ability than on quiet obedience.

Another situation in which social class might affect the child's access to the optimal language-teaching environment involves no such social-class difference in parental goals. Two social-class groups that have identical notions about the importance of verbal training and verbal ability might nonetheless be differentially able to provide the language-teaching environment they both value. Teaching language and enhancing cognitive development must, in any family's list of priorities, come below ensuring basic survival for their children—providing food, preventing and treating illness, guarding against accidents, etc. The family that—whether because of poverty, chronic illness, large numbers of closely-spaced children, long working hours, poor housing conditions, or other factors—is devoting most of its resources to ensuring basic survival of the children can hardly pay much attention to their linguistic and cognitive development, though they might fully recognize the value of doing so. Studies of the educational goals and childrearing values of low-income mothers have produced conflicting results. Some studies (Tulkin & Kagan, 1972) find important differences between middle-class and working-class parents in their ideologies of childrearing, whereas others (Belle, in press) find that low-income women do not differ greatly from middle-class women in their hopes for their children or in their conceptions of the role of the parent in fostering children's development. Even if similar in aims and beliefs, however, low-income women are much more subject to stress-inducing life events (e.g., loss of employment) and life conditions (e.g., poor housing) that are related to depression and anxiety as well as to different patterns of interaction with their children (Belle, in press).

Middle-class and working-class children might also differ in the nature of the linguistic environment available to them if their parents differed greatly in their knowledge of how to produce the ideal linguistic environment. Thus, parents who were equally interested in preparing their preschoolers to achieve and succeed in first grade might nonetheless go about helping their children in very different ways—one by teaching lots of names for things, another by encouraging the child to ask *why* and *how* questions, and yet another by teaching verses and songs and encouraging verbal play and word games. Such differences in style have, for example, been found by Ninio (1980) in a comparison of middle-class and working-class Israeli mothers reading books to their children. She found that middle-class mothers used much more varied labels for actions and attributes, whereas lower-class mothers tended to teach nouns and to stress comprehension rather than production in their teaching of words. Although Ninio reports no data on the parents' ideology, the different styles she reports are both entirely consistent with an ideology that places high value on language development and parental language teaching.

NATURE OF THE OPTIMAL LINGUISTIC ENVIRONMENT

Discussions of the optimal environment for stimulating language development generally identify a pattern of responsiveness or contingency to the child as the crucial variable. Studies by Cross (1978); Furrow, Nelson, and Benedict (1979); and others (Wells, 1978; Wells, Barnes, & Satterly, personal communication) have all found that children learn to talk faster if their mothers are providing a large proportion of conversational responses that are semantically contingent on the children's own utterances and that fall within limits of complexity matched to the child's own language level. Furthermore, mothers who match their children on the aspects of a situation that they are likely to talk about, and who are very accepting of their children's efforts at words and sentences, are less likely to have children whose language acquisition is delayed (Nelson, 1973). Even in the prelinguistic period, high levels of semantic contingency to children's nonverbal behaviors and prelinguistic vocalizations are related to the children's subsequent language acquisition (Snow, 1979b).

Clearly, providing contingent, responsive talk to children is a style of parenting that is dependent both on a particular ideology of childrearing and on having the resources of time and energy to pay close attention to what children are saying and to respond sensitively to their utterances. The contingent, responsive style can be contrasted with a parenting style that relies much more on directives, on direct teaching and teaching by imitation, and much less on ensuring children's comprehension and full participation. This alternative style of parenting (it is, of course, an oversimplification to see the two styles as more than two poles on a continuum) might be characterized as relying extensively on "routines."

Routines in Parent–Child Interaction

Routine is a word that is used with two very different meanings in the child language literature. It is used by Bloom (1970), Gleason (1980), and others to refer to unanalyzed child utterances that have a purely social function; for example, *hello, good-bye* and *thank you*. Child language analysis normally includes in the category of routines child utterances that, though seemingly appropriate and informative, have a stereotyped character, such as answers to questions (*What do you say, sweetie? ans. Thank you very much, mommy*), which are invariant.

The second use of *routine* is to refer to situations or interactions that are highly predictable, stereotyped, and repetitive (e.g., the "peek-a-boo" routine or the bath routine). Such routines are also frequent and important in classroom activities—the clean-up routine, the snack routine—and their function in classrooms has been extensively discussed (Dickinson, 1980).

I would like to suggest that the ambiguity of the word *routine* reflects a connection between the two types of routines. The connection is that routine utterances are learned in the context of routine situations. Such utterances are called routines in recognition of the fact that the child who uses them has no semantic representation for them. They function purely as place fillers in routinized interactions.

Furthermore, I think it can be demonstrated that children learn a great deal of language from routines. The utterances first learned as place fillers can subsequently be submitted to a semantic and a syntactic analysis, which results in their acquiring a semantic and a syntactic representation. In other words, acquiring routines does not obviate the necessity of acquiring rules; it postpones that necessity somewhat but may also facilitate it.

In this chapter, I will discuss three types of routine situations that occur in parent–child interactions during the prelinguistic and language learning period, and demonstrate: (*a*) How they are structured; (*b*) how they develop and become elaborated with development; and (*c*) how they contribute to language acquisition. It is striking that the same formal structure characterizes all these routine interactions, although they occur at very different points in the child's development and the content and explicit goal of the three routines are very different. The three routines I will discuss are formal games played by mothers with infants during the first year of life, instructional games played during the second year of life, and joint book-reading during the third year of life.

Prelinguistic Games

The structure and function of games during the prelinguistic period has been studied most extensively by Bruner and his associates (Bruner, 1975; Bruner & Sherwood, 1976; Ratner & Bruner, 1978), who have emphasized the isomorphism between game structure and crucial linguistic structures the child will encounter. Bruner sees the prelinguistic game-playing as a chance to discover and practice these linguistic contrasts and distinctions while having fun.

It may be, however, that the primary function of game playing for the mother and infant is that of giving them a shared routine, an interaction opportunity that is sufficiently predictable and practiced so that both can take their turns successfully. The value of such a bit of sure-fire interaction to both parent and infant is obvious: The infant finds it "fun," as evidenced by smiles and laughter, and the parent finds it highly rewarding that the infant is learning something and can communicate. In addition, the infant is, in fact, learning to identify a number of slots in the game and how to fill them.

Let us consider a somewhat idealized version of the development of a game structure. This idealization is based on observations of mother–infant interaction carried out in 9 English and 16 Dutch families. Details of the studies, observational procedures, and findings can be found in Snow, de Blauw, and van Roosmalen (1979), and de Blauw, Dubber, van Roosmalen, and Snow (1979). This structure and development are idealized in the sense that all the stages were not observed for a single game with any mother–child pair. The idealization represents a chaining of developmental links seen in several families and with several different games.

The first stage (see Table 3.1) consists of a maternal intervention and an infant response. For purposes of this idealization, I have chosen the most frequently observed game among the English mothers studied— a tickling game that is played by circling the index finger on the baby's palm, then walking one's fingers up the arm, then tickling the underarm while saying the verse:

Round and round the garden   (circling with index finger)
Like a teddy bear
One step, two step   (walking up arm)
Tickle you under there

In the second stage in the development of this game, an initiatory move and a closing move are added; the initiation is made possible by the infant's recognition of the opening move of the game (taking the hand) and response of heightened attention to that move. The closing move opens up the possibility of further infant response (e.g., request for repetition). In the third stage, the mothers introduce a new slot by pausing during the verse, just before the anticipated tickling. This pause heightens

Table 3.1
Development of Prelinguistic Games

I	II	III	IV
M: I'm gonna tickle you. Round and round the garden Like a teddy bear One step, two step Tickle you under there (tickling B under arm) B: (laughs)	M: Wanna get tickled? (taking B's hand) B: (looks at M) M: Round and round the garden Like a teddy bear One step, two step Tickle you under there (tickling B under arm) B: (laughs) M: That was fun, wasn't it?	M: Wanna get tickled? (taking B's hand) B: (looks at M, smiles) M: Round and round the garden Like a teddy bear One step, two step (pause) Tickle you under there (tickling) B: (laughs) M: Was that fun? B: (laughs) M: Again?	M: Raggedy Ann's gonna tickle you! B: (looks) M: Watch out! B: (looks, smiles) M: Round and round the garden Like a teddy bear One step, two step B: (looks at M, smiles and wriggles) M: Tickle you under there (tickling) B: (laughs) M: Was that fun? B: (laughs) M: Again?

the infant's excitement and enjoyment, but also creates an opportunity for an added infant turn, which is realized in Stage four. A further feature of Stage four, and of successful game playing with older infants in general, is the introduction of objects into the game. After about 5 months, infants typically show a decreased interest in face-to-face interaction and a heightened interest in toys and manipulated objects. Thus, keeping the game going and developing during this period often requires using toys as pseudo-agents in the game.

In sum, playing games with preverbal infants can be seen as creating a set of slots and enabling the infant to fill the slots appropriately. These preverbal games develop by opening up new slots, thus increasing the infant's participation, distributing the work of playing the game more evenly between parent and infant, and creating a more elaborated structure that can include openings, closings, and repeat options as well as the basic game moves.

"Round and round the garden" is a simple game, one played with very young infants, and one that is subject to only limited amounts of elaboration. The game forms studied by Bruner and Sherwood (1976), such as "peek-a-boo," are much more sophisticated, complex, and mature. "Round and round the garden" allows only a very limited range of fillers per slot, whereas "peek-a-boo" derives much of its interest from the choice available for filling the slots. For example, the obligatory slot, "cover face," can be filled by covering either the mother's or the child's face; the covering can be effected by hands, a shirt, a diaper, a curtain, or even just by closing one's eyes. The much simpler games such as I have observed with infants from 3 months on are easy for the infants to learn precisely because they are less variable and more predictable. Infants can start to initiate these very simple games at 8–10 months by producing an early move themselves or by assuming the posture typical of the game. It is, of course, the existence of the well-practiced game routine in the interactional history of the parent–infant pair that makes it possible for the infant to take that sort of communicative initiative and for the parent to recognize it. That the games are well practiced is attested to from our observational data—the frequency of game playing was an average of two times per hour at 3 months and four times per hour at 6 months for the 16 Dutch mother–infant pairs we observed. This means that the average infant had experienced about 1000 bouts of game playing by 6 months of age (Snow, 1979a). Since, however, only three to five games were played with any frequency in most families, these 1000 bouts represent intensive practice of only a few game formats for any infant—ample opportunity to learn the game and to elaborate its structure.

Games constitute, then, an optimal context for infants to initiate communication since the routinization characteristic of games facilitates the infants' identification of potential slots and learning of appropriate fillers and optimizes the chance that parents will recognize infant communicative behaviors. It is not surprising, then, that children's first words are very likely to be "game" words (Nelson, 1973) and that the earliest stage of language comprehension consists of comprehension of utterances from well-practiced games (Benedict, 1979). The role of games and routines in developing children's linguistic ability will be discussed more explicitly in the next section.

Instructional Games

In analyzing continuities in patterns of mother–child interaction from 3 through 17 months, we identified a subclass of interactive routines that had many of the characteristics of games, yet could not actually be classified as games because they did not satisfy the criterion of being purely "for fun."[2] We subsequently came to call these interactions *instructional games* to emphasize their formal similarity to the prelinguistic games while at the same time recognizing that they were initiated by the parents for purposes of teaching the child something. Frequently encountered examples of instructional games were labeling games to teach body parts or animal names, social-routine games to teach *hello* and *good-bye*, telephone games to teach the steps in a telephone conversation, and *What does the X say?* to teach animal noises.

The specific instructional game I will use for illustrative purposes is "the body-part game." An idealized version of its structure and development is presented in Table 3.2.

Typically, the first stage in the development of the body-part game is a highly stereotyped question–response pair, which is subject to no variation by either partner. In the second stage, the complexity of the game is increased by requiring the child to indicate one of several body parts in response to its name. The third stage of development adds another level of complexity: not just variable body parts, but also different bodies. At some point after this sort of game has been well learned, the child may start to initiate the game by pointing to some body part, eliciting from the parent a response like *What's that? Your nose?* or *Is that your nose?* Subsequently, the child can answer the question appropriately for the first time in the development of this game by giving a verbal response in what has been, throughout its entire development,

---

[2] This section is based on data primarily analyzed by Clara Dubber, in her master's thesis "Early language and language acquisition."

TABLE 3.2
Development of Instructional Games

I	II	III	IV	V	VI
M: Where's your nose?	M: Where's your $\begin{bmatrix} nose \\ ears \\ eyes \\ hair \\ etc. \end{bmatrix}$?	M: Where's $\begin{bmatrix} mommy's \\ daddy's \\ teddy's \end{bmatrix}$ $\begin{bmatrix} nose \\ ears \\ eyes \\ hair \\ etc. \end{bmatrix}$?	E: (points) M: What's that? Your nose?	B: (points) M: What's that?	B: What's dat? $\begin{bmatrix} nose \\ ears \\ eyes \\ hair \\ etc. \end{bmatrix}$
B: (points appropriately)	B: (points appropriately)	B: (points appropriately)		B: $\begin{bmatrix} nose \\ ears \\ eyes \\ hair \\ etc. \end{bmatrix}$	

a language-teaching game. Some children take the development of the game even one step further by assuming the role of questioner, preparatory either to answering the question themselves or to demanding an answer from the parent. This phenomenon of the child taking over the parent's turn, and thus playing both parts in a conversation, has also been commented on by Scollon (1979).

Instructional games, like the preverbal games discussed above, create slots. The child is now expected to fill in the slots with linguistic responses. Interestingly, the game structure that, for the adult observers, resides strongly in the turn alternation, evidently has a different character for the child. For the child, the slots are not strongly identified with a person—just the opposite, in fact; the slots that had been Mommy's become the child's, to the point that the child will even produce several adjacent turns, totally ignoring the turn-alternation requirement.

Dubber (1978) analyzed the frequency of instructional games in observations of 17-month-old Dutch children and analyzed the similarities among the games played in different families. She found that such games occurred two to four times per hour and that there was little variation, either within or across families, in the types of games played. As for the prelinguistic games discussed previously, then, children have considerable opportunity for practicing the games their parents consider important enough to play.

Book Reading

A third highly routinized situation typical of parent interaction with preschool children consists of looking at picture books. Ninio and Bruner (1978) and Ninio (1980) have documented the routine nature of interaction episodes organized around looking at simple pictures. They identified the steps in the interaction as establishing joint attention (*Look! What's that?*), eliciting response (*What is that? What's that called?*), response (at first, just looking at the picture; later, some other vocalization; still later, a word), and evaluation (*That's right, it's a rabbit*). It was striking how few different maternal utterances were used in each of the various slots and how the required child behavior increased in sophistication.

The Ninio data reveal the same kind of progressive elaboration of child response possibilities and increasing precision of child response as that just discussed for the two types of games. A slightly later stage in book reading, a book-reading style typical of some, but not all, parent–child pairs,[3] consists of a very explicit exploitation of the slot-plus-

---

[3] I am indebted to Courtney Cazden for pointing out, in her discussion of this paper at AERA, the different ways in which book reading can be routinized by different mother–child pairs.

filler format. Consider the following dialogue between a child aged 3:1 and his mother while reading *The Cat in the Hat* (1958) by Dr. Seuss (this excerpt is taken from the middle of the reading because the tape recorder was not functioning during the first few pages of the book; it is, however, typical of the entire sequence):

MOTHER	CHILD
he came down with a bump	
from there on the wall	
and sally and I	
we saw all the things	
	things fall
and our fish came down too	
he fell into a pot	
he said	
do I like this?	
no I do	
	not
this not a good game	
said our fish as he lit	
no I do not like it	
not one	
	eh little bit
now look what you did	
said the fish to the cat	
now look at his house	
look at this	
look at that	
you sank our toy ship	
sank it deep in the	
	cake?
you shook up our house	
and you bent our new	
	rake?
you should not be here when	
our mother is not	
you get out of this house	
said the	
	fish in de pot
turn the page	
but I like to be here	
oh I like it a lot	
said the cat in the hat to	
the fish in the pot	
I will not go away	
I do not wish to go	
and so said the cat in the hat	
	so so so so

I will show you another good
  game that I

               know

turn the page
and then he ran out
as fast as a fox
the cat in the hat came back
  in with a

               box

a big red wood box was

               shut with a hook

now look at this trick
said the cat

               take a look

then he got up on top of the
  tip of his hat

               hat

I call this game

               fun in a box

said the

               cat

in this box are

               two things I will
               will show them to
               you

I will pick up the hook
you will see something new
two things
and I call them

               thing one and
               thing two

I can't read it unless you
  hold it up in your lap.
Okay you have to put it in
  your lap so that you can
  read it and then I can
  read it, too.
There.
these things will not

               bite you

they want to

               have fun

then out of the

               box?

came

               thing two and
               thing one

umm
they said how do you do
would you like to shake hands

               with thing two and
               thing one

and sally and I did not know
what to do
so we had to shake hands

　　　　　　　　　　　with thing one and
　　　　　　　　　　　thing two

have no fear little fish
said the cat in the hat
these things are good things
and he gave them

　　　　　　　　　　　pat

they are tame oh so tame
they have come here to play
they will give you some fun
on this

　　　　　　　　　　　wet wet wet wet day

The above dialogue took place 4 weeks after the child had received a copy of *The Cat in the Hat* and after somewhere between 10 and 20 readings of it with his mother. Clearly, the kind of slot filling demonstrated by him was much supported by the rhyme structure of the book— the majority of the phrases filled in were the second parts of rhymes. However, just 3 months later, the child was capable of supplying much more than rhyming words and short phrases. Consider the following performance, at age 3:4:

MOTHER   CHILD

What's that say?

　　　　　　　　　　　the cat in the hat
　　　　　　　　　　　by doctor seuss
　　　　　　　　　　　the cat in the
　　　　　　　　　　　　hat
　　　　　　　　　　　(slowly with pauses
　　　　　　　　　　　　between words)
　　　　　　　　　　　the sun did not shine
　　　　　　　　　　　it was too wet to play
　　　　　　　　　　　so we sat in our . . . sat in the
　　　　　　　　　　　　house all dat cold cool wet
　　　　　　　　　　　　day
　　　　　　　　　　　I sat dere eh sally
　　　　　　　　　　　sat dere we two
　　　　　　　　　　　eh something to wisheh
　　　　　　　　　　　something to do
　　　　　　　　　　　too wet to go out
　　　　　　　　　　　too cold to play ball
　　　　　　　　　　　so we sat in the house doin'
　　　　　　　　　　　　nothing at all
　　　　　　　　　　　all we could do sit sit sit

> *sit*
> *eh like it one little bit*
> *then something went bump*
>
> *how that bump made us jump*
> *and look eh eh eh . . . it was*
>   *the cat in the hat*
> *why would you sit there like*
>   *dat*
> *I know is eh wet*
> *and know sun is not shining*
> *you can have a good fun*
>   *an have*
> *fish is goin up up with the*
>   *fish*
> *dere's a fish*

Or consider the following excerpt, which covers exactly the same pages as the first part of the passage cited before from 3 months previously:

MOTHER	CHILD
	dat is not all can I do said
	the cat
	then he fell on his head
	came with a bump
	hoppin' on the ball
Sally	
	I saw all the things fall
the fish	
	said
came down	
	fell . . . into a pot
this is not a good game	
	fish said
	what?
I do not	
	I'm finished
you're finished	
	yeah
okay	

Clearly, now the child is providing the majority of the structure for the "reading." His mother fills in until the appropriate slot is created for his next available filler, but she is now producing considerably less of the text than he is (despite the fact that she can read the book, whereas he must work from memory!). Admittedly, his rendition is not perfect—even the initial, memorized chunk shows considerable deletion and restructuring. However, the child does not allow his memory failures to lose him the floor in these performances; he is now in the position of

TABLE 3.3
Development of Book-Reading Routine

	I	II	III	IV	V
C:	*Who's that?*	*Who's that X.*			
M:	*X*	*X, right.*			
		What's X doing?			
C:	*X*	*X doing?*	*X Ying.*		
M:	*X, right.*	*X is Ying.*	*That's right.*		
C:			*X have?*		
M:			*X has a Z*		
C:			*a Z.*	*YZ*	*X has a Z*
M:			*right, a Z*	*right*	*Yes he does*
C:					*Why X has a Z?*
M:					*Because P.*

providing slots and waiting for appropriate fillers from his mother, rather than the other way around.

Another, much more sophisticated kind of routinization of book reading has been discussed elsewhere, based on data from this same child (see Snow, in press). That analysis was based on successive readings of a very different kind of book—Richard Scarry's *Storybook Dictionary* (1967), which presents on each page 10 to 18 different units of pictures and text, each unit in itself highly complex. Snow demonstrates the ways in which this potentially very chaotic book-reading situation is routinized at several levels: (*a*) By adhering to a standard format for reading this book, according to which only one or two pictures per page were discussed; (*b*) by establishing the routine that the child made the picture selections; (*c*) by discussing the same pictures again and again at successive sessions; (*d*) by producing very similar sequences of conversational moves with reference to any given topic.

At the levels, then, of basic format, of picture selection, of topic selection, and of conversational moves during topic discussion, routinization was evident, and the interactions could be seen to be highly structured and predictable. An idealized example of the routinization of the conversation at the level of topic discussion was presented by Snow (in press), and is reproduced here as Table 3.3. It is argued that this kind of routinization enabled the child in question to use these book-reading sessions as a very potent context for learning language.

CONCLUSION

Several years ago, in a study of social class differences in mothers' speech (Snow, Arlman-Rupp, Hassing, Jobse, Joosten, & Vorster, 1976), we found that mothers' speech was more complex in book reading than in a free-play situation. At that time, we suggested that this resulted from the greater contextual support for speech available during book reading; the presence of the book served to focus attention and determine topics, so these tasks need not be fulfilled by maternal utterances. The automatic establishment of joint attention to an agreed-upon topic freed the mother to make more sophisticated, and thus linguistically more complex, comments than would be possible during free play.

Although this explanation cannot be ruled out, I now feel that a much more potent reason for the greater complexity of "book talk" can be found in the accompanying routinization. Routines enable participants to deal with complexity. We think of routines as simple and unsophisticated—the product of memory, not of rule use. But their simplicity allows for the introduction, into the slots created by the routine, of fillers considerably more complex in structure and–or content, than could possibly be dealt with elsewhere. The slot, by its predictability, provides the opportunity for novel, complex, and creative fillers to be inserted.

Relevance to the Child Reared in Poverty

The use of routines in interactions with young children provides a sharp contrast to the style of interaction generally considered most facilitative to language acquisition, a style in which responsiveness, contingency, and fine tuning to the child's level of ability and interest are considered crucial. Routines are not fine-tuned to individual children; they are played off at the mother's initiation, and they can work whether or not children understand or can analyze the utterances used.

There is evidence to suggest that some groups of children growing up in poverty are more likely to be exposed to the extensive use of routines, especially comprehension routines, than to responsive, contingent interaction styles (see, for example, Margaret Ward's *Them Children,* 1971—a study of rural blacks). The argument made here would lead to the conclusion that the exploitation of routine styles of interaction can contribute to language acquisition, much as the use of contingent styles can. Why, then, are poor children at risk for delayed language and for failure at the tasks of reading and writing that require sophisticated language skills?

The answer may have to do with the possibilities for developing, elaborating, and expanding on the routines; positive effects on children's language may come primarily in the later stages of development of any routine, when the child is taking a relatively active role in the routine. Getting the routine developed and elaborated requires having gone through it many times, with considerable time and attention devoted to each run-through. Consider the low-income parent who is caring for several young children; who is singly responsible for cooking, cleaning, and child care, often in addition to holding down a job; who has little access to time- and energy-saving appliances; whose housing conditions are inadequate; who is likely to be suffering from poor nutrition and poor health; and who is at high risk for depression and other mental health problems associated with the combination of poverty and powerlessness (Belle, in press). Is this parent likely to be able to sit and read a book with her 2-year-old for 20 minutes a day? Is this parent likely to interrupt bathing her 1-year-old in order to play "Where's your nose?" Though, out of necessity, her interactions with her children are likely to be controlling and routinized, the potential for elaboration of the routine, which may be crucial in the routine's contribution to language acquisition, is probably absent.

In general, lower-class mothers have been described as being less responsive, less well-tuned to their children (e.g., Hess & Shipman, 1965), and it has been suggested that this deficiency on the part of the parent explains the children's linguistic and cognitive deficits. I think it is clear that this explanation is greatly oversimplified. There are different styles of childrearing, and the highly responsive, contingent, finely tuned, individualized style favored by middle-class North American mothers is not the only way to produce children with well-developed linguistic and cognitive abilities. Cross-cultural studies, which have provided data from groups that do not utilize this style (e.g. Harkness, 1977; Richman, 1980), have made this abundantly clear. However, whatever style might be favored by a given culture or social group, implementation of that style requires considerable resources from the parent. The parent whose resources are directed to ensuring that her children are adequately fed and housed will have little time or energy left over for teaching her child or for playing with him or her. The styles of interaction with one's children may be much less important to the children's development than their access to interaction. Highly indirect methods of solving the consequences of poverty for children have been tried; intervention programs, daycare centers, home training programs, and parent education programs can all be shown to have some positive effect on children's development. It seems very likely that eliminating the stress-inducing aspects of poverty would have at least as great an impact on the children. It is clear that social class is a *package variable,* a shorthand term for describing many differences between groups of children: (*a*) in parents' income, (*b*) in parents' sense of financial security, (*c*) in parental education, (*d*) in the kind of job parents hold, (*e*) perhaps in parents' goals or desires for their children, (*f*) very likely in children's access to interaction with their parents, and (*g*) perhaps also in parents' range of styles of interaction with their children. It is not yet clear to what extent and how these different components of the social class differences may interact; whether, for example, a particular style of interaction with children is caused by financial insecurity or by the parents' ideology. It might be that poor women make poor mothers, not because they are incapable of being good mothers, but because the problems created by poverty prevent them from caring for their children as they would like. In any case, it is clear that children are capable of learning to talk in many different ways and in many different environments. Parental contribution to their children's language acquisition, and to their cognitive development in general, is not limited by any particular style of parenting.

REFERENCES

Belle, D. E. *Lives in stress: A context for depression.* Beverly Hills, California: Sage, in press.

Benedict, H. Early lexical development: Comprehension and production. *Journal of Child Language,* 1979, *6,* 183–200.

Bloom, L. *Language development: Form and function in emerging grammars.* Cambridge, Massachusetts: MIT Press, 1970.

Bruner, J. S. The ontogenesis of speech acts. *Journal of Child Language,* 1975, *2,* 1–21.

Bruner, J. S., & Sherwood, V. Peekaboo and the learning of rule structures. In J. S. Bruner, A. Jolly & K. Sylva (Eds.), *Play: Its role in development and evolution.* Harmondsworth: Penguin, 1976.

Cross, T. Mothers' speech and its association with rate of linguistic development in young children. In N. Waterson & C. Snow (Eds.), *The development of communication.* London: Wiley, 1978.

de Blauw, A., Dubber, C., van Roosmalen, G., & Snow, C. Sex and social class differences in early mother–child interaction. In O. Garnica & M. King (Eds.), *Language, children and society.* New York: Pergamon Press, 1979.

Dickinson, D. *Routines and rituals: The multiple meanings of classroom procedures.* Qualifying paper, Harvard Graduate School of Education, 1980.

Dubber, C. *Vroegtalige periode en taalverwerving (Early language and language acquisition).* Master's thesis, Institute for General Linguistics, University of Amsterdam, 1978.

Furrow, D., Nelson, K., & Benedict, H. Mothers' speech to children and syntactic development: Some simple relationships. *Journal of Child Language,* 1979, *7,* 423–442.

Gleason, J. B. The acquisition of social speech: Routines and politeness formulas. In H. Giles, P. Robinson & P. Smith (Eds.), *Language: Social psychological perspectives.* Oxford, England: Pergamon Press, 1980.

Harkness, S. Aspects of social interaction and first language environment in rural Africa. In C. Snow & C. Ferguson (Eds.), *Talking to children: Language input and acquisition.* London: Cambridge University Press, 1977.

Hess, R., & Shipman, V. Early experience and the socialization of cognitive modes in children. *Child Development,* 1965, *36,* 869–886.

Nelson, K. Structure and strategy in learning to talk. *Monographs of the Society for Research in Child Development,*1973, *38*(1–2), Serial No. 149.

Ninio, A. Picture-book reading in mother–infant dyads belonging to two subgroups in Israel. *Child Development,* 1980, *51,* 587–590.

Ninio, A. The naive theory of the infant and other maternal attitudes in two subgroups in Israel. *Child Development,*1979, *50,* 976–980.

Ninio, A., & Bruner, J. The achievement and antecedents of labelling. *Journal of Child Language,* 1978, *5,* 1–15.

Ratner, N., & Bruner, J. Games, social exchange, and the acquisition of language. *Journal of Child Language,* 1978, *5,* 391–402.

Richman, A. *Gusii mothers and children as caregivers.* Seminar on the Development of Infants & Parents. Fifth Annual Conference on Infancy, Boston, 1980.

Scarry, R. *Storybook dictionary.* London: Hamlyn, 1967.

Schaefer, E. S. Development of adaptive behavior: Conceptual models and family correlates. In M. Begab, H. Garber, & H. C. Haywood (Eds.), *Prevention of retarded development in psychosocially disadvantaged children.* Baltimore, Maryland: University Park Press, in press.

Scollon, R. A real early stage: An unzippered condensation of a dissertation on child language. In E. Ochs & B. Schieffelin (Eds.), *Developmental Pragmatics*. New York: Academic Press, 1979.

Seuss, Dr. (Theodore Geisel). *The cat in the hat*. New York: Beginner Books (Random House), 1958.

Snow, C. E. The role of social interaction in language acquisition. In A. Collins (Ed.), *Children's language and communication: 12th Minnesota Symposium on Child Psychology*. Hillsdale, New Jersey: Erlbaum, 1979.(a)

Snow, C. E. *Are parents language teachers?* Paper presented at the Conference on the Socialization of Children in a Changing World, Cincinnati, April, 1979.(b)

Snow, C. E. Saying it again: The role of expanded and deferred imitations in language acquisition. In K. E. Nelson (Ed.), *Children's language* (Vol. 4). New York: Wiley, in press.

Snow, C. E., Arlman-Rupp, A., Hassing, Y., Jobse, J., Joosten, J., & Vorster, J. Mothers' speech in three social classes. *Journal of Psycholinguistic Research*, 1976, *5*, 1–20.

Snow, C. E., de Blauw, A., & van Roosmalen, G. Talking and playing with babies; the role of ideologies of childrearing. In M. Bullowa (Ed.), *Before speech*. New York: Cambridge University Press, 1979.

Tulkin, S. R., & Kagan, J. Mother–child interaction in the first year of life. *Child Development*, 1972, *43*, 31–41.

Ward, M. *Them children: A study in language learning*. New York: Holt, Rinehart and Winston, 1971.

Wells, C. G. What makes for successful language development? In R. Campbell & P. Smith (Eds.), *Advances in the psychology of language* (Vol. 2). New York: Plenum, 1978.

Wells, C. G., Barnes, S. B., & Satterly, D. Characteristics of adult speech which predict children's language development. Personal communication.

II

Language Use and Schooling

Language as a critical skill for school adaptation and learning has been a theme of much of the research and intervention for poverty children. These three chapters raise important questions about which, if any, specific aspects of language are important for school performance as well as whether any aspect of language is really as important as societal pressures and norms. Marion Blank's chapter is focused on literacy and how particular aspects of oral language development relate to and are different from critical aspects of literacy. Lynne Feagans stresses the importance of the development of narrative skills for understanding and communicating much of the thematic information transmitted in schools. John Ogbu, from an anthropological point of view, discusses the forces within the black poverty culture and the wider society that shape language and general attitudes toward school learning. All three chapters propose different intervention strategies, based on their particular viewpoints, that would help children succeed in school.

4

Language and School Failure: Some Speculations about the Relationship between Oral and Written Language[1]

MARION BLANK

Since the 1960s, there has been a growing interest in the oral language difficulties found among large numbers of children in our population. This movement reflects a complicated network of ideas. In part, it is a by-product of a concern not with oral language itself, but rather with written language; that is, many students in our schools experience deep and pervasive difficulties in both reading and writing. Since success in the written language system is vital to most academic achievement, the failure in literacy impairs students' total scholastic functioning, leaving them at a major disadvantage in our highly complex technological society.

Because of these factors, considerable effort has been mobilized toward developing programs to enhance literacy. The greatest attention, however, has been directed toward early oral language development. Although this development may seem somewhat paradoxical, its cause is not difficult to discern. Our culture maintains strongly held beliefs about the role of early experience in later development. From this per-spective, it is reasonable to seek the basis for written language difficulties in much earlier appearing skills. Support for this orientation is also avail-able in the many empirical studies that have shown a strong correlation between early oral language skills and reading achievement (Benton & Pearl, 1978). These studies reinforce the idea that the key to effective literacy rests with improved oral language functioning.

[1] This work was supported by National Institute of Child Health and Human De-velopment, HD12278.

For purposes of identifying children at risk for failure, the correlation between oral and written language achievement has proven to be meaningful. It enables one to predict, with reasonable accuracy, which children at 4 and 5 years of age are likely to be failing in school when they are 8 or 10 years of age. For purposes of treatment, the correlation is not particularly informative but nevertheless it has been used as if it did reflect both the cause and cure of the problem. Specifically, the correlations have been used to determine the content of the treatment in that any skill correlating with reading achievement is likely to become part of oral language instruction. Thus a typical program designed to reduce school failure might include a segment of syntax training, one on semantics training, and one on story narratives since all of these measures differentiate successful from nonsuccessful achievers.

Many problems result from this approach. First, the instruction follows from the content of tests rather than from a coherent theoretical framework. Essentially, each of the many testable skills of young children is a candidate for inclusion into the curriculum. As a result, teachers are forced to deal with an overwhelming number of discrete and vaguely related skills. No clear rationale is offered to indicate how the skills relate to one another, which of them ought to be treated as central, which as subordinate, and so on. Thus, the teachers are given the heavy responsibility of affecting the children's functioning without having been provided with any coherent system for understanding the extraordinarily complex area of behavior they are supposed to foster.

Second, with the instruction representing the content of a test rather than the content of natural exchange, the language that is used is often artificial making it unlikely that the children will transfer the skills to the noninstructional situation. For instance, in a unit on morphology, the children might deal with 20 consecutive sentences involving the pluralization of nouns. This teaching procedure, which trains the children on the content of tests, often serves mainly to lessen the correlation between the test and school performance, rather than to enhance the children's verbal functioning.

Third, and perhaps of greatest importance, is the fact that although the tested skills may correlate with reading, many of them are probably not causally related to either oral or written language acquisition. As a result, much of the teaching effort is misdirected and unnecessary. This point is difficult to grasp when one remains within the domain of language since, at least, a *prima facie* case can be made to relate any oral language skill to written language achievement. For example, if a child does poorly in vocabulary, one can state that the enhancement of vocabulary is necessary if he or she is to be able to understand the content of a written text.

When one leaves the realm of language, however, the dangers of relying upon correlations between tests become clear. For example, Satz, Taylor, Friel, and Fletcher (1978) have found that a finger localization test in kindergarten is one of the best predictors of reading achievement in the early elementary grades (i.e., with the eyes closed, the child has to recognize which finger[s] has been tapped by a tester). The task is an accepted part of a neurological battery, and the correlation is probably not an artifact but a reflection of a meaningful relationship to reading achievement (e.g., it may reflect developmental immaturity or subtle neurological damage). Training on the test, however, is quite a different matter. Because the task is so clearly different from reading, few would argue that training on finger localization would be a productive path to follow in trying to prevent or overcome the difficulties of poor readers. I believe that similar difficulties arise when one considers tests in the language realm. Although an oral language test may correlate with reading achievement, one cannot thereby conclude that the skill is necessary for reading or that training on the skill will facilitate reading.

Having rejected the approach of training to test performance, we are faced with the key problem of offering an alternative strategy. This issue will form the core of my presentation. I will begin by attempting to reframe the basic question that guides both research and therapy. As indicated by the previous comments, much of the effort until now has been predicated on the question, "What skills in early oral language correlate with later written language mastery?" An alternate approach is to start with the behavior that initially aroused concern (i.e., the failure in literacy) and ask the following: What are the essential characteristics of written language; to what degree are these characteristics found in oral language; and to what extent do these characteristics pose problems for children who are experiencing difficulties in mastering reading? This three-part question will guide the remainder of the material to be presented here.

In dealing with the first part of the question—the essential characteristics of reading—I would like to suggest the following five qualities: (a) the disembedded quality of reading; (b) the sustained, sequential aspect of written discourse; (c) the implicit connectedness of ideas; (d) the conventions of written language; (e) the receptiveness of reading. Each of these will be discussed in turn.

THE DISEMBEDDED QUALITY OF READING

The term *disembedded quality* is one that I have borrowed from Margaret Donaldson. In an interesting book entitled *Children's Minds*

(1978), Donaldson attempts to define the characteristics of classroom discourse—that is, oral language discourse—that may cause difficulty for many children. The quality that she finds most significant is the abstract, "decontextualized" character of much of the language exchange. She puts it as follows:

> It is when we are dealing with people and things in the context of fairly immediate goals and intentions and familiar patterns of events that we feel most at home . . . However, when we move beyond the bounds of human sense, there is a dramatic difference. Thinking which does move beyond these bounds so that it no longer operates within the supportive context of meaningful events is often called "formal" or "abstract.". . . To reduce the risk of confusion . . . I shall speak rather of "disembedded thinking" (with formal being one way of disembedding). The better you are at tackling problems without having to be sustained by human sense, the more likely you are to succeed in our educational system [p. 75, 77].

Donaldson goes on to claim that a child who can handle the formulation, *If p, then q,* will be more successful than a child who can only deal with the formulation when it is in such terms as *If there are houses, then there are doors.*

Although Donaldson considers oral language exchange, many of her comments are valid for the world of written language as well. Reading by its very nature has a disembedded quality. It generally does not go to the contentless extreme of an *If p, then q* formulation. Nevertheless, even when there are supporting pictures, the ideas in a book do not have the power of an actual event. For example, imagine a child who is at home and hungry. In this situation, he could easily and without much reflection say, *I want a sandwich,* or some comparable request. When a similar event is depicted in a book, the child himself no longer has the internal cues (i.e., the feeling of hunger) or external cues (i.e., the kitchen nearby, a supportive figure who complies with requests, etc.) that meaningfully tie the language to the context. In other words, the language is disembedded from the physical context in which it would naturally occur. This single, simple example is trivial. It is offered here only to illustrate the point that disembedding occurs even in the simplest cases of text. Once text becomes more complex, the disembedding becomes increasingly powerful and significant.

In considering the second part of the question posed—namely, to what degree is this characteristic found in oral language—we find an interesting phenomenon. If one analyzes the verbal interactions involving children, it seems clear that much of the language used by children is embedded and context-bound. For example, a child whose finger is bothering her might say to her mother, *I have got a sore finger,* or a child who wants to put on a particular dress might say *I can wear this;* a child who does not want to get on the school bus says, *I am not going to school*. Disembedding clearly and not surprisingly does not represent a dominant mode of verbal exchange for children (and possibly for few adults as well).

In children who are becoming adept at higher level language skills, however, instances of disembedded language begin clearly to emerge. For example, I recently saw a 4-year-old who was asking his mother about "how babies are made." Most surprisingly, from the mother's point of view, his concern was not what she and most adults would have anticipated. As she tried to explain about reproduction, he interrupted and made himself clear by stating, *Not that, I mean: Do they come out just with bones and then someone puts the skin around them?*

The richness of this anecdote allows it to be interpreted in multiple ways. From a Piagetian point of view, it can be used as further evidence for the conceptual limitations of the preschooler. But from the Donaldson point of view, the exchange has major elements of disembedding. There is no immediate physical need or problem confronting the child (i.e., he is not faced with the task of constructing a baby), and there are no contextual cues currently available to support the question (i.e., this particular question was triggered by the child having seen a picture of a human skeleton in an encyclopedia some days before). While this particular question is not nearly as disembedded as an *if p, then q* formulation, it nevertheless appears to have major elements of the de-contextualized thought to which Donaldson refers.

If we now turn to the third part of the question guiding the approach being offered here, we confront the problem: To what extent does this quality pose problems for children who experience reading difficulties? Because of the paucity of research in this area, no firm answer can be offered. However, in studies that my colleagues and I have conducted (Blank, Rose, & Berlin, 1978) we have obtained evidence that disembedded language, represented by questions requiring such processes as prediction (e.g., *What will happen . . . ?*) and justification (e.g., *How did you know . . . ?*), is mastered by children 5 years of age who are likely to succeed in reading but poorly mastered by children who are at risk for failure to read.

This finding is not particularly revealing in itself since so many cognitive tasks, particularly language-based cognitive tasks, yield differences between successful and unsuccessful students. The finding, however, becomes potentially more significant when one recognizes the trend to dismiss this type of language as being irrelevant or unimportant. I first encountered this view some years ago while conducting an intervention program for children who were at risk for school failure (Blank, 1973).

In documenting principles used in the teaching, I offered an example of a child who, upon noticing an adult put on a coat, said, *You're going home.* The adult replied, *Yes, but how do you know I'm going home?* At that point, the child replied, *You're not going home?*

It is the adult's question that has aroused controversy. The claim has been made that the question is "unfair" since the child knew that the adult was leaving. Why should the child have been put through a "test" where she has to justify her observation? The response to this criticism rests with one's view of language. If one feels that language should be limited to descriptions of ongoing events, feelings, and desires (embedded language), then clearly the question is unnecessary and potentially confusing. If one feels, however, that language ought to be used as a symbol system that transcends the immediate physical context, then the question is both necessary and desirable. Furthermore, if one lives in a literate society, I believe that the latter choice is unavoidable. Once a child is past primer-level skills, reading, by definition, requires dealing with a symbol system that transcends the immediate physical context. If, as I propose, *disembedded oral language skills* are precursors to written language mastery, then these oral language skills are not "unfair tests" but an essential foundation for literacy.

THE SUSTAINED, SEQUENTIAL ASPECT OF WRITTEN LANGUAGE

A second feature of written language is its use of long verbal chains. The term *chain* is not meant to represent a behaviorist view of language, but rather the fact that reading involves sentences—with one sentence following another for extended sequences. The sustained, sequential aspect that is so typical of written language is not characteristic of much oral language. As in the examples of children's comments earlier (e.g., *I've got a sore finger,* and *I'm not going to school*), much conversation occurs as one or two relatively isolated utterances. Even when the conversation continues, there is no clear demand for maintaining a continuous theme. Hence, after the comment about a sore finger, a bandage might be applied, and that particular topic might end. Essentially, much of oral language might be seen as representing perceptual–verbal connections in that each utterance is tied to a clear physical context. By contrast, much of written language might be seen as verbal–verbal connections because the language at one point is meaningful only insofar as it is tied to language at a preceding point. This distinction is not meant to represent an all-or-none phenomenon; rather it is intended to highlight a feature that generally distinguishes the two language systems.

As in the case of *disembedded language,* conversation at times shows the sustained, sequential aspect of written language. Susan Isaacs (1930), in her reports on preschool children, has documented the sophisticated skills that can be found in this realm by 4 and 5 years of age. Unfortunately, relatively little attention has been paid to this phenomenon. Considerable research effort in oral language has been devoted to the analysis of language at the level of the word and the sentence, but relatively little at the level of connected discourse. In order to provide some insight into the phenomenon being discussed, the material that follows offers a segment of dialogue between a teacher and a 6-year-old learning disabled boy. A physical object (a book) is present, but the exchange is characteristic of verbal–verbal dialogue in that the language is not tied to a motivating physical context that can elicit the child's active involvement. The book essentially serves as a point of departure for a series of questions, with one question building upon the previous one—hence, a verbal–verbal exchange.

ADULT	CHILD
1. *Jim, look at this, we're going to be talking about this book today* (pointing to a wordless book; for example, a storybook based on pictures alone).	2. (picks up pen from table, then glances over at book)
3. *You know, this is a special book. Look through the pages and tell me how it's different from other books* (points to other books on table).	4. (rolls pen around in hand)
5. (takes pen from child) *Let me put this away. You can play with it later.*	6. (picks up a plastic bowl and moves it around the table)
7. *Look through the pages and tell me how you think it's different.*	
	8. (quickly leafs through pages) *He's fallin' in* (points to picture, then quickly picks up a pen).

As long as the dialogue remained confined to this level, the child remained disinterested, uncomfortable, and taciturn. Once the teacher redirected the exchange so that it involved a perceptual–verbal dialogue (i.e., dramatizing the actions depicted in the book), the child's behavior changed dramatically. The following segment is illustrative of the process.

ADULT	CHILD
1. *Let's try and make something that looks just like this picture* (referring to a boy fishing). *Let's first get a bucket* (points to bucket on table) . . .	2. (reaches over, moves bucket closer to adult) (This action, in contrast to ones in the prior segment is not an attempt to "leave" the exchange; rather it reflects a desire to cooperate with the adult's suggestion)
3. . . . *and fill it with some water. Do you see any place in this room where we could get water?*	4. (looks around room, then points toward sink) *Yeah, over there.*
5. *Could you go over and fill up the bucket?*	6. (goes over to sink and fills up bucket, then returns to table)
7. *Now, I'd like you to pour some of that water in this tub* (points)	8. (starts to pour water in tub) *All of it?* (this is the first instance in the entire lesson of the child initiating an idea. It further suggests his comfort and freedom in this setting).
9. *That's a very good question. Let's see. How about putting up to this line* (draws a line in the tub).	10. *All right* (pours water up to mark) *There's just a teeny bit in there* (referring to remainder left in bucket). (Again the child is initiating

11. *Right, there's
    just a teeny bit
    left over. Where
    is most of the
    water now?*

his own ideas in the
exchange)

12. *In there* (points to
    tub).

These two small segments of dialogue raise interesting questions. The differences in the child's responsivity in the two exchanges might be attributed to motivation so that his seeming limitations in the first segment are seen only as performance variables (e.g., fear, disinterest, etc.) and not as a reflection of any limitations in his verbal competence. In this view, the second segment made him more comfortable, thereby allowing his language behavior to emerge and show its strength.

This argument represents an important and complex issue that cannot be dealt with easily. My own opinion is that the motivation is a consequence and not a cause of the language behavior. Specifically, I believe that verbal–verbal, disembedded exchanges are different for young children and continue to be difficult for the children with problems in the academic setting. They do not understand the organization and rules by which such exchanges are carried on, which causes them to feel confused and defensive. By contrast, the realm of perceptual–verbal, embedded exchanges is clear and more easily mastered. In such a dialogue, one does not have to retain what occurred even one or two exchanges earlier. Instead, the physical context serves as a powerful aid so that each utterance seems clear and meaningful in its own right (talking about the water, the bucket, etc.), and no attention need be paid to the continuity among exchanges. To the degree that continuity exists, it is generally a by-product of the physical context remaining unchanged and not the result of the speaker's effort to maintain a consistent theme. If this hypothesis is correct, it suggests that the strength or extent of a verbal skill cannot be evaluated as an independent entity (e.g., one cannot ask simply, Can person A produce formulation X?). Instead, the context in which the language is used is a critical variable in assessing the verbal mastery that any person has.

This point is closely related to the long-debated issue of generalization in psychology. If a concept can be used over a restricted, as opposed to an extended, domain, serious questions exist about an individual's mastery in that sphere. An interesting example of this phenomenon was made available to me recently in a classroom where a 5-year-old asked her teacher, *What is one thousand and one thousand?*

The teacher replied *Well, what is one apple and one apple?* The child replied, *Two apples.* The adult went on with, *and one chair and one chair, one ball and one ball,* and *one penny and one penny*—all of which the child answered correctly. The teacher then said, *So then, what is one thousand and one thousand?* and the child replied, *I don't know; that's a big number.* Essentially, the child was saying, *My concept of one applies to the concrete world* (the world that Donaldson has termed the *domain of common sense*); *it does not apply when it is in a purely verbal realm for which I have no concrete referent.*

This example, like the segments of dialogue presented previously, confront us with a complex choice. Are we to say that the children have the concepts, the competence, the skill (or whatever other term might be used) and simply do not have it accessible to them in all situations, or are we to say that the limited accessibility reflects a restricted grasp of the skill in question, with the restrictions being governed by the contexts in which the skill might be used? In my view, my latter alternative is the more valid one. Furthermore, these comments have been designed to suggest that a critical variable in language use is the perceptual–verbal versus the verbal–verbal nature of an exchange. Finally, books by definition represent unusually long and complex verbal–verbal sequences. Hence, mastery of sustained verbal exchanges in the oral language sphere might be a vital precursor to written language mastery.

THE IMPLICITNESS OF CONNECTED DISCOURSE

The past decade has seen a major *paradigmatic* shift in the study of reading. In contrast to the long emphasis on skills of decoding, increasing attention is being paid to the fact that most reading involves organized, connected text. Much of the research effort is now focused on studying how readers comprehend the variety of passages with which they must deal (Walker & Meyer, 1980). Central to this view is the idea that reading involves chains that are linked so as to create a coherent set of ideas. We are only now beginning to appreciate the complexity of processing necessary for recognizing that coherence since the unity is often implicit rather than explicit. Even seemingly simple stories for preschoolers demand high levels of implicit connectedness. For example, consider the following page from a nursery story entitled *Squirrel Goes Skating* (Uttley, 1980). The story is from England; therefore the vocabulary may be somewhat unfamiliar. Nevertheless, the text serves to illustrate the point being made. In the story Hare, who lives with Grey Rabbit, is speaking about his chilblain (a type of frostbite):

"Ow, ow,!" exlaimed Hare, rubbing his toe. "Do think of something Grey Rabbit, you don't know how it hurts."
"Moldy Warp once told me to use some snow," said Grey Rabbit. "I'll get some." She ran outside and scraped the frost from the grass. Then she rubbed Hare's foot till the chilblain disappeared. (Uttley, 1980).

The point to note about this deceptively simple passage is the marked change that occurs in every possible parameter from one sentence to the next. The changes encompass length, vocabulary, syntax, and concepts. For example, in terms of speaker intent (a major pragmatic variable), the first utterance is a complaint, followed by a direct request, which is then followed by an implied request. The second speaker responds by reporting some information that has been obtained from another party (*Moldy Warp once told me . . .*). From a purely logical point of view, it seems unnecessary at best, and foolish at worst, for a listener to respond to a request for help by reporting a bit of information representing a third person's idea. Nevertheless, the reply is not seen as illogical but as sensible and possibly interesting.

For people who are fluent in language, the rapid shifts across sentences go almost unnoticed, and the text seems quite coherent. The reason for the coherence, however, is not based on anything that is said in print but rather on what is not said—what is invisible. Unstated, implicit ideas are available to the sophisticated language user that serve to unify the great variation of form and content in the information actually stated. The "sense" of written text paradoxically comes as much, if not more, from the unstated than from the stated.

As with the issues discussed previously, there appear to be oral analogues to this process of implicit cohesion. Again, the oral analogues are not high frequency occurrences, largely because so much of everyday dialogue can take place without concern for cohesion. Nevertheless, cohesion can be found, and major elements of the process seem to be mastered by many preschoolers. For example, in a lunchtime conversation between a mother and her 5-year-old child, the mother said, *Now eat your carrots.* Then she paused and, changing tone, said, *Oh, I forgot to plant the tomatoes.* The conversation continued for a while until suddenly the child altered the flow by saying, *I know why you said tomatoes. When you said carrots, it made you think of tomatoes, and that's why you did it.* In effect, the child was saying that she expects a conversation to be connected, that the grouping of tomatoes and carrots in that context was peculiar but that there must be some logic available by which the combination could be explained—and indeed, she found the logic.

Although coherence between utterances is expected and understood by skilled language users, children who are poor in language present quite a different situation. Those who have not attained mastery of verbal–verbal exchanges do not possess the skills by which to connect the seemingly endless and unstructured variety in the material they confront. In the absence of unstated organizing themes, they have little expectancy as to how the text will proceed. For example, if one could ask the nonverbally sophisticated child, "Which sentence is a more logical one in the exchange between Hare and Grey Rabbit, *She ran outside and scraped the frost from the grass.* or *She ran outside and made some snowballs for throwing?* it is likely that the child would not see one as preferable to the other. Indeed, the snowball one might be seen as better since it both connects more directly to the word *snow* in the previous sentence and it reflects a more desirable activity.

In my view, the children's difficulties in this area are dependent in large measure on the amount of unstated information that must be gleaned to make the test comprehensible. No text can be totally explicit. If the gaps are fairly small, however, the children can cope more effectively. For example, a narrow gap might be exemplified by the following: After Hare says, *You don't know how it hurts,* Grey Rabbit might have said, *Oh, it does hurt and I will help you so that it stops hurting.* The redundancy of the information and the closer semantic links (*hurt–help*) allow the child to avoid dealing with high levels of implicit information.

The issue of implicit versus explicit cohesion has been generally neglected in early reading. Effort has concentrated so heavily on presenting simple words that can be easily decoded that the connectedness of the text is often even more implicit than it is in books for more sophisticated readers. Much connectedness depends on the use of non-content words (e.g., *but, however, then* and *until*), which relate one idea to another (e.g., in the sentence, ***Then*** *she rubbed Hare's foot,* the word *then* implies that the activity followed upon Rabbit's scraping of the frost). Because most noncontent words are both deemed meaningless and marked by difficult grapheme-to-phoneme correspondences, they are often specifically avoided in early texts. As a result, the child is faced with establishing cohesion in the absence of many of the most useful and common cues that permit cohesion.

The following first-grade passage (Makar, 1977) illustrates the phenomenon under discussion. Accompanying the text are pictures of a pup (Tag), a cat (Kit), and a girl (Peg).

> *Tag is a pup.*
> *Kit is a cat.*
> *Kit ran to get Tag.*

Peg has a wig.
The wig is wet.
Peg set the wig on a big log.

Although some of the same words reappear (e.g., *Tag, Peg, wig,* etc.), they generally do not serve to enhance cohesion. The ideas of each sentence are so independent that the reading of one sentence does not sufficiently prepare the reader for the content of the next (e.g., if one were asked to predict the second sentence after reading the first, it seems highly unlikely that the theme, *Kit is a cat,* would be offered). As a result, early texts leave children—particularly children in difficulty—to confront an almost unmanageable linguistic situation. The explicit cues for cohesion are misleading (they repeat content, but the words lack an intrinsic relationship to a theme), and the implicit cues for cohesion are practically nonexistent (the subtle connectives are deleted so that there is no clear organization for relating one sentence to the next). Many of us have long been discouraged by the texts offered to beginning readers. The point emphasized here is that cohesion may be a key factor in explaining our dissatisfaction and, ultimately, in offering better alternatives.

CONVENTIONS IN WRITING

Every social context carries its own linguistic conventions. The setting, the participants, and the purposes of the exchange all have important effects on the language that is used. For example, an interchange between a doctor and a patient has a different tone, pacing, and vocabulary from a conversation between friends. Written language, like oral language, is also marked by its own conventions. For instance, more elaborated and syntactically complex language is required in writing than in talking (Hunt, 1977; Moffett, 1968). Although the differences between the two modes of language are readily acknowledged, insufficient recognition has been given to the fact that the conventions employed in the written mode often violate the rules that the child has learned in the oral mode. For example, books for young children typically contain pictures to accompany the text. The pictures are included so as to make the material more appealing to children and thereby ease the transition from oral to written language. To understand the situation facing the child, imagine a picture—for example, a bird singing on a rooftop. Imagine further that the scene being depicted is not in a book, but represents (as it is supposed to do) a real event. Then make up some sentences about the scene. Under these conditions, adults commonly respond with statements such as the following: *There is a bird on a house, That bird is standing and singing,* and *A bird is wearing a hat and singing.* In fact what the book says is: *Mr. Bird was happy. He was so happy he had to sing* [Eastman, 1968].

The words *was* and *had* have been emphasized not because they are unique to this book but rather because they are so typical of children's stories. Although a visual representation is present that in the nonbook world would be described in the present tense, in the book world the past tense is used. This use of the past tense is counter to almost any use of the past tense that the child has learned. Indeed, in reading this page aloud, a learning disabled child read it as, *Mr. Bird is happy, he was so happy.* (In this connection, it seems reasonable to propose that the common misreading of *was* by young children occurs not because they see it as *saw* but rather because the use of *was* in books is antithetical to their usual use of the past tense.)

These violations of oral language are common in early reading. For example, in the nonbook world when people speak, they simply offer the utterance they have in mind. When their statements are translated into the written mode, they are accompanied by such words as *he said, they shouted,* and *she whispered.* In other words, quotations must be explicitly introduced and identified with devices that generally involve complex pronominal change (e.g., *He said: I am going*). The reasons for this are clear and reasonable, but they nevertheless represent distinctly different uses of language from those that occur with spoken language. Furthermore, these altered uses of language occur in the earliest books that children must read.

As before, the question arises as to whether these written language conventions ever appear in the oral language mode. Examination of young children's experiences suggests that there are two major domains in which these conventions are found. One is clearly in story-reading— that is, when adults read stories to young children, the children are clearly exposed to these sorts of language uses. There does, however, seem to be a second major domain in which they appear. This is the realm of dramatic play. In dramatic play, children employ a number of devices through which they distance themselves from the language in ways reminiscent of the conventions used in books. For example, as they plan and structure their roles, they commonly switch among verb tenses, they assign quotations explicitly to the various participants, and they do not describe the real world but rather a pretend world (e.g., *You said, stand in line. But I'm the teacher, and I'm supposed to say that*).

As might be expected, children who have difficulties in learning to read seem to encounter limitations in both these domains of oral language. For instance, parents of children who function poorly in school commonly report that the children do not enjoy being read to. This is not unexpected in that they are not attracted by long verbal sequences. At the same time, this means that they do learn to deal with the conventions of the written mode. Similarly, these children are also reported to show delay and/or difficulties in dramatic play. Again, they are excluded from a major channel through which their language skills might be enhanced.

THE RECEPTIVENESS OF READING

In recent years research in child language has been marked by a shift in focus from the study of structure to the study of function. In contrast to the previous nearly exclusive concern with syntactic and semantic skills, there is now a growing interest in the uses to which children put their language system. Clearly, a major use of language is as a tool for communication. The introduction of the theme of communication complicates the study of language. For while language structure can be studied as an intraindividual phenomenon, communication cannot; at a minimum it demands the consideration of two participants.

Although the introduction of two participants adds complexity, it also enables us to gain some insight into the demands that reading entails. Written language, like spoken language, essentially involves a communication situation. Nevertheless, the relationship between the two participants is quite different in the two modes. In the oral language mode, both participants are simultaneously present, so that each person assumes the role of both speaker and listener. In the written language mode, only one person is present, and during the act of reading, that person assumes essentially only the role of the listener who follows the logic, reasoning, thoughts, and ideas of an invisible speaker.[2]

The importance of the listener role in reading demands the reconsideration of some commonly held views concerning the relation between oral and written language development. Studies of oral language development have tended to value the speaker role more than the listener role; the more complex the language produced by a child, the more advanced is his or her functioning judged to be. The influence of this orientation can be seen in many areas. For example, expressive language is deemed to be more difficult than receptive language, and production

[2] The act of writing also involves the presence of only one person, with that person serving in the role of the "speaker." If the writing is to be meaningful and coherent, however, the speaker's role is greatly complicated because he or she must anticipate all the needs, interests, and capabilities of the nonpresent listener. Hence, writing, like reading, demands that the communication be formulated in the absence of the feedback that is such a major feature of oral communication.

is seen as more advanced than comprehension. Some have challenged this view (Clark, 1980; Goodman & Goodman, 1977), but it still continues to exert a powerful influence. Thus, many preschool programs encourage children to speak a great deal since extensive speaking is seen not only as indicative of expressive language mastery but as the foundation for effective reading.

Effective communication in both the oral and written mode cannot occur unless one is willing and able to comprehend the verbalizations produced by another person. This emphasis on receptive language may seem strange since receptive language is thought to be relatively simple. Hence, even if one acknowledges its significance, it might be assumed that almost all children are well equipped for the receptive-listener mode that must be adopted for reading. Research that I and my colleagues have conducted (Blank, Rose, & Berlin, 1978), however, has suggested that the discrepancy between expressive and receptive language diminishes, if not disappears, when one controls for problem difficulty. Thus in many tests, receptive language demands are relatively simple (e.g., *touch your nose, pick up the pencil*), whereas expressive language demands are more complex (e.g., *repeat the story you just heard; tell me how you get to school*). When receptive language demands are formulated so as to be of equivalent difficulty to expressive language demands (e.g., *before you touch the chair, I want you to tap the fourth block*), the receptive language skills are not found to be easier than expressive language ones. Indeed, in certain language disorders, receptive language is poorer than expressive language functioning (Blank, Gessner, & Esposito, 1979).

This improbable finding becomes less puzzling when one considers the pragmatics underlying expressive and receptive language. Expressive language can occur as an utterance that is unrelated to any other utterance in a conversation. For example, in the opening of a conversation, one may come into a room and ask, *Has anyone seen my coat?* In utterances of this type, one can concentrate on formulating the particular issue that one has in mind and pay relatively little attention to the thoughts or interests of the person who hears the verbalization. Expressive language, however, can also occur as the response to another person's utterance (e.g., replying to the question above with a comment such as *Yeh, I think you left it in the car*). Thus, expressive language can take on two forms: One is as an elicited response that is part of a communicative exchange; the other is as an utterance that is far more independent of communicative demands. By contrast, receptive language always represents an elicited response (e.g., pointing to a picture in reply to someone saying, *Show me the dog*). Thus, even though the responder may not use any overt language, he or she is responding to a communicative event. In this sense, elicited expressive language and elicited receptive language are similar communicative acts despite their difference in form. By contrast, nonelicited expressive language (i.e., nonelicited in the sense that it is not a reply to another person's utterance) may represent a different, and in many ways, easier behavior. It is easier in the sense that when using this type of language the child "is spared the task of putting himself in the other person's position. . . . The spare attention . . . then may be used for formulating" relatively more complex utterances [Clark, 1980, p. 16]. In other words, the child's comprehension (i.e., where he or she has to both understand language and interpret another person's position) may be less sophisticated than production (i.e., those instances of production where he or she can concentrate on the language alone).

The pattern of the discussion until now has been to ask if children who have difficulty in mastering the reading process also show difficulty in the area of oral language under consideration. Unfortunately, because of the paucity of studies of language, little information can be offered at this time about children's ability to deal with the demands of "receptive" language. We have begun to study this issue in our research (Blank & Franklin, 1980), and hopefully, in the not too distant future, a richer data base will be available. In the interim, it seems important to recognize that the trend in both psychology and education is not only to minimize the significance of "elicited" language skills but actually to view them as counterproductive to a child's sense of self. For example, when a child displays difficulty or disinterest in attending to the language of others, this behavior is often rationalized with the statement, *He just wasn't interested, that's all.* or *Why should he have to listen? He has the right to decide whether or not he wants to get involved.* As in the issues considered earlier, this view has validity: Children cannot be viewed simply as individuals who are to be dominated by others. But to the degree that the behavior represents a pervasive attitude toward situations involving elicited language, then the child is likely to be a seriously impaired communicator in both the oral and written mode. If the children are to be helped, it seems essential to obtain information for both understanding and treating this often-neglected component of language.

A CONCLUDING COMMENT

A number of varied language factors have been raised in this presentation. Underlying all, however, is the concept of discourse. Each component that has been discussed can exist only within the context of a sustained exchange—whether it be in the oral or written mode. Since interest in discourse is relatively recent, this area of language is marked by limited understanding. As a result, a presentation such as this invariably raises more questions than it answers. Among the major ones are the following:

1. What type of evidence can be gathered to show that the oral language factors posited here are in fact critical components of later written language skills?
2. Even if these factors are shown to be necessary, are they sufficient to explain the behavior? If not, what other factors might be involved?
3. The skills discussed here are complex ones that are likely to depend upon earlier prerequisite skills. What might these earlier skills be, and what is the nature of their relationship to the skills under discussion?
4. How might this information be translated into a basis for effective instruction?

The last question is perhaps the most crucial of all. Much of the impetus for analyzing oral written language relationships comes from the difficulties that literacy represents for many in our nation. This situation has created a pressing need for innovative programs which will prevent large numbers in our population from being disenfranchised in our highly complex technological society. Although some ideas in the paper are relevant to teaching and curricula, in-the-main educational considerations have not been dealt with. This omission does not stem from a lack of interest. The enhancement of learning has for many years been one of my primary interests. Effective teaching, however, raises a host of issues which goes far beyond both the time and content constraints of this presentation. Hopefully, another conference of this type will soon take place which will be devoted to the intriguing issue of how knowledge of behavior may be translated into the enhancement of functioning.

REFERENCES

Benton, A. L., & Pearl, D. *Dyslexia: An appraisal of current knowledge.* New York: Oxford University Press, 1978.

Blank, M. *Teaching learning in the preschool: A dialogue approach.* Columbus, Ohio: Merrill, 1973.

Blank, M., & Franklin, E. Dialogue with preschoolers: A cognitively-based system of assessment. *Applied Psycholinguistics,* 1980, *1,* 127–150.

Blank, M., Gessner, M., & Esposito, A. Language without communication: A case study. *Journal of Child Language,* 1979, *6,* 329–352.

Blank, M., Rose, S. A., & Berlin, L. *The language of learning: The preschool years*. New York: Grune & Stratton, 1978.

Clark, R. Errors in talking to learn. *First Language*, 1980, *1*, 7–32.

Donaldson, M. *Children's minds*. New York: Norton, 1978.

Eastman, P. D. *The best nest*. New York: Random House, 1968.

Goodman, K. S., & Goodman, Y. M. Learning about psycholinguistic processes by analyzing oral reading. *Harvard Educational Review*, 1977, *47*, 317–333.

Hunt, K. W. Early and late blooming syntactic structures. In C. Cooper & L. Odell (Eds.), *Evaluating writing: Describing, measuring, judging*. Urbana, Illinois: National Council of Teachers of English, 1977.

Isaacs, S. *Intellectual growth in young children*. London: Routledge & Kegan Paul, 1930.

Makar, B. W. *"The Wig" in primary phonics*. Cambridge, Massachusetts: Educators Publishing Service, 1977.

Moffett, J. *Teaching the universe of discourse*. Boston: Houghton Mifflin, 1968.

Satz, P., Taylor, H. G., Friel, J., & Fletcher, J. Some developmental and predictive precursors of reading disabilities. In H. L. Benton & D. Pearl (Eds.), *Dyslexia: An appraisal of current knowledge*. New York: Oxford University Press, 1978.

Uttley, A. *Squirrel goes skating*. Great Britain: Collins Colour Cubs, 1980.

Walker, C. H., & Meyer, B. J. F. Integrating information from text: An evaluation of current theories. *Review of Educational Research*, 1980, *50*, 421–437.

/

5

The Development and Importance of Narratives for School Adaptation

LYNNE FEAGANS

Children just beginning public school are faced each day with the language demands of the classroom. These demands are different, and probably to varying degrees unlike the demands of the community from which they come. Children of every social strata and cultural background have survived and adapted their language to the culture of their home community, but some of these children do not adapt to the language demands of the classroom. Indeed, the language of learning is often basically different from the language for living (Doughty, Thornton, & Doughty, 1977). Unfortunately for a large portion of the lower socio-economic strata, adaptation to school has been a persistent, and even now a largely unsolved, problem. It seems likely that these children with problems in school often have problems with the mismatch between the use of language in their community and the use of language required in school.

> Pupils are individual human beings who have learnt language in the process of learning how to live the life of their communities; the whole process has taken place in the context of the patterns of relationships, habits and values that make up that specifically human environment. If we are to make sense of the pupil's problems and needs when he comes to use the language he has learnt in the context of the school, then we must be very clear about the processes by which he has learnt it, and the human environment in which the learning has taken place [Doughty, Thornton & Doughty, 1977, p. 169].

THE LANGUAGE OF CHILDREN
REARED IN POVERTY

For those children from lower socioeconomic backgrounds, who disproportionately come from the black population and who have adaptation problems in school, language has been implicated in their failure in school in a variety of studies (Deutsch, Katz, & Jensen, 1968; Raph, 1965), but it is still unclear why they have such problems. It appears that information then is needed in two major areas in order to understand the language problems: First, what language processes are central to adaptation to school, and second, what experiences have these children had in their communities that make this adaptation to school difficult?

Let us say at the outset that there are, of course, other factors that are certainly implicated in the maladjustment and failure of children from lower socioeconomic backgrounds including differing values, motivations, and behavioral styles; but it is argued in this paper that the ability to use language appropriately in school is not only critical for school adaptation but also critical to learning in school.

This chapter will address the following questions: (*a*) What are the language demands of the school situation; (*b*) what are the likely precursors that are needed to meet the language demands in school; and (*c*) what are some of the socioeconomic differences in the acquisition of these language skills that can be related to language problems in the classroom?

This effort will be speculative at times and will rest not only on the research literature but on data that we at the Frank Porter Graham Center have collected in our longitudinal project on poverty children.

DIALOGUE SKILLS

Since this chapter will be discussing the literature on language beyond the sentence level that usually occurs in an interactive situation, the dialogue will be the focus of much of what is discussed.

Dialogue skills are defined here as those abilities that allow for the successful exchange of information and affect in an interactive situation. The skills required for dialogue exchange are numerous and include both nonverbal and verbal skills that are both social and cognitive in nature. For the purpose of this chapter, emphasis is placed on the structure and content of the dialogue, that is, the knowledge and use of the appropriate sequences of turns that partners observe as well as how these sequences are related to each other (Camaioni, 1979; Sacks, Schegloff, & Jefferson, 1974). It is, of course, clear that all children learn the dialogue rules that are adaptive for their home community. It is not clear that these rules are always the ones that are adaptive for instructional settings in school.

NARRATIVE SKILLS

Narrative skills are defined as those abilities that allow for the understanding and exchange of event-structured material. These skills include the knowledge of such information as introductions, setting information, character descriptions, theme information, event sequences, reactive events, and conclusions (Rumelhart, 1975; Stein & Glenn, 1979). In addition, these skills include the knowledge of how to sequence the information to form a coherent narrative. These parts of a narrative are structured in a particular way, at least in "middle-class" America, as has been shown in the history of the experiments on event-structured material in adults and children (Mandler & Johnson, 1977; Schank & Abelson, 1977; Stein & Glenn, 1979; Thorndyke, 1977). The series of events in the dialogue are usually logically related to each other and may lead to a climactic event and final resolution.

These narrative sequences are most typically presented to children in the form of stories. Both dialogue and narrative skills are combined in the use of intraconversational narratives in such school activities as "show and tell" and relating experiences and historical events. These are typical of the teacher–child interactions during instructional activities in the early elementary school years—activities in which a theme or topic is developed in interactional sequences.

The narrative will be defined much as Labov and Fanshel (1977) defined it.

> We define narrative as one means of representing past experience by a sequence of ordered sentences that present the temporal sequences of these events by that order. A narrative event is not the kind of experience that is captured easily in a single sentence, and a turn at speaking that embodies a narrative means that a speaker will hold the floor for more than one sentence. [p. 105].

This structure can be represented in a variety of ways by either positing a story or narrative grammar with rewrite rules or a tree structure indicating the relationship among the parts of the narrative or story. Since a variety of ways have been developed to examine the structure of stories and narratives, Figure 5.1 is a schema that is a summary and conceptualization of the narrative and story grammars proposed by others (Labov & Fanshel, 1977; Stein & Glenn, 1976; Thorndyke, 1977).

Labov and Fanshel (1977) have described the narrative as containing first an *abstract,* which signals to the speaker that a narrative is to begin. In many cases this can be a statement of the theme of the narrative or a statement of the goal or moral to be learned.

The second aspect of the narrative is the *orientation,* which intro-

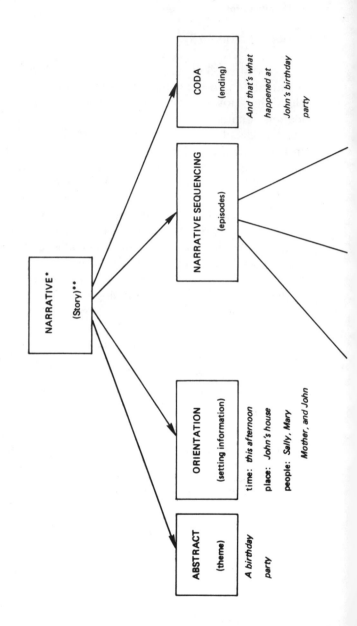

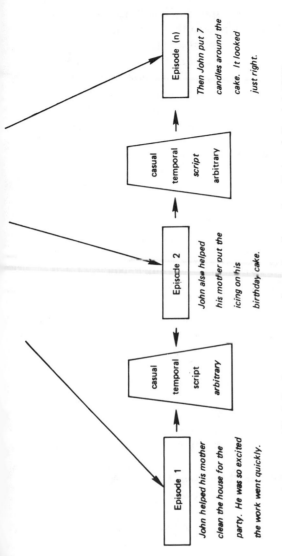
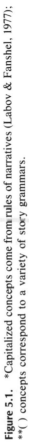

Episode 1

John helped his mother clean the house for the party. He was so excited the work went quickly.

casual
temporal
script
arbitrary

Episode 2

John also helped his mother out the icing on his birthday cake.

casual
temporal
script
arbitrary

Episode (n)

Then John put 7 candles around the cake. It looked just right.

Figure 5.1. *Capitalized concepts come from rules of narratives (Labov & Fanshel, 1977);
**( ) concepts correspond to a variety of story grammars.

duces time, place, and characters. It corresponds closely to the setting information in a story that helps to introduce to the hearer the relevant aspects of the situation around which events take place.

The third aspect of the narrative is the *narrative sequencing,* which involves the recounting of events or episodes. These episodes usually contain an action by one or more of the leading characters in the narrative followed by some result and/or internal reaction by the characters.

These episodes in the narrative are connected either *tightly* or *loosely,* depending on the type of linkage between episodes. In the tightest situation there is a direct causal link between one episode and the next, that is, the first episode precipitates the next episode in a causal chain.

The linkage could also be *temporal.* This linkage produces tightly connected episodes, not because the episodes are causally linked but because they must precede each other temporally. For instance, an event about an early experience of a child precedes an event about an experience as an adult, not because of any causal link but because of our knowledge of temporal ordering. The third linkage is a "script" linkage; one that is predictable from past information about the connection of episodes. For instance, the sequence of episodes in an event like a birthday party is predictable because of the cultural experience of the sequential ordering. Thus this linkage between episodes is also tight, given that the person is familiar with the "script" in question.

The last link is less often found in narratives or stories but does occur. This last link is called an *arbitrary link* because there is no inherent reason for the sequence or connection of episodes. These arbitrary links are often signaled in narratives or stories by the conjunction *and* between episodes, indicating no necessary ordering. Many children's stories contain this arbitrary ordering.

The final aspect of the narrative is the *coda.* This signals the end of the narrative by conventional phrases, as in stories (*and they lived happily ever after*) or by verbal statements that can bring the listener back to the present (*and I guess even now many people have experiences like that*).

The description of narrative information given in Figure 5.1 can then be used to describe the kind of event-structured information in stories in written or oral form, as well as much of the thematic information communicated in an interactive situation. The development of the knowledge about and structure of narrative material certainly develops in all children and adults, but the way in which this knowledge is acquired as well as how this knowledge is structured must certainly influence the way in which we understand and communicate narrative events. We will explore these differences in the next sections of this chapter.

WHAT IS DEMANDED IN THE CLASSROOM?

Information in the classroom is communicated through the use of oral language by the teacher, especially in the lower grades. But how can we describe the language that children must understand and use to adapt and learn in school? Past language evaluations and programs for children from lower socioeconomic levels having problems in school have focused on the syntactic structures of such children as well as their semantic or conceptual development. Ervin-Tripp (1971), Labov (1970) and Hymes (1979) have all questioned whether the syntactic complexity or the semantic–conceptual knowledge of these children is problematic for real world or classroom learning. Although a certain base level of syntactic and semantic development is indeed necessary for school adaptation, it is argued here that language beyond the sentence level occurring in dialogues, and especially within a narrative framework, characterizes the language in school. It is these uses of syntax and semantics that every child must acquire to do well in school. These discourse skills incorporate not only knowledge of the language but of the rules and format for sequencing the discourse.

Unfortunately, there is little research on the structure and content of dialogues in the classroom. There is certainly a whole literature in education that examines teacher and pupil styles and classroom management techniques (Flanders, 1970; Gallagher & Aschner, 1963), but little is known about the actual language demands in the classroom.

Some basic research has been done on the structure and content of dialogues in the classroom during instructional periods. Bellack, Kliebard, Hyman and Smith (1966) and, more recently, Sinclair and Coulthard (1975) have tried to capture generalizations about the form of the discourse in classrooms. Sinclair and Coulthard (1975) have said that learning to speak and learning to behave according to the rules of the interaction are inseparable. For instance, they give an example of a teacher who is giving a lesson in the classification of objects and also in the rules for making appropriate moves in the discourse. The teacher, during this instructional discourse would not respond to student answers, even if they were correct, if the answers were "shouted out." She would say: *Can't hear if you shout.* This link between linguistic and discourse behavior is explicitly stated in this example, although most rules of discourse are not stated explicitly in teacher–pupil interactions.

Within this framework, Sinclair and Coulthard (1975) have described at least three kinds of transactions initiated by the teacher in an instructional setting: (*a*) informing, (*b*) directing, and (*c*) eliciting. *Informing* transactions are those in which the teacher initiates a dialogue with a group of children or one child for the purpose of imparting some thematic information. Thus the teacher's initial move is very lengthy. *Directing* transactions are those in which the teacher wants the child to perform some act that is often nonverbal. *Eliciting* transactions are those in which the teacher tries to encourage pupil verbal responsiveness to her initial move. This in no way allows the child to become the initiator in the exchange, but he is encouraged to elaborate on the topic.

Occasionally, pupils initiate transactions, but this is rare in the instructional setting. They are often employed for points of clarification or for personal requests by the child. In general, they do not lead to lengthy exchanges.

All these transactions begin with preliminary or introductory remarks and end with a final exchange. In between a series of medial moves are optional, and these moves generally elaborate on the topic introduced. This framework is similar to the basic structure of a narrative—the narrative being a special case of the general framework of dialogues in the classroom—since the narrative involves the sequence of complicating events that some dialogues in the classroom, such as managerial ones, do not. Yet, it is argued here that knowledge of the use of these dialogues that contain a narrative structure, called *intraconversational narratives* (Umiker-Sebeok, 1979), is critical for the understanding and expression of much of the information to be learned in school. In fact, it is probably the case that information exchanges and the building of abstract knowledge depends on the knowledge of how to use a sequence of moves in a dialogue to give and get thematic information to and from another.

Those language demands in the classroom are not explicitly stated and teachers do not attempt in any systematic way to teach dialogue skills for learning. The teacher assumes that all children understand the sequence of moves and the structure of a dialogue for learning. Thus, if children fail to learn, it is often assumed that they are inattentive or have some language problem. This, of course, could be disastrous to a child who comes from a home community where the use of language in dialogues is different from the use of language in dialogues in school because the problem has been misdiagnosed.

PRECURSORS

Although the production of narratives has been found to begin as early as age 3 (Umiker-Sebeok, 1979), the precursors of these skills are likely to be found much earlier in the child's development of dialogue within the broad framework of language and social development. This is because the development of language and the development of social skills are both a part of the larger development of the communicative system in the child, which moves from preverbal interactions to the acquisition of language. Language and social development in the context of interaction have to do with the development of dialogue. At a 1977 conference, Bruner spoke of the role of dialogue in the language development of the child:

> Consider the essentially social way in which the acquisition of knowledge of language must occur. We use language in order to communicate with others, and as John Searle somewhere remarked, we could possess a quite rich and full knowledge of syntax and semantics and still be rather a hopeless idiot as far as communicative competence is concerned. Communicative competence has to do with dialogue [Bruner, 1978, p. 244].

The communicative context for the development of the infant has focused on the mother–caretaker dyad and, in particular, on the interactions that occur there. Stern (1977) has described in detail the development of the dialogue structure in the mother–infant dyad. "In other words, he (infant) is being taught how to take speaking turns that normal conversational exchange requires [p. 197]." The mother, in dialogue with an infant unable to appropriately respond, leaves pauses for the infant to respond and may even respond for the infant and then carry on with her own conversation. The mother acts as if the baby were responding (Snow, 1977; Stern, 1977), and thus may be teaching the infant the structure and rhythm of the adult dialogue. This is not trivial information to be learned.

Although the immediate purpose of these conversational exchanges is for the pure enjoyment of the interaction, important information can be learned by the infant about the structure of the communicative exchange. These interactive episodes provide information to the infant about the regularity, repetitiveness, and rhythm of the dialogue. They are often repeated and become ritualized so that both infant and caretaker can predict the sequence as in the "peek-a-boo" game. Garvey (1977) describes these ritualized interactions in this way.

> Sequences of nonsense syllables move to chants built on recognizable word shapes with fairly regular patterns of stress and pitch. But in all these types of playful vocalization the meaning of the words is secondary or nonexistent and it is only the sound and rhythm that are enjoyed or that enhance the accompanying activity [p. 62].

Both Garvey and Stern describe these routines, which are often idiosyncratic to the dyad but which epitomize the interactional and repetitive qualities of the early interactive dialogues.

Other researchers have also emphasized the role of these ritualized games in the development of the mother–child dyad (Bruner & Sherwood, 1976; Gustafson, Green, & West, 1979; Schaffer, 1979). They have described the development from the passive infant to the more active infant as games become less ritualized and more amenable to innovations by child and mother. Discussions in these works often allude to the importance of these games and interactions for future development, in particular language and communicative competence.

Although there is a growing literature about the importance of these early interactions on the development of language, there is no clear link to the language development research. The child who begins to speak in words is no longer characterized in the same way. Research in this area focuses on the cognitive or referential nature of the "word"; it is devoid of the emphasis on the rhythmic and affectual nature so reminiscent of the early infant interactions. It is true that ritualized routines are not as characteristic of children acquiring their first words, especially in those referential children studied by Brown (1973) or Bloom (1970, 1973), whose children spoke quite referentially from the beginning of data collection. Primary emphasis has been on the semantic–syntactic development because of the obvious salience to the adult and to the researchers of the one- and two-word stage of language development. Recently, some interest has been generated in investigating the importance of interactive routines and individual differences in language development.

A few studies have begun to investigate the early dialogue routines of mother and children. Ninio and Bruner (1978) and Ninio (1980) have described the joint book-reading routine in which mother and child engage in picture identification and explanations by the mother. This routine was shown to facilitate labeling and the acquisition of naming. In addition, this routine revealed a rather sophisticated dialogue structure, beyond the normal characterization of the child's dialogue exchanges.

But what do these routines and games imply about the development of narratives? The development of dialogue structure is closely related to the development of narrative skills and, as will be argued here, is a precursor to later narrative skills. For instance, Snow (see Chapter 3) has also investigated joint book-reading skills in a child from 2 to $3\frac{1}{2}$ years of age. The description of the structure of the routine reveals the beginnings of a narrative structure. The child first points, introducing the topic; the mother responds by naming the object; and the child imitates or confirms the name. In more complicated sequences the mother may elaborate on the object as to its action or history. As can be seen, this primitive dialogue routine contains the elements of an introduction, with setting and character information as well as the development of some event or action sequence. This joint book-reading skill may not only foster naming and the structure of dialogue but may actually be the precursor for later narrative skills. Ninio (1980) has found that there are striking social-class differences in the frequency and type of joint book-reading activities engaged in by mother–child dyads. Middle-class mothers more frequently use this book-reading routine and use it more effectively. Thus they may be using a more narrative framework in their book reading. Ninio's study suggests that children from lower socioeconomic backgrounds may not have had the prerequisite experiences to develop the intraconversational narrative structures needed in school.

Intraconversational narratives specifically have been studied in middle-class children (Umiker-Sebeok, 1979) from 3 to 5 years of age. This study found that at 3 years of age children indeed had the beginning of a narrative structure. Of the six narrative elements modeled after Labov and Waletzky (1966) and Kernan (1974), children at 3 years of age used 1.7 types on the average in their narratives, generally including introductions and complicating events; while 4- and 5-year-olds used between 2.4 and 2.8 types, including introductions, complicating events, and orientations.

Stein and Glenn (1976, 1979) have formulated a story schema that is similar to Figure 5.1. They have conducted a series of experiments on children from first to fifth grade to determine the parts of the schema that are remembered as well as how the connections between episodes (causal or acausal) affected what was remembered. They found that even the youngest children were better able to remember the sequence of episodes when those episodes were causally related. In addition, they found that major settings, consequences, and initiating events were recalled most often by the children, whereas attempts, reactions, minor settings, and internal responses were less often recalled. In a later study, Glenn (1980) systematically varied stories, so that some contained episodes that were causally related and others contained stories that were arbitrarily temporally linked. The causally linked stories were better recalled by both first- and third-graders than the arbitrarily linked ones. The stories that had arbitrarily linked episodes produced both omission of episodes and inversion of episodes by the children with much greater frequency than did the stories in which the episodes were logically related.

Social-class differences in the development of narratives have not really been investigated. One study (Hall, Cole, Reder, & Dowley, 1977) examined the effect of setting on children's ability to recount narrative information about a visit to a grocery store. A comparison was made between Head Start children's ability to relate this narrative information to the teachers while in the grocery store setting (informal) or in the school setting (formal). They found that the amount of speech produced was a function of the setting, but the quality of speech did not differ in the two settings. Dore (1978), in a further analysis of these data using his own coding scheme for conversations, found that the quality of discourse for some children was improved in an informal setting, but this certainly was not true for all the children in the study. Yet, even this one study made no comparison to the performance of other groups of children or to a model narrative.

LANGUAGE INTERACTION AND POVERTY

Although there is little direct information about social-class differences and narrative skills in children, there is some research on dialogues. Since dialogue skills and narrative skills are often intertwined, argued here to be an essential element, some research on dialogues is reviewed briefly; but is found in more detail in Farran (see Chapter 2).

It has been demonstrated in multiple language studies that the poverty child functions poorly on tasks that require verbal interaction (Bernstein, 1961; Raph, 1965; Robinson, 1971). These studies described the language of the low-income child as deficient because the child did not express abstract concepts, did not answer questions pointedly, assumed much information on the part of the hearer in verbal explanations, and used more nonverbal cues in communication. Bernstein (1961) initially hypothesized that low-income speakers used language for primarily social purposes and not for exchange of abstract information. Raph (1965) reported that this deficit in expressive language appeared to contribute heavily to the lower intellectual functioning of these children.

One explanation of social-class differences in discourse skills is that poverty children have had less opportunity to engage in active dialogue with adults, and the quality of that dialogue, when it occurs, is different from that of middle-income children. Ward (1971), Slobin (1968), and Robinson and Rackstraw (1967) have all described the low frequency of verbal interaction between children and adults in poverty groups. Not only do such interactions appear to occur infrequently, but they differ qualitatively in relation to what topics are discussed, who determines what topic is discussed, and what functions language typically serves. In general, such speech has been anecdotally described as differing from middle-class mothers' speech in that it is predominately "administrative," in the sense of assisting in carrying out daily business (e.g., *Where are your shoes?*) and focuses on topics that the mother has determined. But does this mean that rich and complicated information is not exchanged within poverty homes or that the frequency of these exchanges between adults and children appears to be less?

Children in poverty environments are also often confronted with a large number of people and little space (Stack, 1974). Thus the children have ample opportunities for interaction, but these interactions may often be short. In order to engage in lengthy dialogues in which a topic is developed, two people must have a fairly lengthy exchange. In many poverty homes, the opportunities for such dialogues may be few, merely because of the number of people in the environment. In addition, the strain for survival may not give a high priority to verbal interaction.

Feagans and Haskins (in preparation) have tape recorded the language of 20 low-income and 20 middle-income children in their neighborhoods. No differences have been found in the amount or complexity of language. There were differences in the length of a dialogue, that is, middle-income children were involved in conversations in which the number of exchanges on a topic was greater than that of low-income children, especially low-income girls. It should be noted also that there were many more adults and children in the neighborhoods of these low-income children in comparison to the middle-income children; again indicating lack of opportunity for sustained interactions. Yet, as Snow has stated (see Chapter 16), the economics of survival must often preclude other factors. If a family is struggling to pay the rent and to eat, then the development of certain school-like skills must be necessarily secondary.

In studies of middle-income adult–child dialogues, it has been found that children at 3 years of age use contingent information in formulating messages. That is, they are able to share the same topic with an adult and add information to a prior utterance of an adult. Bloom, Lightbowm, and Hood (1975) found that 70% of the child utterances that occurred immediately following an adult utterance were contingent in this sense. In contrast, Garvey and Hogan (1973) have emphasized that children in peer verbal interactions use repetition and social routines, patterns that occurred infrequently in the adult–child data presented by Bloom. Because low-income children have been reported to interact more often with peers and less often with adults (Ward, 1971), their more typical interaction patterns may be less like middle-class adult–child interchanges. Those children may have less practice with such adult–child interchanges.

LANGUAGE, SCHOOL AND POVERTY

There has always been an emphasis on language skills and school success (Cazden, John, & Hymes, 1973). Children from poverty backgrounds have been found to be less able to understand and use language to meet the demands of the classroom situation (Cazden *et al.,* 1973). In the past, emphasis has been placed on remedying these language problems by instituting programs that emphasize syntactic skills (complex syntactic structures, dialect switching) and semantic or conceptual skills. It has become increasingly clear that these skills may play less of a role in the successful adaptation to school than has previously been thought. More importantly, the use of language for dialogue exchange and for narratives may be of far greater importance because such skills are used by teachers and expected of school-age children. As Shuy (1979) explains:

> In terms of the mismatch between child language and school language a great deal needs to be learned about functional language. It is my opinion that mismatches in this area offer considerably greater interference than anything researched in the past. We have ample evidence that phonological interference is not very important. Grammatical interference seems to be possibly important, but no where nearly as much as functional language interference [p. 34].

Children who enter school, then, with functional language skills that are not adaptive for the classroom setting will have a difficult time.

A few studies have examined, either in production or comprehension tasks, the child's ability to decode or encode discourse or narrative material. Robinson (1971) and Rackstraw and Robinson (1967) provided information about the low-income child's expressive language performance on tasks that either required the child to tell a story about a series of pictures or to answer open-ended questions on a specific topic. The low-income child consistently gave less precise answers to questions, made inappropriate assumptions about the listener's knowledge, and used fewer abstract linguistic structures than did the middle-income child. Bernstein (1972) explained this apparent deficiency of the low-income child in terms of the functions of language employed by children of different social classes. For example, Bernstein explained that it was clear from low-income children's stories about the pictures they were shown that they understood the content of the stories and that they had linguistic skills at their disposal to tell the stories in a complete fashion. The reason the children may not have used these skills in the situation was a lack of understanding of the demand characteristics of the task or unfamiliarity with this narrative function of language.

Milgram, Shore, and Malasky (1971) found that in the recall of an illustrated story read aloud to disadvantaged and advantaged kindergarten children, the advantaged group was more verbal but produced no more of the essential elements than did the disadvantaged group. The authors speculated that the pictures provided the structure necessary for the disadvantaged group to do well and that without the clues from the pictures, the disadvantaged children might not have done as well.

Indepth studies of the child's use of language in school-like situations have been done in a series of research projects in England. Tough (1977), in a longitudinal comparison of middle- and low-income children in England, reported that at 3 years of age there were differences between the two groups on linguistic structures and the functions of their language. The low-income child used less complex structures; had a shorter mean length utterance; and used language less often to talk about past and future experiences, to give explanations, or to reflect on feelings. By 7 years of age it became clear that in a variety of familiar situations (talking with peers), the low-income children could and did use complex structures and long sentences. The differences between the two groups at 7 years of age lay in their use of language. The low-income children more often assumed that the listener shared their viewpoint, and they tended to be less explicit and to reflect less on their own past experiences.

Tough contended that differences in the functions of language hinder the low-income child in school. Because low-income children used language in different ways, they did not respond in the way the teacher had expected on the tasks set for them.

Blank (1975) has argued that children who enter school without knowing certain abstract functions of language are at a great disadvantage and fall progressively further behind their peers. These *intangibles of language,* as she calls them, such as understanding what is demanded from a *why* question, were investigated among poorly and well-functioning black children. She found that 12-year-old poorly functioning children were performing like 5-year-old well-functioning children. This large gap indicates not only the progresssive decline that poorly functioning children may encounter but also indicates how inadequate our schools are to deal with language differences in such children.

Another aspect of this unfamiliarity with the language demands of the classroom on the part of children from lower socioeconomic backgrounds is what is called the *unteachable response*. Blank, Rose, and Berlin (1978) have explained that poverty children often answer the teacher's overtures in a dialogue with an irrelevant response, one that gives such vague information about the reply that the teacher cannot decide even if the child understood the question. These *unteachable responses* appear to be the result of the child's lack of understanding of the use of such question–answer dialogues and the teacher's failure to understand and be able to help such children.

Recently, several studies of poverty children have suggested that experience in school may minimize some of the social-class differences as children learn school language functions. Bruck and Tucker (1974) found that lower- and middle-income kindergarten children differed significantly on tasks of expressive grammatical and communicative language at the beginning of the school year. By the end of the year, however, the differences between the groups had markedly decreased on the grammatical tasks, but they remained strong on the communicative tasks. Analyzing errors on the tasks, Bruck and Tucker hypothesized that gains by low-income children were due to the specific acquisition of linguistic skills and not to increasing knowledge of the demand characteristics of the tasks. Such findings suggest that middle-income children may enter school with knowledge of certain functions of language exchange related to narrative school-like tasks, whereas low-income children do not. Williams and Naremore (1969) have made a similar suggestion on the basis of their results with production tasks requiring elicitation of connected discourse.

The functional language skills needed for school (adaptive language skills) are being studied at the Frank Porter Graham Child Development Center. The children studied here come from a longitudinal intervention project that examines children at high-risk for sociocultural retardation (The Carolina Abecedarian Project). The children in this project are being followed from birth through 8 years of age. Families have been identified as high-risk by a number of criteria reported in Ramey and Smith (1977), including maternal IQ, education, and income. After the infants are born, the families are pair-matched on a number of variables, and then a member of each pair is randomly assigned to an educational daycare program or a nonintervention group. Both groups of children receive social work services and medical and nutritional supplements. Thus the significant difference between the groups is an intervention program. The intervention daycare infants attend the program 8 hr per day, 5 days per week, 50 weeks per year until they enter public kindergarten. At school entry each intervention daycare child (experimental) and nonintervention child (control) is matched on sex with a low-risk child (middle-class) from the public school classroom.

Two experiments were designed that examined both narrative and communicative skills that appeared to be important for school (Feagans & Farran, in press). These experiments were administered in the fall of the kindergarten year in two sessions. At this point in the study approximately 45 high-risk and 45 low-risk children have been tested. The three aspects of each experiment were comprehension, verbal communication, and verbal flexibility.

The first experiment (instructional box) was accomplished in sessions involving three tasks: (a) the child was given an attractive wooden puzzle box and was instructed either verbally or nonverbally about how to open it. If the child failed to open it correctly, the procedure was repeated until the child achieved perfect comprehension. Thus trials to criterion was the comprehension measure; (b) the child was asked to explain to an adult confederate how to open the box—communication measure; and (c) the child was then required to clarify the instructions by verbally responding to a set of rephrasing requests, such as *tell me more* or *I don't understand*—verbal flexibility measure.

The second experiment (stories) involved reading three kinds of stories to the child that contained episodes that were (a) causal or script related; and (b) arbitrarily related; and (c) related by temporal-causal connectives like *before* and *after* (see Figure 5.1). Like the first experiment, there were three tasks: (a) the child was read a story until he or she could act the story out with the props provided—comprehension measure; (b) the child was asked to paraphrase that same story—production measure; and (c) the child was asked a series of questions about the story—verbal flexibility measure.

Results from the comprehension part of both experiments indicated that the experimental group performed somewhat better than the control group on two of the five comprehension measures, but that both groups performed more poorly on all measures of comprehension in comparison to the middle-class group.

Results from the verbal production part of Experiment II indicated that the groups did not differ on the proportion of complex sentences, total number of words, or on mean length utterance (MLU). Thus there were no structural output differences among the groups.

Both groups of high-risk children were less able to paraphrase the important episodes in the stories and to communicate information about the box in comparison to the low-risk children. On the story task both groups of high-risk children lost twice as much information in the paraphrase as did the middle-class children, and on the instructional box task the middle-class group produced twice as many informational units as the high-risk groups. The high-risk groups were also less able than the middle-class group to answer abstract questions about the stories (*how, when,* and *why*) and less able to rephrase a communication when the adult pretended not to understand.

Error analyses performed on the production part of the story task (Feagans & Farran, 1980) indicated that although all children's errors were due to missing elements in the story, the high-risk children added proportionately more irrelevant events in their paraphrases, used more nonreferential language, and more often referred to the sequence of episodes in a story in the wrong order. By examining the pattern of forgetting, it appeared that all groups tended to forget similar events, thus indicating no differences in the kind of events forgotten. It did appear, though, that both high-risk groups less often gave setting information in their stories and that the nonintervention group, especially, did not introduce the characters of the story. Errors of these types could be attributed (a) to the lack of experience in the use of language for narratives, indicating a less complete story schema by the high-risk children; and/or (b) to the possibility that the high-risk children did not understand the implicit demand characteristics of the tasks. These implicit demand characteristics could include the following:

1. Tell only the story told to you in a paraphrase. Do not add irrelevant information.
2. Tell the events in a story in the order in which they were told to you. Do not get the events out of order.
3. Be explicit. Be sure to tell information about the characters and setting as well as events in a story.

Experiments are now in progress to try to separate out these two possible explanations by varying the demand characteristics of the situation.

It is also clear from these experiments that the major variables from these tasks are related to achievement in kindergarten as measured by the Peabody Individualized Achievement Test and to teacher ratings of communication skills in the classroom. It is still to be seen whether these skills are predictive of later school adjustment and achievement when the children are in the later elementary school years.

CONCLUSIONS

It is clear that children from poverty families need assistance in using their language to adapt to the language material characteristic of school classrooms. The importance of gaining these skills cannot be overemphasized since teacher–pupil interaction as well as instructional materials require the child to both understand and verbally display these skills in order to succeed and learn in school, no matter what the cultural or economic background. But there is much we still do not know about social-class and/or cultural differences. More information is needed in order to better understand and help children whose language is not well adapted to the language functions at school. Hymes (1979) has formulated the problem in this way:

> I want to suggest that the problem of language in education is not to go back to basics, but to go forward to fundamentals. We must consider questions such as: (a)

how does language come organized for use in the communities from which children come to schools? (b) what are the meanings and values associated with use of language in the many different sectors and strata of the society? (c) what are the actual verbal abilities of children and others across the range of settings they naturally engage? (d) what is the fit (and misfit) between abilities and settings—where is an ability, frustrated for lack of a setting, a setting unentered for lack of an ability, in what ways are patterns of personal verbal ability shaped by restrictions of access to settings, on the one hand, culturally supported aspirations, on the other [p. 16]?

We have only begun to answer questions such as those raised by Hymes. What little we do know about the development of discourse and narrative skills indicates that, indeed, we need to seriously examine the development of dialogue skills in children from lower socioeconomic backgrounds in their community and in school. It appears to be particularly important to examine the sequence of moves and events in dialogues, especially those that are of a narrative type because it seems clear that teachers and schools will continue to expect and demand that children be able to use their language to understand and express their ideas within a narrative framework.

This chapter has tried to argue that the knowledge of the structure of "school-like" narratives particularly, and dialogues in general, are critical skills needed for the successful adaptation to the classroom and for the acquisition of school transmitted information.

Unfortunately, the thrust of language research and programs for poverty children has not focused on these areas of language. Teachers are still using materials that drill such children on syntax and vocabulary skills, hoping that this will somehow improve their understanding of classroom language. The teachers' inability to deal with unteachable responses and/or to understand their own use of narrative structure in conversation prevents them from helping these children.

What is needed, then, is a reanalysis of our programs and research for poverty children. We must first document carefully the development of dialogue and narrative skills in the natural community of both advantaged and poverty children. If, as has been argued here, there are differences in the structure and frequency of these interactions, intervention strategies for such poverty children would be quite different from previous ones. Much emphasis would be placed in preschool and school-age programs on developing one-to-one interactions that foster the sequence of moves needed to understand and express narrative information. This would, of necessity, require conversations to be lengthy and to remain on the same topic for an extended period of time. In addition, material presented to children would emphasize the thematic and narrative elements, with less emphasis on breaking materials into single words or sentences. Thus, to understand the development of this skill and the differences in the development among different groups of children helps us to help them, not only in adjusting to school but in learning the material they need to function well in this society.

REFERENCES

Bellack, A. A., Kliebard, H. M., Hyman, R. T., & Smith, F. L. *The language of the classroom.* New York: Teachers College Press, 1966.

Bernstein, B. Social structure, language and learning. *Educational Research,* 1961, 163–178.

Bernstein, B. A critique of the concept of compensatory education. In C. B. Cazden, V. L. John, & D. Hymes (Eds.), *The functions of language in the classroom.* New York: Teachers College Press, 1972.

Blank, M. Mastering the intangible through language. In Ira D. Aaronson & R. W. Rieber (Eds.), *Developmental psycholinguistics and communication disorders.* New York: The New York Academy of Sciences, 1975, 44–58.

Blank, M., Rose, S. A., & Berlin, L. J. *The language of learning: The preschool years.* New York: Grune & Stratton, 1978.

Bloom, L. M. *Language development: Form and function in emerging grammars.* Cambridge, Massachusetts: MIT Press, 1970.

Bloom, L. M. *One word at a time: The use of single word utterances before syntax.* The Hague: Mouton, 1973.

Bloom, L. S., Lightbowm, P., & Hood, L. Structure and variation in child language. *Monographs of the Society for Research in Child Development,* 1975, *40,* (2, Serial no. 160).

Brown, R. *A first language: The early stages.* Cambridge, Massachusetts: Harvard University Press, 1973.

Bruck, M., & Tucker, G. R. Social class differences in the acquisition of school language. *Merrill Palmer Quarterly,* 1974, *20,* 205–220.

Bruner, J. S. The role of dialogue in language acquisition. In A. Sinclair, R. J. Jarvella, & W. J. M. Levelt (Eds.), *The child's conception of language.* New York: Springer-Verlag, 1978.

Bruner, J., & Sherwood, V. Peekaboo and the learning of rule structures. In J. Bruner, A. Jolly, & K. Sylva (Eds.), *Play: Its role in development and evolution.* Hammondsworth, England: Penguin, 1976.

Camaioni, L. Child–adult and child–child conversations: An interactional approach. In E. Ochs & B. B. Schieffelin (Eds.), *Developmental pragmatics.* New York: Academic Press, 1979.

Cazden, C. B., John, V. P., & Hymes, D. (Eds.), *The functions of language in the classroom.* New York: Teachers College Press, 1973.

Deutsch, M., Katz, D., & Jensen, A. R. *Social class, race, and psychological development.* New York: Holt, Rinehart and Winston, 1968.

Dore, J. Variation in preschool children's conversational performances. In Keith K. Nelson (Ed.), *Children's language* (Vol. 1). New York: Gardner Press, 1978.

Doughty, P., Thornton, G., & Doughty, A. *Language study: The school and the community.* New York: Elsevier, 1977.

Ervin-Tripp, S. Social backgrounds and verbal skills. In R. Huxley & E. Ingram (Eds.), *Language acquisition: Models and methods.* New York: Academic Press, 1971.

Feagans, L., & Farran, D. C. How demonstrated comprehension can get muddled in production. *Developmental Psychology,* in press.

Feagans, L., & Farran, D. C. *Story comprehension and recall as a function of story structure.* Paper presented at the Sixth Biennial Southeastern Conference on Human Development, Alexandria, Virginia, 1980.

Feagans, L., & Haskins, R. *Dialogues in the neighborhoods of low- and middle-income children.* Manuscript in preparation, 1981.

Flanders, N. A. *Analyzing teaching behavior.* Reading, Massachusetts: Addison-Wesley, 1970.

Gallagher, J. J., & Aschner, M. J. A preliminary report on analyses of classroom interaction. *Merrill-Palmer Quarterly,* 1963, *9,* 183–194.

Garvey, C. *Play.* Cambridge, Massachusetts: Harvard University Press, 1977.

Garvey, C., & Hogan, R. Social speech and social interaction: Egocentrism revisited. *Child Development,* 1973, *44,* 562–568.

Glenn, C. G. Relationship between story content and structure. *Journal of Educational Psychology,* 1980, *72,* 550–560.

Gustafson, G. E., Green, J. A., & West, M. J. The infant's changing role in mother–infant games: The growth of social skills. *Infant Behavior and Development,* 1979, *2,* 301–308.

Hall, W. S., Cole, M., Reder, S., & Dowley, G. Variations in young children's use of language: Some effects of setting and dialect. In R. O. Freedle (Ed.), *Discourse production and comprehension* (Vol. 1). Norwood, New Jersey: Ablex, 1977.

Hymes, D. Language in education: Forward to fundamentals. In O. K. Garnica & M. L. King (Eds.), *Language, children and society.* New York: Pergamon Press, 1979.

Kernan, K. T. *Some elements of structure in the narratives of Black American children.* Paper presented at the annual meeting of the American Anthropological Association, Mexico City, 1974.

Labov, W. The logic of non-standard English. In F. Williams (Ed.), *Language and poverty.* Chicago: Markham, 1970.

Labov, W., & Fanshel, D. *Therapeutic discourse: Psychotherapy as conversation.* New York: Academic Press, 1977.

Labov, W., & Waletzky, J. Narrative analysis: Oral versions of personal experience. In J. Helm (Ed.), *Essays on the verbal arts.* Seattle: American Ethnological Society, 1966.

Mandler, J. M., & Johnson, N. S. Remembrance of things parsed: Story structure and recall. *Cognitive Psychology,* 1977, *9,* 111–151.

Milgram, N. A., Shore, M. F., & Malasky, C. Linguistic and thematic variables in recall of a story by disadvantaged children. *Child Development,* 1971, *42,* 637–640.

Ninio, A. Picture-book reading in mother–infant dyads belonging to two subgroups in Israel. *Child Development,* 1980, *51,* 587–590.

Ninio, A., & Bruner, J. The achievement and antecedents of labelling. *Journal of Child Language,* 1978, *5,* 1–15.

Rackstraw, S. J., & Robinson, W. P. Social and psychological factors related to variability of answering behavior in five-year-old children. *Language and Speech,* 1967, *10,* 88–106.

Ramey, C. T., & Smith, B. J. Assessing intellectual consequences of early intervention with high risk infants. *American Journal of Mental Deficiency,* 1977, *81*(4), 318–324.

Raph, J. B. Language development in socially disadvantaged children. *Review of Educational Research,* 1965, *35,* 389–400.

Robinson, W. P. Social factors and language development in primary school children. In R. Huxley & E. Ingram (Eds.), *Language acquisition: Models and methods.* New York: Academic Press, 1971.

Robinson, W. P., & Rackstraw, S. J. Variations in mothers' answers to children's questions as a function of social class, verbal intelligence test scores, and sex. *Sociology,* 1967, *1,* 259–276.

Rumelhart, D. E. Notes on a schema for stories. In D. G. Bobrow & A. M. Collins (Eds.), *Representation and understanding: Studies in cognitive science.* New York: Academic Press, 1975.

Sacks, H., Schegloff, E., & Jefferson, G. A simplest systematics for the organization of turn-taking in conversation. *Language,* 1974, *50,* 696–735.

Schaffer, H. R. Acquiring the concept of the dialogue. In M. H. Bernstein & W. Kessen (Eds.), *Psychological development from infancy.* Hillsdale, New Jersey: Erlbaum, 1979.

Schank, R. C., & Abelson, R. P. *Scripts, plans, goals, and understanding: An inquiry into human knowledge structures.* Hillsdale, New Jersey: Erlbaum, 1977.

Shuy, R. On the relevance of recent developments in sociolinguistics to the study of language learning and early education. In. O. K. Garnica & M. L. King (Eds.), *Language, children and society.* New York: Pergamon Press, 1979.

Sinclair, J. McH., & Coulthard, R. M. *Towards an analysis of discourse.* Oxford, England: Oxford University Press, 1975.

Slobin, D. I. *Questions of language development in cross-cultural perspective.* Manuscript prepared for language learning in cross-cultural perspective. Michigan State University, East Lansing, 1968.

Snow, C. E. The development of conversation between mothers and babies. *Journal of Child Language,* 1977, *4,* 1–22.

Stack, C. B. *All our kin: Strategies for survival in a Black community.* New York: Harper & Row, 1974.

Stein, N. L., & Glenn, C. G. An analysis of story comprehension in elementary school children: A test of schema. *Resources in Education,* 1976, *2*(8), 1–68.

Stein, N. L., & Glenn, C. G. An analysis of story comprehension in elementary school children. In R. Freedle (Ed.), *New directions in discourse processing.* Norwood, New Jersey: Ablex, 1979.

Stern, D. S. *The first relationship: Infant and mother.* Cambridge, Massachusetts: Harvard University Press, 1977.

Thorndyke, P. Cognitive structures in comprehension and memory of narrative discourse. *Cognitive Psychology.* 1977, *9,* 77–110.

Tough, J. Children and programmes: How shall we educate the young child? In A. Davies (Ed.), *Language and learning in early childhood.* London: Heinemann, 1977.

Umiker-Sebeok, J. D. Preschool children's intraconversational narratives. *Journal of Child Language,* 1979, *6,* 91–109.

Ward, M. C. *Them children.* New York: Holt, Rinehart and Winston, 1971.

Williams, F., & Naremore, R. C. On the functional analysis of social class differences in modes of speech. *Speech Monographs,* 1969, *36,* 77–102.

6

Societal Forces as a Context of Ghetto Children's School Failure

JOHN U. OGBU

This chapter will focus on language problems of black school children. Although both research and intervention efforts tend to treat the language problems of blacks as similar to those of the poor in general, we shall argue that they are not. We shall maintain that there is a distinction between class and racial, or castelike, stratification that has important implications for language development and language use in community and school. For unlike poor whites, poor blacks bear the burden of both class and racial stratification to which they have developed language and other coping strategies. It is probably for this reason that black and white children from "the same" social class do not necessarily behave alike in school and test situations. Consider the well-documented fact that at every socioeconomic level, black children perform less well than their white peers on standardized "intelligence" and academic achievement tests; moreover, these gaps begin as early as the age of 4 and increase in subsequent years (Baughman, 1971; Broman, Nichols, & Kennedy, 1975, cited in Haskins, 1980; Haskins, 1980; Jensen, 1969; Mayeske, Okada, Cohen, Beaton, & Wisler, 1973, cited in Weinberg, 1977; U.S. District Court for Northern California, 1979). Some prefer to attribute the performance gaps to genetic differences (Jensen, 1969); we offer a structural explanation, both for the school-age and preschool performance gaps between black and white children.

Our structural explanation is intended as a context for reinterpreting

117

THE LANGUAGE OF CHILDREN
REARED IN POVERTY

the "language" and related problems of school failure. It will not focus on language per se because research on language development and language use has, to date, been preoccupied with transactional rather than structural questions. However, it is our opinion that both language development and language use, in the black community and among black pupils in school, are affected by the double stratification of class and race and that an effective remedial or intervention effort must recognize this double reality among urban black poor.

Before we develop our structural argument, we shall briefly summarize some of the current explanations of black language problems. Following that, we shall distinguish class from racial or castelike stratification and examine the implication of the latter for black schooling. Some implications of our perspective for intervention efforts will be considered at the end of the chapter.

SOME CURRENT PERSPECTIVES ON THE LANGUAGE PROBLEMS

Two major perspectives on the language problems of black school children have emerged since the early 1960s, namely, deficit and difference perspectives. The research approach to the first is primarily developmental, whereas historical and sociolinguistic ethnographic approaches are used in connection with the second. There are, of course, differing views within each perspective as well as changes over time. But each perspective has promoted a distinct notion of the language problems, their causes, and their remedies.

Deficit Perspective

The deficit perspective holds that black children come to school with inadequate language for successful teaching and learning. Specifically, ghetto black children are said to be verbally "deprived": They cannot speak complete sentences, do not know names of objects, cannot form concepts, or convey logical thoughts. Their language is said to be mainly concrete rather than abstract, to have little capacity for conceptual learning, and to be context-bound (Bereiter, 1965; Bereiter & Engelmann, 1966; Bereiter, Osborne, Engelmann, & Reidford, 1965; Deutsch, 1964; Deutsch, Bloom, Brown, Deutsch, Goldstein, John, Katz, Levinson, Peisach, & Whiteman, 1967; Jensen, 1968; Labov, 1972; Whiteman & Deutsch, 1968). The deficit perspective explained the verbal deprivation by what I have elsewhere (Ogbu, 1978, 1979) called the *failure-of-socialization hypothesis*. According to this hypothesis, nonwhite ghetto children are verbally deprived because their parents do not provide them with the same amount and quality of verbal stimulation as do white middle-class parents for their children in the suburbs. Specifically, non-white ghetto children are said to be retarded in language development because they receive little verbal stimulation and hear very little well-formed language (Labov, 1972). The intervention strategy resulting from this hypothesis emphasized teaching ghetto children the proper English of the white middle-class and teaching ghetto parents how to stimulate their children verbally, as their white middle-class counterparts do. Educational psychologists and other proponents have substantially modified their thesis, partly because of severe criticisms from historical dialectologists and socioanthropological linguists and partly because their intervention programs have not produced expected results.

Archival and field studies by historical dialectologists, linguists, and anthropologists have now provided sufficient evidence for rejecting the concept of verbal deprivation on the grounds that it is inapplicable to black children in the ghetto (Baratz, 1970; Baratz & Baratz, 1970; Labov, 1972; Mitchell-Kernan, 1972; Stewart, 1970). It is ironic to label ghetto children as "verbally deprived" when verbal skills are among the most highly prized in their community (Abraham, 1972; Foster, 1974; Kochman, 1972; Perkins, 1975). The importance of verbal skills for ghetto people is obvious in the following description of the role of verbal abilities in a Washington ghetto study by Hannerz (1969):

> The skill of talking well and easily is widely appreciated among ghetto men; although it is hardly itself a sign of masculinity, it can be very helpful in realizing one's wishes. "Rapping," persuasive speech, can be used to manipulate others to one's own advantages. Besides talking well is useful in cutting losses as well as in making gains. However, all prestige accrued from being a good talker does not have to do with the strictly utilitarian aspect. A man with good stories well told and with quick repartee in arguments is certain to be appreciated for his entertainment value, and those men who can talk about the high and mighty, people and places, and the state of the world may stake claims to a reputation of being "heavy upstairs" [pp. 84–85].

Even a cautious version of the deficit model leaves many questions unanswered: If ghetto adults possess discourse and narrative skills, when and how did they learn them? Labov (1972), Kochman (1972), and others show that teenagers in the ghetto are well versed in discourse skills. Where, when, and how did they learn their skills?

In the author's own Ibo culture of Nigeria, for example, there is no picture-book reading; children and adults are in an extended family setting with many adults present. Yet, children learn discourse and narrative skills from conversations with adults, listening to adults, participation in folk tales, etc. What is not clear from the deficit perspective is whether the problem stems from ghetto children not possessing discourse and narrative skills when they come to school or merely not demonstrating such skills in classroom and test situations.

The Difference Perspective

The difference perspective argues that blacks possess a distinct English dialect that children acquire in the normal course of their growing up in the ghetto, just as their white middle-class peers acquire the white middle-class English dialect or the "standard English" in their own normal course of growing up in the suburb. According to this view, the two dialects are structurally equal, "since any verbal system used by a speech community is a well-ordered system with predictable sound patterns, grammatical structure, [and] vocabulary [Williams, 1970]."

The existence of a distinct black English dialect was discovered partly through the method of historical dialectology (Dillard, 1972; Stewart, 1970) and partly through ethnographic research (Labov, 1972). Stewart and other historical dialectologists traced the origins of black English dialect from the eighteenth-century West African pidgin English dialect, through the evolution of the latter into the Creole English dialect of the plantation South and the process of decreolization following emancipation, leading finally to the present-day form. On the basis of his ethnographic research, Labov (1972) acknowledged the validity of some aspects of the Creole hypothesis but emphasized the fusion of southern and northern black English dialects in the evolution of the present-day black ghetto dialect. The point to stress is that both groups agree that a distinct ghetto black English dialect exists that is structurally equal to the white middle-class English.

Black ghetto children learn the ghetto dialect because it is the language of their community rather than because their parents are incapable of teaching them the white middle-class dialect. This point is made by Williams (1970) when he states that languages are learned in the social contexts of their environments. Ibo children, for example, learn to speak Ibo not because their fathers are in the home or their mothers read books to them but because it is the language they hear continually from whatever sources and it is the language to which individuals in their environment respond. By the time children are 5 years old, they have developed language (i.e., have learned the rules of the speech community).

Proponents of the different-dialect hypothesis initially attributed the disproportionate school failure of ghetto blacks, especially their failure to learn to read at the same pace and with the same ease as their white middle-class peers, to structural interference when black children are trying to use the standard English. On this point Baratz (1970) writes:

> When the middle-class child starts the process of learning to read, his problem is primarily one of decoding the graphic representations of a language he already speaks. The disadvantaged black child must also "translate" them into his own language. This presents him with an almost insurmountable obstacle since the written words frequently do not go together in any pattern that is familiar or meaningful to him [p. 20].

The intervention strategy arising from this explanation places the burden of change on the school rather than on the ghetto child. As summarized by Simons (1976), it was initially proposed that the black dialect should be permitted in the classroom and that books and other curricula materials should be written in black dialect. Alternatively, some researchers (Goodman, 1965, cited in Simons, 1976) proposed presenting instructional materials and text books in the standard English but letting children produce black dialect responses. These remedies did not, however, produce expected results (i.e., they did not result in improved reading achievement among black children).

Critics charged that the hypothesis and resulting intervention strategy focused too much on materials and their effects on the teachers and on the teachers' responses to black children and that the hypothesis failed to specify the mechanisms by which the interference or mismatch occurred. Some critics proposed two types of interference: One was phonological (i.e., it was hypothesized that differences in pronunciation might interfere with the acquisition of word recognition skills). Subsequent research showed, however, that this was not a significant factor (Simons, 1976; Rentel & Kennedy, 1972). The second was grammatical, namely, that there might be a mismatch between a black child's syntax and the standard English syntax of the texts used by the teacher (Baratz, 1970; Stewart, 1969). But research has revealed no significant differences between black children who read materials written in standard English grammar and those who read materials written in black dialect grammar. The overall conclusion drawn from these studies is that black dialect is not the source of the failure of black ghetto children to learn to read (Simons, 1976).

Since the early 1970s anthropologists and others working from the difference perspective have moved away from a purely linguistic framework to a sociolinguistic one as a basis for understanding communicative interaction in the classroom. In their research they employ the theory of speech acts, which focuses on the intent of utterances as well as the effect of utterances on their hearers. The following summary is based on Simons' (1976) interesting paper.

The theory of a speech act distinguishes between the literary meaning of what is said and the effect it is intended to have upon the hearer. An example is a teacher's statement to students, *We don't sit on the tables,* which literarily refers to the fact that people do not sit on the tables but could also mean a request or a command not to sit on the tables. The correct interpretation of such a speech act depends partly upon shared background information and partly upon the ability of the hearer to make inferences.

Gumperz expanded the theory beyond an individual utterance by adding the notion of *situated meaning* (cited in Simons, 1976; see also Gumperz & Herasimchuk, 1972). A situated meaning is the intent of a speaker in a particular context. *Context* "includes the speaker's perception of a social situation and social relations, the type of speech activity, and the relation of the utterance surrounding it and the discourse as a whole [Simons, 1976, p. 18]." In order to understand the situated meaning of an utterance, the hearer must know both the literary meaning and the appropriate metacommunication cues or contextualization cues that suggest the meaning of the utterance in a particular social situation. Among commonly identified contextualization cues are (*a*) intonation, (*b*) code switching, (*c*) stress, (*d*) choice of lexical items and syntactic structure, (*e*) rhythms, (*f*) loudness and softness, and (*g*) utterance sequencing strategies. Both communicative strategies and meanings of contextualization cues are culturally determined, that is, people from different cultural backgrounds (e.g., ghetto blacks and suburban whites) will not share the same communicative background and will therefore differ in their communicative strategies and interpretation of the situated meaning of a given passage or utterance. This difference in communicative background is hypothesized to result in miscommunication between people from different cultures.

The language problems of ghetto black students, according to the theory, are essentially those of miscommunication of the situated meaning between teacher and student due to the fact that students and their teachers do not share the same communicative background or culture.

However, it is what is communicated by the classroom environment that is at issue rather than differences in cultural backgrounds or in the language of the teacher and students per se. And the goal of research is to isolate the processes that are meaningful to the participants in classroom communicative interchange. Phillips' notion of *participant structure* (1972) provides the conceptual framework for research. Basically, a participant structure is "a constellation of norms, mutual rights and obligations that shape social relationships, determine participants' perceptions about what is going on, and influence learning [Simons, 1976]." It is hypothesized that the participant structure of the home and the school are different for ghetto blacks. The generally poor school performance of these children is attributed to the discontinuity between their home participant structure and that of the school. Several studies have been conducted to show that what is learned in the classroom is influenced by the differences in participation structures or the values and presuppositions learned in the home (Erickson & Mohatt, 1977 cited in Koehler, 1978; Philips, 1972).

A more severe difference perspective survives in the notion that black ghetto children come to school with some language skills that are different from those required to do well in school. A strong case for such problems is made by Feagans in this volume (see Chapter 5). She argues that both teacher–pupil interaction and instructional materials require the child to know and demonstrate discourse and narrative skills. According to her, one aspect of these children's problem is that they do not possess such skills when they come to school because they grow up in communities where they do not have the opportunity for sustained adult–child conversations on the same topic. As a remedy, she advocates teaching these children intraconversational narrative skills: "Much emphasis would be placed in preschool and school-age programs in developing a one-to-one interaction that foster the sequence of moves needed to understand and express narrative information [Feagans, Chapter 5, p. 113]."

Feagans's argument that children effectively learn discourse and narrative skills in sustained one-to-one conversations with adults may be true of Western middle-class culture; however, other cultures, including the black American ghetto, may provide other means of learning discourse and narrative skills that have not yet been discovered by researchers. Nor is it necessarily true that the presence of many adults in a culture prevents a one-to-one sustained adult–child conversation. As I mentioned in the example from the Ibo culture, narratives are learned from a variety of adults and children.

The difference perspective has made two major contributions toward our understanding of the language problems but has not gone far enough. The first contribution is the discovery of a distinct black English dialect. Yet the historical dialectologists do not fully answer the question of why the separate dialect evolved and persists, despite centuries of apparent contact with speakers of standard English. Some evidence in Stewart's accounts (1970) strongly suggests the need to explore the influence of caste or racial barriers in the evolution and perpetuation of the dialect. The influence of racial isolation and other barriers on black language patterns during slavery points to this need. For example, according to Stewart, house slaves who had greater contacts with speakers of standard English quickly acquired a more standard variety of English than the Creole of the field hands as did the educated blacks (Stewart, 1970; Labov, 1972). Immigrant groups who did not face such barriers gave up their "pidgin" and other varieties of English to acquire the more standard form. Moreover, if, as Stewart (1970) suggests, social mobility in American society requires and encourages standard English, then caste barriers that have traditionally limited social mobility among blacks (Ogbu, 1978) have also limited their opportunities to acquire standard English as a functional language.

The second contribution of the difference perspective lies in the microenthnographic studies of classroom communicative interchange. These studies have enriched our understanding of how ghetto black and similar subordinate-group children fail. They describe one set of mechanisms by which the school failures, and reading failures in particular, are achieved within the classroom. This knowledge is quite useful in at least two important ways: developing intervention programs (e.g., for preparation of teachers) and in encouraging cautious interpretation of quantitative studies of children's academic performance.

However, these microethnographic studies as presently formulated are too simplistic and, in some cases, misleading. In the first place, the mismatch explanation is based on research on one type of minority-group children that we have designated elsewhere as *castelike minorities* (Ogbu 1978). The mismatch hypothesis has not been applied to immigrant minorities and other groups who differ from their public school teachers in communicative strategies and interpretation of situated meanings but nonetheless are more successful in school and in learning to read than black Americans. An adequate explanation must be based on broader comparative data. Second, the mismatch hypothesis ignores historical and societal forces that may actually generate the observed patterns of classroom communicative interaction. Finally, although insights from these studies can be used for remedial programs (Erickson 1978; Simons 1976), they cannot lead to a significant social change that would, in turn, eliminate the need for such remedial efforts in subsequent generations of black children (Ogbu 1980a, in press, a). Implicit in our presentation in the next section are two points relevant to the contributions of the difference perspective: that caste barriers played a major role in the evolution of the black English dialect as an alternative to the standard English; and that caste barriers and relations make classroom communicative interchange a problem area.

CASTELIKE MINORITY STATUS AND LOWER-CLASS STATUS

In our previous work (Obgu, 1978) we suggested that black Americans are a special type of minority group, a castelike minority. We also suggested that castelike stratification is different from stratification by social class and that it has different educational implications. Therefore, it is erroneous to treat black language and other school problems either as minority problems or as lower-class problems. There are important distinctions.

A *castelike minority group* is one incorporated into a society involuntarily and permanently and whose only means of escape from this enforced subjugation is through "passing" or emigration—routes that are not always open. Black Americans, for example, were brought to the United States as slaves. Membership in a castelike minority group is acquired more or less permanently at birth. Members of a castelike minority group generally have limited access to the social goods of society by virtue of their group membership and not because they lack training and ability or education. In particular, they face a job ceiling—that is, highly consistent pressures and obstacles that selectively assign blacks and similar minority groups to jobs at the lowest level of status, power, dignity, and income while allowing members of the dominant white group to compete more easily for more desirable jobs above that ceiling. We use the term *castelike minority* as a methodological tool to emphasize the structural base of the history of black subordination. We are not suggesting that black Americans are a caste group in the classical Hindu Indian sense.

Black castelike minority status is different from the status of the lower-class white. What is the distinction? There is no generally accepted definition of social class, though we can distinguish broadly the Marxist and the non-Marxist definitions. The non-Marxists define a social class as a segment of society's population differentiated by education, occupation, and income—the interaction of which is believed to result in a common lifestyle and power relation. Social classes here are synonymous with socioeconomic groups. In contrast, the Marxists define social classes on the basis of their relations to the means of production and power struggle.

Neither of the two definitions can be used to provide adequate explanation of the language and other school problems of black Americans. For example, as earlier indicated, gaps in IQ and academic achievement remain when blacks and whites from the same socioeconomic status are compared. We have seen no comparisons of blacks and whites on IQ and academic achievement based on the Marxist definition of class. We therefore retain the non-Marxist definition of class as a socioeconomic group in the rest of our discussion. And we shall compare caste and class stratifications on the basis of: (a) closure; (b) affiliation; (c) status summation; (d) social mobility; and (e) cognitive orientation.

Closure and Affiliation

The basis of class stratification is economic relations, an acquired characteristic, whereas castelike stratification is based on "status honor," regarded as an inborn quality. Although social classes are more or less permanent entities, they have no clear boundaries and their membership is not permanent since people are continually moving in and out of them. Moreover, children of an interclass mating can affiliate with the class of either parent. Castes are, on the other hand, permanently hierarchically organized into more or less endogamous groups. Intercaste marriage is often prohibited, but where intercaste mating or marriage is allowed there is usually a formal or an informal rule as to which parent group the children belong—throughout the history of the United States to the present all children of known black–white matings are automatically defined as black. In very rare cases do some blacks covertly become whites through the painful and nonlegitimated process of "passing."

Status Summation

In a class system, social, occupational, and political positions are often based on training and ability. This phenomenon is much less so for caste and racial minorities, which explains why blacks and similar minorities are preoccupied with the civil rights struggle for equal social, economic, and political opportunities.

Social Mobility

Vertical social mobility is built into class stratification as legitimate, and the means of moving from a lower status group into a higher one is usually prescribed. Mobility from one social stratum to the next is prohibited in a castelike stratification.

Cognitive Orientation

Classes and castes differ in their cognitive orientations. Castelike minorities do not accept their low social, political, and occupational status as legitimate outcomes of their individual failures and misfortunes. Black Americans, for example, see racial barriers in employment, education, housing, and other areas as the primary causes of their menial positions and poverty. Most blacks share this orientation of "blaming the system" rather than themselves for failure to get ahead, a cognitive orientation that forms the basis of their collective struggle for equal opportunities through civil rights.

In contrast, in the United States at least, there is neither a conscious feeling among white members of a given class that they belong together in a corporate unity, nor that their common interests are different from those of other classes (Myrdal, 1944). Even white lower-class Americans do not share a collective perception of their social and economic difficulties as stemming from the system. What distinguishes poor ghetto blacks from the lower-class segment of the dominant white group is not their objective material condition but the way the two groups perceive and interpret that condition. This differential perception and interpretation has far reaching implications for formal education.

Castelike minorities (e.g., black Americans) and dominant groups (e.g., white Americans) are, of course, internally stratified by social class. However, black and white social classes are not equal in development and are qualitatively different. They are unequal in development because, traditionally, blacks have less access to the number and variety of jobs and training associated with class differentiation and mobility. For example, the black upper class has been traditionally made up of people in a limited number of professions such as law, medicine, business, teaching, and preaching, with the last two comprising almost two-thirds of the upper class before the 1950s. These are professions that serve primarily the needs of the black community. Until recently, blacks were largely excluded from other higher-paying professions such as architecture, civil engineering, accounting, chemistry, and management. In general, a castelike minority upper class tends to overlap with the middle-class segment of the dominant group, and minority middle class overlaps with the upper lower-class segment of the dominant group. The minority lower class is made up of an unstable working class, the unemployed, and the unemployables (Drake & Cayton, 1970; Ogbu, 1978, 1974).

Castelike minority social classes are qualitatively different because the historical circumstances that created them and the structural forces that sustain them are different from those that created and sustain the social classes of the dominant group. For example, the narrow base of class differentiation among black Americans began with slavery rather than with differences in education and family background. After slavery, racial barriers in employment—a job ceiling—continued for generations to limit their base of class differentiation and mobility (Higgs, 1980;

Ogbu, 1978). These collective experiences resulted in the evolution of a shared perception of lack of equal opportunity for blacks of any class (i.e., the perception that it is much more difficult for blacks than whites to achieve economic and social self-betterment in the conventional economy and sociopolitical system). Another reason for the qualitative difference is the forced ghettoization of blacks (Drake, 1968; Ogbu, 1978). Even after emancipation and urbanization, whites created and maintained clearly defined residential areas of the cities where they restricted the black population until recent decades. Many relatively well-to-do blacks who would prefer to live elsewhere were forced to share the ghetto with less fortunate blacks. This involuntary common residential experience also generated a common sense of oppressed people.

The cumulative effects of the common experiences of the job ceiling and enforced ghettoization might have resulted in the following equally cumulative effects that qualitatively differentiate social classes of blacks from those of the dominant whites: an evolution of an orientation toward blaming the system for black economic and social problems; an evolution of a greater sense of "peoplehood" or a common identity among blacks of all social classes than can be found among whites; and an evolution of a coping lifestyle shared by members of all social classes but most pronounced among lower-class blacks because of extreme poverty and fewer chances for advancement. The coping lifestyle includes some dimensions of black dialect that allow blacks to express frustrations, exploit their marginal environmental resources, and manipulate relationships with the dominant group in a way that permits them to retain their safety and identity. In order to show how the cumulative effects of the job ceiling and ghettoization enter into the language and school problems of black children from preschool through school age, we shall now introduce the concept of the *status mobility system*.

STATUS MOBILITY SYSTEM OR SOCIETAL FORCES AFFECTING BLACK SCHOOL PERFORMANCE

A status mobility system is the approved method and folk theory of self-betterment in a society or social group. Members of a society or social group share this theory about how their status mobility system works, and the theory includes the range of available status positions (e.g., types of jobs open to people), rules for eligibility for competition for the available positions, and how to qualify for successful competition. The status mobility system works insofar as the actual experiences of a large proportion of the population confirms the folk beliefs about the system. The way the system works generally influences the values and practices of parents and other adults entrusted with the upbringing of children as well as the way children strive to be as they get older. The native theory of how their status mobility system works is the cognitive basis of their behavior in childrearing (and schooling) and in their quest for self-betterment (Ogbu, 1980b, 1980c, in press, b).

When a society is stratified, especially by caste or race, there tend to be different status mobility systems for different social strata. The status mobility system of castelike minorities in such a society usually has two unique features. First, it offers access to fewer social goods like high-paying occupations than the status mobility system of the dominant group; and second, it embodies two sets of rules of behavior for achievement: one imposed by the dominant group and the other evolved within the subordinate population. In the United States whites impose both educational credentials and "Uncle Tomming" or clientship as qualifications for blacks to get ahead, whereas blacks have evolved survival strategies, including collective struggle and hustling, as alternative means of getting ahead. Members of the minority groups employ these two sets of rules or qualifications differentially according to their circumstances.

Childrearing and schooling in a castelike society reflect the multiple nature of the status mobility system. They are organized to prepare differentially dominant-group and minority-group children to participate in their respective status mobility system. Therefore, a clue to the basis of minority education problems, particularly their disproportionate school failure, lies in the nature of their status mobility system. Partly because the minority's status mobility system contains access to fewer jobs requiring high-level schooling, and partly because it embodies two sets of rules of behavior for achievement or qualification, minority schooling is usually characterized by the following factors that contribute to their disproportionate school failure: (a) inferior education; (b) disillusionment and lack of effort arising from low educational payoffs; (c) incongruence between minority survival strategies and school requirements; and (d) conflict and distrust between the minorities and the schools.

Inferior Education

Inferior jobs and other adult positions available to castelike minorities and the dominant group's perceptions of the minority's status mobility system shape the kind of education considered appropriate for the minorities. In general, castelike minorities do not get the same kind of quality education available to the dominant group. And inferior education results in inferior performance.

Thus while slavery lasted, American blacks received occasional education in the Bible because their masters believed that it would make them more obedient and faithful workers. After the Civil War, blacks remained in the peon-like status of sharecroppers or in the "Negro jobs" of domestic and unskilled labor, and education followed suit. The ruling white elites believed that the tenant system would break down if black children, as future laborers, received the same kind of education as did whites since such education would encourage them to question the high rates of interest and exploitative methods of account-keeping used by the planters in dealing with illiterate tenants. Consequently, academic training for blacks was deemphasized, and black education was starved of funds (Bond, 1966; Bullock, 1970).

As the South urbanized, blacks initially were provided with some industrial education, chiefly for cooking and low-grade building skills. But then many desirable factory jobs began to require special training. Ironically, the curricula of black schools could emphasize classical or academic programs but not the kind of industrial training that white schools began to emphasize.

We can conclude that, historically, if blacks did not qualify for desirable jobs, it was because their education was designed to disqualify them rather than because they were incapable of qualifying for the jobs. Until perhaps the 1960s American society never seriously intended for blacks to achieve equal social and occupational status with whites through education.

Even now, subtle mechanisms continue to underscore the different futures facing ghetto black and suburban white graduates. One subtle mechanism now receiving increasing attention is the disproportionate number of black children who are labeled as having "learning handicaps" and are channeled into special education, which prepares them for inferior occupations. For example, in a recent court case brought by blacks against the San Francisco school district, evidence was presented showing that black children, who made up only 31.1% of the school enrollment in 1976–1977, constituted 53.8% of all children in the educable mentally retarded classes. In the same year, in 20 California school districts that enrolled 80% of all black children in the state, blacks comprised 27.5% of the school population but constituted 62% of the educable mentally retarded population. The judge in the case found against the San Francisco school district, noting that the disproportionate placement of blacks in the special education classes could not have been by chance. The figures for San Francisco are similar to those in other large American cities like Chicago and New York.

Black Response

It would appear, from their long history of collective struggle for equal education, that blacks see formal education as a means of improving their social and occupational status. But their expectations have not been met partly because their education has not been designed to do this. Blacks appear to have responded to inferior education and the job ceiling in a number of ways that have actually tended to promote school failure and educational preparation for marginal economic participation. Among these responses discussed next are conflict with the schools, disillusionment and lowered efforts, and survival strategies.

Conflict with Schools

Throughout the history of public school education in America, blacks have perceived their exclusion from superior education as being designed to prevent them from qualifying for the more desirable jobs open to the dominant white group. Consequently, a significant part of their collective struggle has gone toward forcing whites and the schools to provide them with equal education.

Thus, initially, blacks fought against total exclusion from the public schools. Now for over a century they have been fighting against inferior education in segregated and in integrated schools. Where and when they attend segregated schools, the latter are theoretically "their" schools, so that one might expect them to identify and work with such schools. But the identification and cooperation have usually been undermined by simultaneous perceptions of segregated black schools as being inferior to white schools. This results in attention and efforts being diverted toward integration and equalization of education. In this relationship there emerges a general feeling that the public schools cannot be trusted to educate black children well because of their gross and subtle mechanisms of discrimination. These conflicts also force schools to deal with blacks defensively, to resort to various forms of control, paternalism, or even to "contest"; all of which divert efforts from the task of educating black children. It is reasonable to assume that this type of relationship, riddled with conflict and suspicion, makes it more difficult for blacks to accept and internalize the goals, standards, and instructional objectives or approaches of the public schools; it is a situation that must contribute to the educability problems of black children.

Job Ceiling, Disillusionment, and Lowered Efforts

Castelike minority children perceive their future adult opportunities as limited by the job ceiling, and these perceptions influence their perceptions of and response to schooling. For example, the junior and senior high school students we studied in Stockton, California, saw the local student body as academically stratified into above-average, average, and below-average groups, with themselves (blacks and chicanos) falling into the average and below-average groups. These students explained that in order to be a part of the above-average group, a student must have serious attitudes toward school and work hard in school. Local blacks and chicanos, they also explained, do not behave in this manner because they do not expect to get the same jobs and other educational benefits open to whites (Ogbu, 1974).

Castelike minority children learn about the job ceiling and other caste barriers partly from observing older members of their community and partly from the unconscious teaching of their parents. They live in a world in which they daily observe unemployed and underemployed adults as well as drug abuse, alcoholism, and crime. Although ghetto black parents tell their children that it is important to get a good education, they may also subtly convey to them the idea that society does not fully reward blacks for their educational efforts and accomplishments when they discuss before their children their own employment experiences and frustrations due to the job ceiling or the frustrations and experiences of relatives, friends, neighbors, and other members of their community. The children increasingly learn to blame the system as their parents do. Eventually the children become disillusioned about their ability to succeed in adult life through educational credentials, and they begin to have doubts about the real values of schooling. As they get older and become more aware of the status mobility system of the ghetto, they become less and less interested in school, less serious about their schoolwork, and less willing to exert the efforts necessary to do well in school. And they rationalize their subsequent failures by blaming the system (Frazier, 1940; Ogbu, 1974; Schulz, 1969).

Survival Strategies and School Requirements

Economic, social, political, and other discriminations experienced by generations of adult blacks and similar minorities force them to develop alternative or survival strategies for coping with their situation and for self-advancement. These survival strategies become an integral part of ghetto culture and the ghetto status mobility system. They are learned normally, and partly unconsciously, by children during the preschool years as they learn other aspects of their culture.

Some survival strategies like *collective struggle* or civil rights activities teach the children to blame the system, including the schools, for their individual and group problems—to externalize the causes of their school problems. Other survival strategies like *clientship* or *Uncle Tomming* teach the children that one key to achievement or self-betterment in that part of the universe open to blacks is through white favoritism, not merit; that the way to solicit that favoritism is by playing some version of the old "Uncle Tom" role, by being compliant, dependent, and manipulative. Still other survival strategies like *hustling* and *pimping* teach ghetto children an inverted version of the conventional work ethic; they learn to view every social interaction, including classroom interaction, as a setting for interpersonal contest and exploitation (Ogbu, 1980c).

We suggest that the survival strategies may contribute to the educability problems of ghetto children in two ways. First, the necessity to teach and learn the survival strategies reduces the time and effort the group invests in teaching and learning skills relevant to school success. Second, the incongruence between the competencies for survival strategies and the competencies required by the school may interfere with actual teaching and learning in the classroom.

Ghetto children generally begin to learn the survival strategies during the preschool years, so that by the time they arrive at school, the potential for learning problems already exists. Preschool children do not, of course, know that there are learning attitudes and skills connected with the survival strategies; nor do ghetto parents deliberately set out to teach their preschool and older children attitudes and skills required by the survival strategies. Nevertheless, it is our contention that preschool children begin to learn these aspects of their culture as they learn any other, before they are old enough to know what they are. We have at least one ethnographic report (Young, 1974) that suggests that low-income black parents use childrearing techniques that may encourage their children to develop the type of contest skills and other competencies associated with survival strategies. As the children get older they become aware of the values of the survival strategies and consciously seek to acquire them. Thus Pouissant and Atkins (1973) report that one study found children as young as age 9 in Harlem already knew that hustling and pimping were essential survival strategies. Some studies report that elementary school children already manifest attitudes and behaviors associated with the survival strategies (Perkins, 1975; Silverstein & Krate, 1975) and that by adolescence many inner-city black youngsters have acquired personal attributes required by the survival strategies (Foster, 1974; Perkins, 1975). It is the influence of these survival strategies that may help to account for the low IQ and achievement scores of preschool, kindergarten, and early-elementary school children in the ghetto—children not old enough to understand job and other adult opportunities. The perceptions of the job ceiling and other adult barriers in relation to the perceptions of their schooling further add to the problems of older children.

Considering the above factors in the context of the ghetto status mobility system—inferior education, conflict and distrust between blacks and the schools, disillusionment and lack of persevering efforts because of a job ceiling, and the influence of survival strategies—we conclude that the disproportionate school failure of ghetto children is an adaptation: The school performance is just at a level appropriate to prepare them for inferior jobs and other positions traditionally open to adult members of their community. These jobs and other positions neither require much education nor bring much reward for educational efforts and accomplishments.

CONCLUSION

Although the classroom is the "scene of the battle" (Robert, 1971), where the school failure is achieved, the causes of the war lie beyond that field and include the historical and structural forces we have considered in this chapter. These important forces cannot be captured easily by research designs that focus on language and communication at home or in the classroom. Even if ghetto children come to school without discourse and narrative skills, there still remains the question of why they do not learn enough of these skills in school to perform like white children from similar socioeconomic backgrounds who may also come to school without the same skills.

It is true that ghetto blacks come to the public school with a different communicative background from that of their teachers, in terms of communicative strategies and interpretations of situated meanings. But probably so do other groups of children—for example, Chinese, Filipinos, Japanese, and other foreign students in American universities and colleges who come from diverse cultures. Why do the latter groups' communicative backgrounds not result in learning problems similar to those experienced by ghetto blacks? The answer lies in both the historical development of ghetto blacks' communicative competencies as well as in their structural position, both of which are different from those of the immigrant groups. Black Americans developed their communicative strategies and interpretations of situated meanings as alternatives to white American communicative strategies and interpretations of situated meanings. The communicative style of each racial group arose to meet the functional requirements of their social and economic realities. In the past, whites often monopolized certain strategies for solving subsistence and other problems of living, forcing blacks to work out alternative strategies or solutions that might be opposite to the white solutions. In some domains, behaving like the whites was not even safe—it might result in beating, imprisonment, or death. So rather than learn how to behave like whites, blacks often learned how to deal with white folks— how to manipulate whites and their institutions with sufficient care to maintain their identities and safety. Black children who acquire this type of communicative etiquette and situated meanings may consciously and unconsciously resist learning the school communicative etiquette and situated meanings that represent "the white ways." In contrast, immigrant minorities and foreign students do not bring to American classrooms communicative etiquette developed in opposition to the whites' and do not find their identities threatened by learning the communicative strategies and situated meanings of the whites. As a matter of fact, they go to school anticipating doing just that in order to succeed.

If one wished to reverse the present situation of ghetto children, the approach that seems most logical from our analysis would be a policy designed (a) to increase the orientation of ghetto children toward academic work, and perseverance in academic work and test-taking situations; (b) to reduce the conflict and distrust between blacks and the public schools; and (c) to harness the competencies of the survival strategies for classroom teaching and learning.

An inevitable part of increasing black academic orientation and efforts is breaking the job ceiling—improving overall black job and other economic opportunities. Provided that the external forces—such as the job ceiling—are changing in the right direction, and the change is so experienced and perceived by blacks, the reversal would also require a kind of internal mobilization of social movement within the black community itself, with a strong ideology and practice supporting "making it" in the mainstream way. It is easier to improve black academic orientation and perseverance when the black way of doing things is no longer seen as opposite to the white way and when it is not threatening to adopt the white way. In this context, some means must be devised to bring blacks and the schools together in ways that make for mutual acceptance of standards, goals, and rules of behavior.

REFERENCES

Abrahams, R. D. Joking: The training of the man of words in talking broad. In T. Kochman (Ed.), *Rappin' and stylin' out: Communication in urban black America.* Urbana, Illinois: University of Illinois Press, 1972.

Baratz, J. Teaching reading in an urban Negro school system. In F. Williams (Ed.), *Language and poverty: Perspectives on a theme.* Chicago: Markham, 1970.

Baratz, S., & Baratz, J. Early childhood intervention: The social science base of institutional racism. *Harvard Educational Review,* 1970, *40,* 29–50.

Baughman, E. *Black Americans.* New York: Academic Press, 1971.

Bereiter, C. Academic instruction for preschool children. In R. Cobin & M. Crosby (Eds.), *Language programs for the disadvantaged.* Champaign, Illinois: National Council of Teachers of English, 1965.

Bereiter, C., Osborne, J., Engelmann, S., & Reidford, P. A. An academically oriented preschool for culturally deprived children. In F. M. Hechinger (Ed.), *Preschool education today.* New York: Doubleday, 1965.

Bereiter, C., & Engelmann, S. *Teaching disadvantaged children in the preschool.* Englewood Cliffs, New Jersey: Prentice-Hall, 1966.

Bond, H. M. *The education of the Negro in the American social order.* New York: Octagon, 1966.

Broman, S. H., Nichols, P. L., & Kennedy, W. A. *Preschool IQ, prenatal and early developmental correlates.* Hillsdale, New Jersey: Erlbaum, 1975.

Bullock, H. A. *A history of Negro education in the South: From 1619 to the present.* New York: Praeger, 1970.

Deutsch, C. Auditory discrimination and learning: Social factors. *Merrill-Palmer Quarterly,* 1964, *10,* 277–299.

Deutsch, M., Bloom, R. D., Brown, B. R., Deutsch, C. A., Goldstein, L. S., John, V. P., Katz, P. A., Levinson, A., Peisach, E. C., & Whiteman, M. *The disadvantaged child: Selected papers of Martin Deutsch and associates.* New York: Basic Books, 1967.

Dillard, J. L. *Black English: Its history and usage in the United States.* New York: Random House, 1972.

Drake, St. C. The ghettoization of Negro life. In L. A. Ferman, J. L. Kornbluh, & J. A. Miller (Eds.), *Negroes and jobs.* Ann Arbor, Michigan: University of Michigan Press, 1968.

Drake, St. C., & Cayton, H. R. *Black metropolis: A study of Negro life in a northern city* (Vols. 1 & 2). New York: Harcourt, 1970.

Erickson, F. *Mere ethnography: Some problems in its use in educational practice.* Past presidential address delivered at the annual meeting of the Council on Anthropology and Education. Los Angeles, California, November, 1978.

Erickson, F., & Mohatt, J. *The social organization of participant structure in two classrooms of Indian students.* Unpublished manuscript, 1977.

Foster, H. L. *Ribbin', Jivin', and Playin' the Dozens: The unrecognized dilemma of inner-city schools.* Cambridge, Massachusetts: Ballinger, 1974.

Frazier, E. F. *Negro youth at the crossways: Their personality development in the middle states.* Washington, D.C.: American Council on Education, 1940.

Goodman, K. G. Dialect barriers to reading comprehension. *Elementary English,* 1965, *42,* 853–860.

Gumperz, J. J., & Herasimchuk, E. Conversational analysis of social meaning. In R. Shuy (Ed.), *Sociolinguistics: Current trends and prospects. Georgetown University*

Monographs in Language and Linguistics. Washington, D.C.: Georgetown University Press, 1972, 99–134.

Hannerz, U. *Soulside.* New York: Columbia University Press, 1969.

Haskins, R. *Race, family income, and school achievement.* Unpublished manuscript, 1980.

Higgs, R. *Competition and coercion: Blacks in the American economy, 1865–1914.* Chicago: The University of Chicago Press, 1980.

Jensen, A. R. Social class and verbal learning. In M. Deutsch, I. Katz, & A. R. Jensen (Eds.), *Social class, race, and psychological development.* New York: Holt, Rinehart and Winston, 1968.

Jensen, A. R. How much can we boost IQ and scholastic achievement? *Harvard Educational Review,* 1969, *30,* 1–123.

Kochman, T. (Ed.). *Rappin' and stylin' out: Communication in urban black America.* Urbana, Illinois: University of Illinois Press, 1972.

Koehler, V. Classroom process research: Present and future. *The Journal of Classroom Interaction,* 1978, *13,* 3–11.

Labov, W. *Language in the inner city: Studies in the black English vernacular.* Philadelphia, Pennsylvania: University of Pennsylvania Press, 1972.

Mayeske, G. W., Okada, W., Cohen, M., Beaton, A. E., Jr., & Wisler, C. E. *A study of the achievement of our nation's students.* Washington, D.C.: U.S. Government Printing Office, 1973.

Mitchell-Kernan, C. Signifying, loud talking, and marking. In T. Kochman (Ed.), *Rappin' and stylin' out: Communication in urban black America.* Urbana, Illinois: University of Illinois Press, 1972.

Myrdal, G. *An American dilemma: The Negro problem and modern democracy.* New York: Harper & Row, 1944.

Ogbu, J. U. *The next generation: An ethnography of education in an urban neighborhood.* New York: Academic Press, 1974.

Ogbu, J. U. *Minority education and caste: The American system in cross-cultural perspective.* New York: Academic Press, 1978.

Ogbu, J. Social stratification and socialization of competence. *Anthropology and Education Quarterly,* 1979, *10,* 3–20.

Ogbu, J. U. *An ecological approach to minority education.* Unpublished manuscript, 1980. (a)

Ogbu, J. U. *Literacy among subordinate minorities: The case of black Americans.* Unpublished manuscript, 1980. (b)

Ogbu, J. U. *A cultural ecology of ghetto competence.* Unpublished manuscript, 1980. (c)

Ogbu, J. U. School ethnography: A multi-level approach. *Anthropology and Education Quarterly,* in press. (a)

Ogbu, J. U. Origins of human competence: A cultural ecological perspective. *Child Development,* in press. (b)

Perkins, E. *Home is a dirty street.* Chicago, Illinois: Third World Press, 1975.

Philips, S. U. Participant structure and communicative competence: Warm Springs children in community and classrooms. In C. B. Cazden, V. P. John, & D. Hymes (Eds.), *Functions of language in the classroom.* New York: Teachers College Press, 1972.

Pouissant, A., & Atkinson, C. Black youth and motivation. In E. G. Epps (Ed.), *Race relations: Current perspectives.* Cambridge, Massachusetts: Winthrop, 1973.

Rentel, V., & Kennedy, J. Effects of pattern drill on the phonology, syntax, and reading achievement of rural Appalachian children. *American Educational Research Journal,* 1972, *9,* 87–100.

Robert, J. I. *The scene of the battle: Group behavior in urban classrooms.* Garden City, New York: Doubleday, 1971.

Schulz, D. A. *Coming up black: Patterns of ghetto socialization.* Englewood Cliffs, New Jersey: Prentice-Hall, 1969.

Silverstein, B., & Krate, R. *Children of the dark ghetto: A developmental psychology.* New York: Praeger, 1975.

Simons, H. D. *Black dialect, reading interference and classroom interaction.* Unpublished manuscript, 1976.

Stewart, W. A. On the use of Negro dialect in the teaching of reading. In J. Baratz & R. Shuy (Eds.), *Teaching black children to read.* Washington, D.C.: Center for Applied Linguistics, 1969.

Stewart, W. Toward a history of American Negro dialect. In F. Williams (Ed.), *Language and poverty: Perspectives on a theme.* Chicago: Markham, 1970.

U.S. District Court for Northern California. *Opinion: Larry P. vs. Riles.* San Francisco, California, 1979.

Weinberg, M. *A chance to learn: A history of race and education in the United States.* New York: Cambridge University Press, 1977.

Whiteman, M., & Deutsch, M. Social disadvantage as related to intellectual and language development. In M. Deutsch, I. Katz, & A. R. Jensen (Eds.), *Social class, race and psychological development.* New York: Holt, Rinehart and Winston, 1968.

Williams, F. (Ed.). *Language and poverty: Perspectives on a theme.* Chicago: Markham, 1970.

Young, V. A black American socialization pattern. *American Ethnologist,* 1974, *1*, 415–431.

III

Language Evaluation

The evaluation of poor children in intervention programs has traditionally been with standardized intelligence tests. Many people believe that the IQ test is actually testing verbal ability' and thus that IQ scores reflect language skills.

Two of the chapters in this part are discussions of alternative ways to view children's performance in an IQ test. Elsie Moore's chapter includes a review of the difference–deficit controversy concerning the lower IQ scores of poor children, especially black poor children. She then reports on her study of transracially and traditionally adopted black children, in which she evaluated their response to the test as well as their mothers' socialization practices. The different patterns she found are similar to ones found in the pilot work by Grace Massey, Asa Hilliard, and Jean Carew, which placed black toddlers in a testing situation. Roger Shuy and Jana Staton have written a chapter that concerns language assessment specifically. Many of the factors of language usage that they identify as important skills for children are similar to the language response styles that Moore and Massey, Hilliard, and Carew describe in the test situation.

7

Language Behavior in the Test Situation and the Intelligence Test Achievement of Transracially and Traditionally Adopted Black Children

ELSIE G. J. MOORE

Poor children and those from isolated ethnic groups consistently show lower levels of academic achievement than their middle-class white peers. Although the reality of these between-group differences in school performance is generally acknowledged by social scientists, considerable disagreement exists over what factors contribute to the differences and how the factors are mediated by social-class and ethnic-group membership. At the center of the controversy is the question of whether the children's achievement difficulties stem primarily from deficiencies in their ability to benefit from formal school instruction or the failure of the educational system to provide them with adequate instruction.

The fact that minority-group children achieve lower average intelligence test scores than their more successful peers has figured prominently in this debate. The theoretical and practical significance of the scoring differences between groups arises from two important assumptions underlying the traditional use of intelligence tests to assess children's intellect and their educational potential. The first is that intelligence tests yield valid and reliable measures of the intellectual functioning of all American children; and, secondly, that the apparent differences in functioning indexed by test scores play an important causal role in differential school achievement (Eckberg, 1979). Theorists who subscribe to these assumptions view the lower average scores observed for minority group children as evidence of deficits in their intellectual competence.

141

THE LANGUAGE OF CHILDREN
REARED IN POVERTY

Therefore, proponents of this deficit perspective locate the problem of school achievement with the children (Bereiter & Engelmann, 1966; Bernstein, 1961; Hess & Shipman, 1965; Jensen, 1969, 1972; Karnes, Wollersheim, Stoneburner, Hodgins, & Teska, 1968; Whiteman & Deutsch, 1968).

The tenability of the test assumptions when applied to the interpretation of minority-group children's test scores has been challenged by a number of investigators on the grounds that intelligence tests are ethnocentric in content and in criteria for judging performance as "normal." These theorists posit that children from different social-class and ethnic groups vary in their learning experiences, behavioral styles, language, attitudes toward learning, and achievement orientations as a result of the socialization provided by their group (Baratz & Baratz, 1970; Cole & Bruner, 1971; Gay & Abrahams, 1974; Ginsburg, 1972; Labov, 1970, 1972; Mercer, 1971, 1974). However, the most widely used intelligence tests assay children's familiarity with the conformity to a single cultural tradition—that of Anglo-Americans. This places children socialized in different cultural traditions at a significant scoring disadvantage because they are not given credit for knowledge derived from their particular subcultural experiences, and assessment procedures are not adjusted to accommodate their characteristic response styles. Therefore, the average lower performance observed for minority-group children is artifactual of the test content and procedures and is not indicative of deficits in the children's fundamental cognitive ability. Furthermore, the apparent relationship between intelligence test scores and school achievement arises from the fact that the public school system's curricula, values, and modes of instruction are similarly biased to favor children socialized in the dominant culture.

Clearly, the controversy over whether minority-group children's average lower performance in educational and testing contexts is consequent to intellectual deficits or cultural differences will not approach resolution until there is more systematic inquiry into what subcultural variations exist between groups and the process by which they impact children's achievement. To date, most of the research on between-group differences in this area has been guided by the deficit perspective. The purpose of this chapter is to consider how ethnic groups may differ in their socialization of language behavior and the consequences of differences in this area of socialization for children's intelligence test performance. The specific focus is how black children adopted by middle-class white families differ in their use of language in the test situation from black children adopted by middle-class black families and the significance of the differences for the two groups' test achievement.

STUDIES OF BETWEEN-GROUP IQ DIFFERENCES

The existence of performance differences on standardized intelligence tests among children from various ethnic and socioeconomic status (SES) groups is well established in the research literature. Children from the lower socioeconomic segments of our society generally achieve mean intelligence test scores that are significantly lower than those observed for children from the middle-class (Bayley, 1965; Golden, Birns, Bridger, & Moss, 1971; Jones, 1954; Lesser, Fifer, & Clark, 1965). Investigations that have compared the average intelligence test achievement of different ethnic groups from both higher and lower social classes report significant effects of ethnicity within social class. Black children typically achieve lower scores than their white peers when social class is controlled (Nichols & Anderson, 1973; Sitkei & Meyers, 1969).

The consistent finding of both social-class and ethnic-group influences on intelligence test performance has led some investigators to posit genetic arguments to account for the between-group scoring differences (Burt, 1955; Eysenck, 1971; Herrnstein, 1971; Jensen, 1969) and others to posit environmental arguments to account for the variance (Bernstein, 1961; Dave, 1963; Hess & Shipman, 1965; Hunt, 1961; Whiteman & Deutsch, 1968; Wolf, 1964). Though these positions represent highly divergent views of the source of the variance in observed between-group differences in scoring, they do share a basic assumption regarding the meaning of such differences. Both positions have traditionally assumed that intelligence test scores are relatively pure indices of quality in mind functioning and that low performance on such measures is indicative of defects in children's general competence or specific skill development.

The hereditarians, who conceptualize measured "intelligence" as a general ability underlying all specific cognitive functions, have attempted to document that the defects that characterized the lower scoring groups are genetic in origin by focusing on the concordance rates of individuals with varying degrees of genetic similarity (family relatedness) for IQ test performance. These correlational studies indicate that as the degree of family relatedness increases, concordance rates of test scores increase (Burt, 1966; Erlenmeyer-Kimling & Jarvik, 1963; Jensen, 1970). Since the obtained correlations conform to theoretical estimates for heritable traits, these investigators argue that intelligence as inferred from test scores is genetically determined. Therefore, socioeconomic and ethnic-group differences in IQ are indicative of innate differences between groups in mental ability.

Although theorists in the area generally agree that these correlational data suggest a heritability component to observed within-group differences in intelligence test performance, the efficacy of extrapolating models of genetic transmission and variability derived from analyses of within-group variance on the trait to account for between-group differences has been stringently challenged. This dissent has been particularly strong in the interpretation of ethnic-group performance differences. Ethnic-group comparisons are particularly problematic because there are no empirical strategies available by which one can make inferences about distributions of genotypic IQ between the groups (Thoday, 1969). Additionally, as Scarr-Salapatek (1975) has pointed out, one must be able to assume that within two populations the same environmental factors affect the development of genotypic intelligence in the same way and that a complete identity in the distribution of the environmental variables within the populations exists before between-group comparisons are reasonable. Since most investigators have been reluctant to accept the latter assumption, in particular, the genetic explanation of these differences remains an issue of scholarly debate.

Investigators who subscribe to the traditional environmental arguments to account for between-group differences on this trait have focused on the positive correlation between socioeconomic status and test scores in the formulation of hypotheses regarding factors that contribute to such differences. Socioeconomic status is conceptualized from the environmentalists' perspective as a variable that indexes some important complex of stimulation and experiences provided by the rearing environment that affects the development of intellectual skills. Differences in socioeconomic status are presumed to index differences in home environments in the provision of this complex of stimulation and experiences. Therefore, these investigators have sought to identify the specific skills that are most vulnerable to environmental influences, the essential components of the environment that affect the development of intellectual abilities and how different socioeconomic status groups differ in these components.

This approach to the explanation of between-group differences in IQ has generated a voluminous literature that generally concludes that deficits in the home environment contribute to deficits in children's intellectual skill development. For example, children from the lower socioeconomic levels differ from their middle-class peers in verbal ability, specifically with regard to vocabulary size (Deutsch, Fishman, Kogan, North, & Whiteman, 1964; Lesser *et al.,* 1965; Stodolsky, 1965), problem-solving skills (Sigel & Anderson, 1966; Sigel & McBane, 1967), and cognitive tempo (Mumbauer & Miller, 1970). Additionally, a number of emotional and social characteristics are found to distinguish poor and middle-class children and are related to intelligence test performance.

These include wariness of adults in the testing situation (Deutsch *et al.*, 1964; Rosenhan, 1966), level of self-esteem (Berry, 1974; Whiteman & Deutsch, 1968), level of achievement motivation (Rosen, 1956; Zigler & Butterfield, 1968), and belief in outer versus inner control of events and one's actions (Gruen, Korte, & Baum, 1974; Stephens & Delys, 1973).

These differences in cognitive abilities and socioemotional development are related to the amount, variety, and complexity of animate and inanimate stimulation provided by the home (Dave, 1963; Tulkin & Kagan, 1972; Whiteman & Deutsch, 1968; Wolf, 1964; Yarrow, 1972); differences in the patterning of stimulation to organize information for the child (Hess & Shipman, 1965; Hess, Shipman, Brophy, & Bear, 1969); and differences in the style of social interaction, specifically as related to language behavior (Bee, Van Egeren, Streissguth, Nyman, & Leckie, 1969; Bernstein, 1961; Streissguth & Bee, 1972). Since there is a positive relationship between socioeconomic status and the quality and quantity of such stimulation provided by the home, these investigators conclude that the middle-class home is more conducive to optimal intellectual development. Another conclusion that can be drawn from these data is that complete identity in the distribution of environmental variables related to measured intelligence does not exist between different social-class groups or ethnic groups since there is a disproportionate occurrence of the low-scoring ethnic groups in the lower socioeconomic strata (Dreger & Miller, 1968).

ENVIRONMENTALISTS, HEREDITARIANS, AND BLACK–WHITE IQ DIFFERENCES

Differences between black and white children's performance on standardized intelligence tests are of particular interest to investigators in the area. These two populations differ not only in ethnicity but generally in socioeconomic status. Black children are disproportionately represented among the nation's poor. Due to the conjoining of the influence of ethnicity and socioeconomic status on this between-group difference, it has attracted the interest of both environmentalists and hereditarians.

Black children score, on the average, about one standard deviation (15 points) lower than white children on standardized intelligence tests (Jensen, 1969; Loehlin, Lindzey, & Spuhler, 1975). This between-group difference first appears around 2 years of age. However, the scoring difference between the groups increases with age, culminating in the average difference just cited (Jensen, 1970; Kennedy, 1969; Sattler, 1974).

The environmentalists have generally concluded that the differences in black and white children's scoring is attributable to the poverty that prevails in the black community, that is, the home environments of a disproportionate number of black children are deficient in the complex of stimulation and experiences necessary for optimal cognitive skill development. The children's home environments act to suppress the development of cognitive skills, and this, in turn, has the effect of lowering the children's performance on intelligence tests.

Following this same line of reasoning, the environmentalists' argument would also predict that when the effects of socioeconomic status are controlled, the average difference between the two groups' scoring would diminish. This, however, is not the case. Researchers report substantial differences in the IQ test scores of blacks and whites within the same socioeconomic strata (McQueen & Browning, 1960; Nichols & Anderson, 1973; Sitkei & Meyers, 1969).

The hereditarians use this finding as support for their hypothesis that genetic factors are involved in black–white differences in IQ (Eysenck, 1971; Herrnstein, 1971; Jensen, 1972; Shockley, 1972). These theorists argue that when socioeconomic status is defined in the same way for both blacks and whites, *identity* for the environmental variables that appear to influence measured intelligence is established. Therefore, any observed variance between the two groups within a particular socioeconomic stratum is attributable to genetic differences between blacks and whites for intelligence. Since whites achieve higher average scores than blacks at each socioeconomic level, the hereditarians conclude that differences between the two groups' scoring are genetic in origin.

Certainly, one assumption of the early conceptualizations of the influence of environment on intelligence is that traditional indices of social class (such as parents' education, father's occupation, family income, dwelling area and type, number of reading materials in the home, and the like) indicate the relative presence of process variables related to IQ for all ethnic groups. The similarity of the within-group correlation between IQ and socioeconomic status observed for blacks (.39) and whites (.46) has been used to support this assumption (Mayeske, Tetsuo, Beaton, Cohen, & Wisler, 1973). However, if environmentalists do not acknowledge the potential significance of subcultural variations as intervening variables in ethnic-group scoring differences, their challenge to the hereditarians' conclusion that genetic factors are involved is substantially diminished.

The use of socioeconomic status indices as the exclusive basis for making inferences about the stimulation potential of home environments has been questioned by investigators in the area. This is due, in part, to research findings that indicate that some dimensions of the home environment that are related to children's intellectual performance such as the affectional–emotional quality and achievement attitudes cannot be predicted from socioeconomic status indices (Caldwell, 1970; Caldwell & Richmond, 1967; Yarrow, 1963). There is also evidence to suggest that traditional indices of social class do not indicate the presence of factors positively correlated with IQ for all ethnic groups. The work of Trotman (1977) directly addresses this issue.

Trotman investigated the effectiveness of SES indices for predicting the level of "intellectuality" of the home environments of black and white middle-class ninth-grade girls and the relationship between the intellectuality of the home environment and intelligence test performance for the two groups. The intellectuality of the girls' homes was measured using Wolf's (1964) interview schedule and rating scale for assessing the presence of process variables related to intellectual performance. The home variables measured included intellectual aspirations, intellectual expectations, emphasis on language use, provisions for enlarging vocabulary, and provisions for home and outside learning. Trotman reported that, despite the similarity of black and white families on traditional indices of socioeconomic status, the intellectuality of the two home environments differed significantly. The white homes showed a higher level of intellectuality than did the black homes. There was an overall positive correlation between this measure and the girls' intelligence test scores. Furthermore, the relationship between the intellectuality of the home environment and the girls' academic achievement was as strong as that observed for their intelligence test performance.

Trotman's findings strongly support the view that traditional socioeconomic status indicators are not efficient predictors of the presence in the home environment of those process variables related to measured intelligence and school achievement across ethnic groups. Therefore, even when the socioeconomic status of blacks and whites is defined in the same way, it cannot be concluded that *identity* for those environmental variables related to IQ is established.

Although the Trotman findings suggest one explanation for why black children score lower than their white peers on standardized intelligence measures, even when the effects of socioeconomic status are controlled, some important questions remain. Is the conclusion to be drawn that, even among middle-class blacks, the home environment is deficient in the stimulation and experiences necessary for optimal intellectual development, or do these findings indicate the tenability of the cultural-difference interpretation of black–white scoring differences?

CULTURAL DIFFERENCE AND
BLACK–WHITE DIFFERENCES IN IQ

In the measurement of intelligence it is assumed that all children are equally motivated to do well and have a similar understanding of the importance of the exercise. However, the "cultural-difference" explanation of between-group performance differences posits that children from different subcultural groups enter the test situation with skills that are different from those assayed by the test. Equally important, the test situation may evoke attitudes and strategies for negotiating the testing session that are different from those assumed by the test developers and administrators. Cole and Bruner (1971) and Labov (1971) hypothesize that it is the discontinuity between the skills and perspectives different children bring to the situation, and the demands and expectations of the testing situation, that is the most significant contributor to consistently observed between-group differences on standardized intellectual measures. This discontinuity between what children from different social groupings bring to the test situation and what the situation expects presumably results from subcultural variations that have not been controlled in the development and standardization of intelligence tests.

In order to test the cultural-difference hypothesis of between-group IQ differences, data is required that shows not only "how well" children from different subcultural groups achieve but also "how" the children respond to the test situation. Hertzig, Birch, Thomas, and Mendez (1968) have provided this type of data for preschool middle-class white and working-class Puerto Rican children. These investigators conclude that differences in the two groups' styles of responding to the demands of the Stanford-Binet scale were significant contributors to observed differences in their achievement. That is, the greater tendency of the Puerto Rican children not to work when confronted with a test demand, to be less responsive to verbal tasks, to delimit their work responses, and to follow initial work responses with "not-work" responses all contributed to the lower average score observed for the group. Based on qualitative explorations of the two groups' home environments, these researchers hypothesize that the stylistic differences between the Puerto Rican children and their middle-class white peers were consequent to differences in the *cultural styles* of their families.

Though a considerable amount of research has been focused on the identification of the factors that contribute to differences in black and white children's test achievement, there have been few studies that have focused on how black children respond to the testing situation and the significance of this factor for their scoring. In most comparative studies of black and white children's test performance, "how well" the black children perform relative to whites before and after some particular intervention has been the primary focus. Investigators who have looked at this dimension of black children's test achievement generally conceptualize their observations in terms of the deficit model.

Vosk (1966) expressed strong reservations about the effectiveness of standardized tests for the discrimination of ability levels among the Harlem first-graders whom she tested. She observed that her pre-test interactions with the children indicated that they were very different in personality and temperament and that most did not appear to suffer intellectual defects. However, once the formal testing session began, a characteristic style of responding emerged for all the children. The children were unresponsive to test demands; when they did respond, their responses were so vague and superficial that no clear-cut judgment of accuracy could be made; the children made stereotyped responses (i.e., the same response to different questions); they tended to rattle-off the first answer that came to mind; and, although each was capable of verbalizing his or her errors, they did not appear to consider the errors important.

Vosk's observations on black children's response styles to the testing session clearly demonstrate that the children's behavior was not conducive to the achievement of high test scores and that their behavior does not conform to the implicit assumption of test developers and administrators that the test items will evoke similar affective and cognitive structures in all children tested. Of course, one may question the representativeness of Vosk's observations since they were made on a subpopulation of black children who had been identified as deviant by school officials prior to testing (i.e., they had been referred for testing because their teachers viewed them as either "behavior problems" or "nonlearners"). However, investigators who have tested "normal" poor black children report observations on their test behavior that suggest that factors other than competence contribute to their lower average score. These factors include willingness to settle for lower levels of success than middle-class white children (Gruen & Zigler, 1968; Zigler & Butterfield, 1968), fearfulness of being tested, and wariness of the adult tester (Zigler, Abelson, & Seitz, 1973). Experimental manipulations of the test situation aimed at mitigating the effects of these factors have been successful in raising black children's test scores, thereby substantiating the significance of such factors for their average lower achievement. Although these investigators interpret their findings as evidence of deficits in the children's socioemotional functioning, the cultural-difference hypothesis offers a reasonable alternate interpretation of the data.

The available research does suggest that children's intelligence test achievement is influenced by the ethnicity of the rearing environment, independent of social class, though no one study has controlled for all potential sources of variance or generated the data required to conceptualize how the ethnicity of the rearing environment influences children's performance on standardized measures. Scarr and Weinberg (1976) report that transracially adopted black children (i.e., black children adopted by white families) achieve a mean intelligence test score that is approximately one standard deviation above that observed for black children reared by their biological parents. These investigators attribute the significant increase in the children's scoring to the "enrichment" provided by the white home environments, as indicated by the above average educational attainment that characterizes these adoptive families. Scarr and Weinberg assume that the higher scores achieved by the transracially adopted children indicate greater cognitive skill development among them than occurs with black children reared in black homes. However, if stylistic differences between groups in the way their members respond to the test demands are significant contributors to observed variations in the test achievement of different groups, as the work of Hertzig *et al.* (1968) suggests, then it seems reasonable to assume that differences in the way black and white families socialize their children to use their skills represent another important source of variance.

Entwisle (1975) has presented a model of how differences between subcultural groups in their use of language may influence their school achievement, or what she terms *educability*. From this investigator's perspective, the family's socialization of language behavior may be as important a factor in children's cognitive performance as linguistic or grammatical competence. The research literature indicates that subcultural groups differ in their verbal demands for cognitive performance; the way they use language to guide their children's problem-solving efforts, particularly in the extent to which they encourage children to generate alternate hypotheses in the face of uncertainty; the use of verbal rewards to support their children's achievement efforts; and the opportunities they provide their children to learn to adjust their language behavior to different contexts. Entwisle believes that these differences between groups affect children's cognitive styles, world views, and language performance, which, in turn, influence teachers' expectations of their ability to master the skills taught in school and their effectiveness in negotiating the requirements of the learning situation. Children whose language behavior conforms to the expectations and values of their middle-class teachers and who are capable of using language to mediate their affective response to important dimensions of the learning context (such as frustration and uncertainty when asked to perform difficult tasks and to solve new problems) would be predicted to show high achievement in the school system.

Our comparative work with transracially adopted black children (black children adopted by white families) and traditionally adopted black children (black children adopted by black families) indicates that the two ethnic groups differ in their socialization of language use and that differences in this dimension of children's behavior play a significant role in intelligence test achievement (Moore, 1980). The two groups of adopted black children were administered the Wechsler Intelligence Scale for Children (WISC) to determine if the ethnicity of the rearing environment effected differences in their achievement. Detailed protocols of their behavior and verbalizations in the testing session were also made to assess whether or not the two groups differed in any systematic way in their response to the task requirements of the test and if any observed differences in their behavior were empirically and conceptually related to variations in their average scoring. The children's adoptive mothers were also observed, as they helped their children perform a difficult task, to determine if any direct links were evident between the way the mothers attempted to facilitate their children's task performance and any stylistic differences between the two groups of children in their test behavior. The analyses of the data indicated significant stylistic differences between the children in response to the tasks of the test, particularly with regard to the way the two groups of children and their mothers used language to negotiate the problem-solving situations.

A COMPARATIVE STUDY OF TRADITIONALLY AND TRANSRACIALLY ADOPTED BLACK CHILDREN

IQ Test Achievement

As a matter of policy, adoption agencies attempt to place children in the "best home available," both in terms of the socioemotional and socioeconomic status characteristics of the prospective adoptive homes. This practice reduces the variation generally observed between black and white families on environmental indices correlated with measured intelligence. Therefore, if these factors are efficient indices of processes related to IQ for all ethnic groups, one would predict that black children adopted by black families under circumstances similar to those of white adoptive families (i.e., through an agency) would also be similar in measured intelligence. However, if the ethnicity of the family influences children's test achievement, independent of socioeconomic status, as

Trotman's (1977) findings suggest, then one might predict significant differences in the scoring of black children as a function of their adoptive status.

Our testing of 23 socially classified black children (10 males and 13 females) adopted by white families and an equal number of black children adopted by black families (14 males and 9 females), whose average age at the time of testing was 8.6 years for each group, revealed significant differences between the groups in average Wechsler Intelligence Scale for Children (WISC) achievement. (All testers were black females.) These differences occurred even though both groups of adoptive families were defined as middle-class, using Warner's (1949) Index of Status Characteristics (ISC), with the adoptive mothers being roughly equal in average educational attainment (white mothers = 16 years; black mothers = 15.7 years).

The transracially adopted children achieved a mean full scale score of 117.1, with a standard deviation of 9.4 and a range of 104 to 138. The traditionally adopted children obtained a mean full scale score of 103.6, with a standard deviation of 11.3 and a range of 84–129. The 13.5-point scoring difference observed between the two groups of adopted black children is significant and of the magnitude typically found between the average scoring of black and white children. However, the mean score of the traditionally adopted children is substantially higher than that observed for black children in general.

Test-Taking Behavior

Performance by the children in the two adoptive subsamples was of interest in this work, but the specific focus was how the children reared in the two ethnic environments responded to the test demands and whether this was a significant variable in their scoring difference. To this end, the behavior protocols taken for each of the children during the testing session were scored, using the response categories identified by Hertzig *et al.* (1968). The two major scoring categories for each of the children's test responses are *work* and *not-work*. Each of these response categories is further specified as either *verbal* or *nonverbal*. Verbal and nonverbal work responses are then scored as either *spontaneous extensions* on the task or *delimitations* (work responses limited to the requirements of the task). Verbal not-work responses are also specified as *negations* (direct refusals to work), *substitutions* (child offers irrelevant verbalization rather than engaging in the task requirements), *refusals in terms of competence* (child makes statement referring to limitation in ability to perform the task), or *requests for aid* (child asks tester for help). Nonverbal not-work responses are also detailed as either *motor substitution* (child engages in irrelevant motor activity rather than perform the task), *motor requests for aid* (as when child shoves task toward tester and says *let me see you do it*) or *passive not-work* (child just sits and stares at the tester or looks to the ceiling when asked to perform a task).

The analyses of these data indicate that the transracially adopted children made a higher proportion of work responses than did the traditionally adopted children. A higher proportion of the transracially adopted children's work responses were accompanied by both verbal and nonverbal spontaneous extensions. The two groups were also found to differ significantly in their characteristic style of making not-work responses. The transracially adopted children showed a greater tendency to refuse to work on the basis of competence (i.e., *I haven't learned to do that yet*). This was their modal not-work response, whereas the traditionally adopted children were more likely to use negation (*I'm tired of doing this, it's boring*), verbal and nonverbal substitutions (*Isn't it time for lunch* or looking under the table), and requests for aid (*Let me see you do this one*) as their form of not-work response. The transracially adopted children followed a higher proportion of their initial not-work responses with work responses than did the traditionally adopted children and were less likely to follow an initial work response with a not-work response.

The observed differences in the two groups' response styles to the performance demands of the WISC have important implications for the interpretation of the scoring difference observed between them. First, if children consistently elect not to work when confronted with a test demand, and to terminate an initial work response with a not-work response, their scores are necessarily lowered because they cannot possibly receive any credit for the items, whereas an attempt at an appropriate answer might yield some credit. These response tendencies also decrease children's opportunities to respond to subsequent demands of the test for which they might easily generate correct responses because the procedures of the WISC require that after X number of incorrect responses or no responses in a particular section of the test, the administrator must move on to the next part. In the tally of the child's score, as well as the application of test procedures, a terminal not-work response is treated as an incorrect answer.

However, although the terminal not-work response is processed as an incorrect response by the tester, it does not really provide any empirical documentation of what the child knows or does not know, what the child can do or cannot do. The only empirically based information is that the child did not attempt a response. Though some investigators might argue that the child's failure to respond when confronted with a test demand can be appropriately used as an indicator of the child's "not-knowing," there is no support for this inference, particularly when the not-work response is invoked by the child with a high frequency. The not-work response may not be as much an index of the child's ability as an index of the child's willingness to expend the energy to retrieve information on demand or solve problems on demand. Differences between the children in this regard may well reflect variations between the two rearing environments in the orientations to and training in problem-solving that they provide; the types of problems for which thoughtful, careful attempts at solution are specifically encouraged (such as problems that are instrumental in nature versus those that are socioemotional in nature); and the identification of contexts in which problem-solving behavior will be rewarded.

The child's tendency not to work after an initial work response to a test demand may also reflect the child's judgment (upon analyzing what is being requested and what is required in terms of cognitive energy investment to generate an appropriate response) of the relative gain that results from attempting to solve the problem. This sort of "cost/benefit" analysis will necessarily involve the child's previous experience in solving a particular type of problem—hence the relative ease with which he or she feels the problem can be solved—and past reward experiences for work on such problems.

Language Behavior in Test-Taking

Although differences between the children in the proportion of work responses provided to test demands have important implications for the interpretation of their scoring difference, we were particularly impressed with the importance of language differences between the children in making both work and not-work responses. As already noted, the transracially adopted black children provided significantly more spontaneous extensions in their work responses, especially verbal spontaneous extensions. The tendency of these children to provide spontaneous extensions provides important clues to their level of involvement in task performance, strategies for solving the problems and generally negotiating the test situation to their advantage, and level of adjustment to the test situation. For example, the child may not know the dictionary definition of the word *hero* but may be familiar with the word from some experiential context. Typically, if the child can place the word in appropriate context, then he or she may infer the meaning of the word sufficiently to gain some credit for the response, if not full credit. For example, in response to this particular question, one of the children in the sample solved the problem in the following manner: *Um, hero* (pause), *oh someone who does something special—helps somebody who is in trouble, like Superman* (child hums the Superman theme song) . . . *he saved the lady from the car, and everybody said he was a* **hero!** (Emphasis is the child's.)

The child's elaboration on his definition of *hero* may serve a number of other purposes to benefit his subsequent test performance. By noting the tester's reaction to his reasoning, he can gain feedback on the efficiency of his problem-solving strategies (in this case, association) for generating appropriate responses and may confirm that the tester understands why he views his construction of the definition of *hero* as accurate.

Since the child must be able to cope, emotionally, with not knowing or not being sure of the answers to a series of questions, given test procedures, children's spontaneous extensions may serve as a mechanism of tension release. In providing the spontaneous extension of their responses, particularly when a test demand has challenged them, children verify for themselves that, based on their understanding of the problem, their response is reasonable and should be acceptable, whether it is scored so or not by the tester.

Not infrequently, the transracially adopted children used spontaneous extensions in an attempt to persuade the tester to provide credit for their responses. In providing the spontaneous extension, children may well raise the amount of credit given their responses, depending upon the particular criteria for scoring a particular item.

In addition to providing more spontaneous extensions on their work responses, the transracially adopted children made a higher proportion of their not-work responses in terms of competence. Typically, the response was of this sort: *I haven't learned that yet; I don't think kids my age are supposed to know that, but I bet my mommy knows; Where did you get that word from, I never even heard of it; I don't think anybody could find anything missing in that picture;* and so on. As these excerpts from the children's records suggest, these types of refusals to work in terms of competence place the inability to generate an appropriate response in experiential terms (i.e., *I don't know the answer because I haven't had the opportunity to learn it*) and do not blame their own capacity or potential to know. If children take an experiential attitude, they will not be dismayed at not knowing the answers to five consecutive questions—which they must do to hold down interference from test anxiety—and will continue to strive for correct responses to questions that they believe are within their ability range.

If children make the refusal to work on the basis of competence in terms of some deficiency in their capacity to know, which a simple *I don't know* may indicate, then these children may be dismayed by a series of questions for which they cannot provide what they may view as an acceptable response. These children may become negative about the testing session and essentially give up. They may then assert their not-work responses in terms of *I don't like to do this* or just shake their heads to indicate *No*. This type of motor substitution is particularly difficult to assess because it is not clear whether the child is indicating *I don't know* or *I'm not going to work anymore, so you may as well stop the test now*. The modal refusal in terms of competence of the traditionally adopted children was in the form of a simple *I don't know*.

To summarize, the transracially adopted children were more effective than the traditionally adopted children in negotiating the test situation because they were able to offset the effects of uncertainty, to construct responses on experiential grounds, and to test problem-solving strategies with the test administrator through the use of language. The children in this group elected these test behaviors spontaneously and were particularly effective in using language to mediate challenging task requirements. The transracially adopted children's use of language in the test situation helped to make them better test-takers. They approached the test, in general, as some sort of game that they wanted to win. They were engaged in the exercise most of the time and could easily be brought back to task focus by the tester's restatement of the problem. The traditionally adopted children showed a greater tendency to disengage from focusing on the task and were much harder to bring back to focus.

ADOPTIVE MOTHERS' SOCIALIZATION OF LANGUAGE IN THE PROBLEM-SOLVING CONTEXT

To assess whether or not the two groups of adoptive mothers differed in their socialization of problem-solving behavior, all mothers were asked to observe their children's work on a difficult block design and were told that they could give as much or as little help as they chose. (Observers were black females.) Although the two groups of mothers did not differ in the amount of help that they gave the children, they did differ in the type of help provided. The white adoptive mothers provided most of their help verbally, in the form of hints or general suggestions to the child. In contrast, black adoptive mothers were more likely to actually place blocks in the design for the child, and when verbal help was provided, it tended to be quite specific in nature.

The two groups of mothers also differed in the strategies they used to encourage their children's continual work on the designs and their independent striving for achievement. The white adoptive mothers showed a greater tendency to cheer as the children solved individual parts of the design and generally attempted to support their children's efforts by expressing approval, even when the children's strategies took them away from solution. They cheered every work effort. In contrast, the black adoptive mothers attempted to encourage their children's performance by expressing disapproval of their strategies when they took children away from solution but said very little as long as their children's work took them toward task solution.

These differences between the two groups of adoptive mothers in their socialization of problem-solving behavior, specifically the use of language to mediate problem-solution, would be expected to contribute to differences in their children's work styles and their language use in the problem-solving situation. The white mothers encouraged their children to explore various hypotheses for task completion by expressing approval and cheering these behaviors on the part of their children. The black adoptive mothers somewhat discouraged this type of behavior by expressing disapproval when the children began to explore solution options that took them away from task completion.

SUMMARY AND CONCLUSIONS

Significant differences in the intelligence test achievement of black children adopted by black and white families were observed despite the similarity of the two groups of adoptive families on traditional indices of socioeconomic status. The magnitude of the scoring differences between the two groups of adopted black children is comparable to that generally observed between black and white children reared by their biological parents. However, both groups of adopted black children achieved mean test scores that were significantly higher than the average achievement of black children in the general population.

In addition to differences between the two groups of adopted black children in average test achievement, significant variations were observed between them in their response styles to the cognitive demands of the Wechsler Intelligence Scale for Children, particularly with regard to the way the two groups used language to mediate their test performance. The transracially adopted black children made significantly more work responses to the test demands than the traditionally adopted children, accompanied their work responses with significantly more spontaneous elaborations—both verbal and nonverbal, and were much more likely to follow initial not-work responses with work responses than the traditionally adopted children. The transracially adopted children made more of their not-work responses in terms of competence than did the traditionally adopted children. The traditionally adopted children were more likely to not work by providing substitutions, negations, and requests for aid in response to test demands.

Our observations indicate that the transracially adopted children were generally more involved in the test situation and actually imposed conditions on the testing session to make it more pleasant for themselves, such as the game orientation they took on the test demands. The traditionally adopted children manifested behavior in the testing situation that indicated that they were much less interested in their performance in the situation than were the transracially adopted children, who appeared less relaxed, and searched for escapes from the process by posing irrelevant substitutions in response to test demands or by starting to work on a problem and then abruptly asserting, *I can't do that*. The transracially adopted children generally showed more tenacity when working on the WISC tasks.

The two groups of children differed significantly in the way they used language in the testing session. The transracially adopted children used language to generate and test hypotheses, to alleviate tension and anxiety, to persuade the tester to give them credit when they were unsure of an answer, and to generally keep themselves focused on the task— all of which helped them to remain task focused. The traditionally adopted children did not show the same level of resourcefulness in their use of language in the testing situation. They were much more passive and reticent in the testing session.

The differences between the children in their styles of responding to test demands and their use of language to facilitate their performance was related to the socialization of language provided by their adopted mothers. The white adoptive mothers encouraged their children to use language to mediate their cognitive task performance by cheering their children every time they developed a new strategy for solving difficult block designs on their own and offering help to them in the form of verbal hints and suggestions. In contrast, the black adoptive mothers were not as encouraging of their children's exploration of different problem-solving strategies. They would say nothing when they agreed with their children's work plan but would express disapproval of hypotheses tested by their children that would not contribute to the problem solution. These mothers also tended to provide help to their children in the form of specific information on how to solve the tasks.

The data from our work suggest that black and white families differ in their socialization of problem-solving skills, especially as this relates to the use of language to facilitate problem solving in the standardized test situation. The differences in the families' socialization of problem-solving skills were reflected in the children's stylistic responses to the test demands and their final test performance. The findings from our work conform to the cultural-difference hypothesis of between-group performance differences. Some might interpret them as more evidence of cultural deprivation in the black community; I do not see how such an interpretation could be justified. Clearly, all children were progressing well, in terms of intellectual performance, in both adoptive situations; however, the ethnicity of the rearing environment did contribute to differences in their scoring. From our perspective, the differences lie in the way the two groups socialize their children to use language skills in particular, and not in a general deficit in skill development for the lower scoring groups.

REFERENCES

Baratz, S., & Baratz, J. Early childhood intervention: The social science base of institutional racism. *Harvard Educational Review*, 1970, *40*, 29–50.

Bayley, N. Comparisons of mental and motor test scores for ages 1–15 months by sex, birth order, race, geographical location, and education of parents. *Child Development*, 1965, *36*, 379–411.

Bee, H. L., Van Egeren, L. F., Streissguth, A. P., Nyman, B. A., & Leckie, M. S. Social class differences in maternal teaching strategies and speech patterns. *Developmental Psychology*, 1969, *1*, 726–734.

Bereiter, C., & Engelmann, S. *Teaching disadvantaged children in the preschool*. Englewood Cliffs, New Jersey: Prentice-Hall, 1966.

Bernstein, B. Social class and linguistic development. In A. J. Halsey, J. Floud, & C. A. Anderson (Eds.), *Education, economy and society*. New York: Free Press, 1961.

Berry, G. L. Self-concept and need factors of inner city high school adolescents and dropouts. *Child Study Journal*, 1974, *4*, 21–31.

Burt, C. Evidence for the concept of intelligence. *British Journal of Educational Psychology*, 1955, *25*, 158–177.

Burt, C. The genetic determination of differences in intelligence: A study of monozygotic twins reared together and apart. *British Journal of Psychology*, 1966, *57*, 137–153.

Caldwell, B. M. The effects of psychosocial deprivation on human development in infancy. *Merrill-Palmer Quarterly*, 1970, *16*, 260–277.

Caldwell, B. M., & Richmond, J. B. Social class level and stimulation potential of the home. In J. Hellmuth (Ed.), *Exceptional infant: The normal infant* (Vol. 1). Seattle, Washington: Special Child Publications, 1967.

Cole, M., & Bruner, J. Cultural differences and inferences about psychological processes. *American Psychologist*, 1971, *26*, 867–876.

Dave, R. H. *The identification and measurement of environmental variables that are related to educational achievement*. Unpublished doctoral dissertation, University of Chicago, 1963.

Deutsch, M., Fishman, J., Kogan, L., North, R., & Whiteman, M. Guidelines for testing minority children. *Journal of Social Issues*, 1964, *20*, 129–145.

Dreger, R. M., & Miller, K. S. Comparative psychological studies of Negroes and whites in the United States—1959–1965. *Psychological Bulletin Monograph*, 1968, *70*, 3.

Eckberg, D. L. *Intelligence and race*. New York: Praeger, 1979.

Entwisle, D. R. Socialization of language behavior and educability. In M. Maher & W. Stalling (Eds.), *Culture, child and school*. Monterey, California: Brooks/Cole, 1975.

Erlenmeyer-Kimling, L., & Jarvik, L. Genetics and intelligence. *Science*, 1963, *142*, 1477–1479.

Eysenck, H. *The I.Q. argument*. LaSalle, Illinois: Library Press, 1971.

Gay, G., & Abrahams, R. Does the pot melt, boil, or brew? Black children and white assessment procedures. In B. Phillips (Ed.), *Assessing minority group children*. New York: Behavioral Publications, 1974.

Ginsburg, H. *The myth of the deprived child*. Englewood Cliffs, New Jersey: Prentice-Hall, 1972.

Golden, M., Birns, B., Bridger, W., & Moss, A. Social class differentiation among black preschool children. *Child Development*, 1971, *42*, 37–45.

Gruen, G., & Zigler, E. Expectancy of success and the probability learning of middle-class, lower-class, and retarded children. *Journal of Abnormal Psychology*, 1968, *7* (4), 343–352.

Gruen, C. E., Korte, J. R., & Baum, J. K. Group measures of locus of control. *Developmental Psychology*, 1974, *10*, 683–686.

Herrnstein, R. I.Q. *Atlantic Monthly*, 1971, *228*, 44–64.

Hertzig, M., Birch, H., Thomas, A., & Mendez, O. Class and ethnic group differences in responsiveness of preschool children to cognitive demands. *Monographs of the Society for Research in Child Development*, 1968, *33*(1).

Hess, R., & Shipman, V. Early experience and the socialization of cognitive modes in children. *Child Development*, 1965, *34*, 869–886.

Hess, R., Shipman, V., Brophy, J., & Bear, R. *The cognitive environments of urban preschool children: Follow-up phase*. Chicago: Graduate School of Education, University of Chicago, 1969.

Hunt, J. McV. *Intelligence and experience*. New York: Ronald Press, 1961.

Jensen, A. How much can we boost I.Q. and scholastic achievement? *Harvard Educational Review*, 1969, *39*, 1–123.

Jensen, A. IQs of identical twins reared apart. *Behavior Genetics*, 1970, *1*(2), 133–146.

Jensen, A. *Genetics, educability, and subpopulation differences*. London: Methuen, 1972.

Jones, H. The environment and mental development. In L. Carmichael (Ed.), *Manual of child psychology* (2nd ed.). New York: Wiley, 1954.

Karnes, M. B., Wollersheim, J., Stoneburner, R., Hodgins, A., & Teska, J. A. An evaluation of two preschool programs for disadvantaged children: A traditional and highly structured experimental preschool. *Exceptional Children*, 1968, *34*, 667–676.

Kennedy, W. A follow-up normative study of Negro intelligence and achievement. *Monographs of the Society for Research in Child Development*. 1969, *34*(126).

Labov, W. The logical non-standard English. In F. Williams (Ed.), *Language and poverty*. Chicago: Markham Press, 1970.

Labov, W. Academic ignorance and black intelligence. *Atlantic Monthly*, 1971, *229*(6), 59–67.

Labov, W. *Language in the inner city: Studies in the black English vernacular.* Philadelphia, Pennsylvania: University of Pennsylvania Press, 1972.

Lesser, G., Fifer, G., & Clark, D. Mental abilities of children from different social class and cultural groups. *Monographs of the Society for Research in Child Development,* 1965, *30,* 1–115.

Loehlin, J., Lindzey, G., & Spuhler, J. *Race differences in intelligence.* San Francisco, California: W. H. Freeman, 1975.

Mayeske, G. W., Tetsuo, O., Beaton, A., Cohen, W., & Wisler, C. *A study of the achievement of our nation's schools.* Department of Health, Education, and Welfare, Publication No. (OE) 72-131. Washington, D.C.: Government Printing Office, 1973.

McQueen, R., & Browning, C. The intelligence and educational achievement of a matched sample of white and Negro students. *School and Society,* 1960, *88,* 327–329.

Mercer, J. Institutionalized anglocentrism: Labeling mental retardates in public schools. In P. Orleans & W. Russell, Jr. (Eds.), *Race, change, and urban society.* Los Angeles, California: Sage Publications, 1971.

Mercer, J. Latent function of intelligence testing in public schools. In L. Miller (Ed.), *The testing of black students.* Englewood Cliffs, New Jersey: Prentice-Hall, 1974.

Moore, E. *The effects of cultural style on black children's intelligence test achievement.* Unpublished doctoral dissertation, Committee on Human Development, University of Chicago, 1980.

Mumbauer, C., & Miller, J. Socioeconomic background and cognitive functioning in preschool children. *Child Development,* 1970, *41,* 471–480.

Nichols, P. L., & Anderson, V. Intellectual performance, race, and socioeconomic status. *Social Biology,* 1973, *20,* 367–374.

Rosen, B. Race, ethnicity, and the achievement syndrome. *American Sociological Review,* 1956, *14,* 47–60.

Rosenhan, D. L. Effects of social class and race on responsiveness to approval and disapproval. *Journal of Personality and Social Psychology,* 1966, *4,* 253–259.

Sattler, J. *Assessment of children's intelligence.* Philadelphia, Pennsylvania: Saunders, 1974.

Scarr-Salapatek, S. Genetics and the development of intelligence. In F. D. Horowitz (Ed.), *Review of child development research,* Vol. 4. Chicago, Illinois: The University of Chicago Press, 1975.

Scarr, S., & Weinberg, R. I.Q. test performance of black children adopted by white families. *American Psychologist,* 1976, *31,* 726–739.

Shockley, W. Dygenics, geneticity, raceology. *Phi Delta Kappan,* 1972, *53,* 297–307.

Sigel, I. E., & Anderson, L. M. Categorization behavior of lower- and middle-class Negro preschool children. Differences in dealing with representation of familiar objects. *Journal of Negro Education,* 1966, *35* (3), 218–229.

Sigel, I. E., & McBane, B. Cognitive competence and level of symbolization among five-year-old children. In J. Hellmuth (Ed.), *Disadvantaged child* (Vol. 1). Seattle, Washington: Special Publications, 1967.

Sitkei, E., & Meyers, C. Comparative structure of intellect in middle and lower class four-year-olds of two ethnic groups. *Developmental Psychology,* 1969, *1,* 592–604

Stephens, M. W., & Delys, P. External control expectancies among disadvantaged children at preschool age. *Child Development,* 1973, *44,* 670–674.

Stodolsky, S. *Maternal behavior and language and concept formation in Negro preschool children: An inquiry into process.* Unpublished doctoral dissertation, University of Chicago, 1965.

Streissguth, A. P., & Bee, H. L. Mother–child interactions and cognitive development in children. In W. W. Hartup (Ed.), *The young child: Reviews of research* (Vol. 2). Washington, D.C.: Association for the Education of Young Children, 1972.

Thoday, J. M. Limitations to genetic comparisons of populations. *Journal of Biosocial Science,* 1969, Supplement, 3–14.

Trotman, F. Race, I.Q., and the middle class. *Journal of Educational Psychology,* 1977, *69,* 266–273.

Tulkin, S., & Kagan, J. Mother–infant interaction in the first year of life. *Child Development,* 1972, *43,* 31–41.

Vosk, J. Study of Negro children with learning difficulties at the outset of their school careers. *American Journal of Orthopsychiatry,* 1966, *6,* 32–40.

Warner, W. L. *Democracy in Jonesville.* New York: Harper & Row, 1949.

Whiteman, M., & Deutsch, M. Social disadvantage as related to intellective and language development. In M. Deutsch, I. Katz, & A. Jensen (Eds.), *Social class, race, and psychological development.* New York: Holt, Rinehart and Winston, 1968.

Wolf, R. The measurement of environments. In A. Anastasi (Ed.), *Testing problems in perspective.* New York: American Council on Education, 1964.

Yarrow, L. J. Research in dimensions of early maternal care. *Merrill-Palmer Quarterly,* 1963, *9,* 101–114.

Yarrow, L. J., Rubenstein, J., Pederson, S., & Jankowski, J. Dimensions of early stimulation and their differential effects on infant development. *Merrill-Palmer Quarterly,* 1972, *18,* 205–218.

Zigler, E., Abelson, W., & Seitz, V. Motivational factors in the performance of economically disadvantaged children on the Peabody Picture Vocabulary Test. *Child Development,* 1973, *44,* 294–303.

Zigler, E., & Butterfield, E. Motivational aspects of changes in I.Q. performance of culturally deprived nursery school children. *Child Development,* 1968, *39,* 1–14.

8

Test-Taking Behaviors of Black Toddlers: An Interactive Analysis

GRACE C. MASSEY
ASA G. HILLIARD
JEAN CAREW

The following chapter reviews the controversy over IQ testing among black children, with particular emphasis on the fact that standardized IQ tests lack educational relevance. That many other factors contribute to an individual's score is demonstrated in a pilot study presented here of the test-taking behaviors of black toddlers. Although these are preliminary data, they serve to highlight the problems of using IQ scores as valid measures of actual intelligence.

IQ TEST CONTROVERSY

Historical Context

The current debate over test bias versus cultural bias in testing has deep roots and will very likely continue for some time (Block & Dworkin, 1976; Hilliard, 1979a; Jensen, 1980; Kamin, 1974). The heart of the argument over the cultural bias of common IQ tests is related to the matter of equity for cultural groups who are compared unfairly with some normative cultural behavior of selected white Americans. Therefore, as might easily be predicted, the norm-group test-takers have the unfair advantage of having had a lifetime to practice the use of cultural materials that serve as vehicles for interrogation. On the other hand, the cultural-

163

THE LANGUAGE OF CHILDREN
REARED IN POVERTY

group members, whose lives have been spent practicing different cultural material, are forced to abandon such experiences and to rely upon experiences that may be quite alien to them. As important as this debate may be, it obscures a more fundamental issue—that intelligence has not been measured for either group.

The phenomenon of intelligence and the IQ tests that were designed to measure the phenomenon were fabricated and applied in education prior to the time that mental functions were even described clearly. Measure of intellectual capacity went from research through development to general application in an amazingly short time. Public school policymakers needed something like IQ tests, and—presto!—such tests were there (Levine, 1976). Intelligence then, as now, was said by IQ test advocates to be measured precisely before it could even be defined operationally in a common way by the community of scientists. There was not then, nor has there been since, any general professional requirement that intelligence be measured in a uniform and rigorous way or that it be measured with instruments that yield comparable data. IQ tests are generally divided into various subtests, each designed to measure some aspect of intelligence. However, the subtests on various IQ tests follow every conceivable pattern (i.e., not all IQ tests contain the same subtests). Some have verbal and quantitative divisions; others have block designs, repeating numbers, similarities, etc. Does each represent a component of intelligence? If not, then what is the meaning of a subtest? If so, does intelligence vary with the test? No matter how poor a construct, instrument, or procedure for measuring ability appeared to be, any serious educator, psychologist, or researcher would overlook the flaws if using the instruments resulted in improved performance in teaching and learning. This has not happened, and there are few professional researchers who seem willing to raise these issues.

Current Uses of the IQ Test

In spite of the fact that the constructs, instruments, and procedures are flawed, researchers and practitioners persist in using them, though they have the potential for being damaging. Test results can cause normal children to be labeled as mentally retarded, which could change the type of teaching "treatment" they receive in school (Mercer, 1971). The IQ tests that purport to measure intelligence are used almost universally in the public schools, where most black children are enrolled. Unfortunately, such testing is done mainly for sorting children, disregarding both their sociohistorical context and their individuality. Among the current popular uses for IQ tests are the following:

1. To determine a child's readiness for kindergarten.
2. To predict a person's future academic performance.
3. To classify a pupil for placement in special schools or programs.
4. To determine if a child is socially competent.
5. To diagnose learning difficulties.

Yet we may ask again: Are teaching and learning improved as a consequence of the use of IQ tests? One discovers, when trying to answer this question, that there are no generally accepted criteria by which answers to the question can be judged. When the IQ was developed, it was viewed as an essentially static measure of some permanent characteristic of the individual, thus, one should not logically use the test results as a measure of the child's progress. But if the test results are responsible for placing the child into a particular educational program, one may well ask: On what basis can that placement ever be changed? It is really not clear how, under even ideal circumstances, one could aid the child's learning with the use of the test.

IQ Test Assumptions

The view of the child represented in IQ tests as they are constructed is antithetical to the view of the child held by an educator. However, the full range of assumptions upon which professional discourse is based is seldom made explicit. Where implicit assumptions can be inferred, they are hopelessly confused. For example, the use of standard questions in tests assumes that questions have a common meaning for all test-takers. Yet, it can be demonstrated that both semantics and assumptions for a given question can vary greatly among intelligent test-takers, causing varied but reasonable outcomes (Donaldson, 1978). Consequently, it cannot be determined with certainty whether a "wrong" response represents a lack of mental ability or simply the fact that a given subject used different data, different assumptions, or both.

Discussants sometime assume that intelligence test scores represent fixed mental abilities and therefore should not be expected to vary much. At the same time, IQ tests are sometimes used as measures of program effects in program evaluation studies. For example, IQ tests have been used to evaluate program effects in Head Start (Roupp, Travers, Glantz, & Collen, 1979). This confusion is evident, as discussants in the intelligence and IQ-testing debate slide back and forth from one set of assumptions to another, giving little evidence that they are aware that the shifts have been made.

Professional Confusion

IQ testing may be used for a variety of school purposes. They may be used for the diagnosis of learning difficulties, for the development of individual educational plans, for research on thinking, and for screening to identify those children qualified for additional educational opportunities. It is not clear how a given IQ test can be used to serve all these diverse needs. If, for example, IQ test advocates are challenged to demonstrate prescriptive or pedagogical validity (Gallagher, 1976) for the test for a particular purpose, arguments that more logically support an entirely different purpose may be marshalled. More explicitly, if an IQ test is found to be weak in predictive validity (Hilliard, 1979b) for certain cultural minority groups, justification often shifts from its use as a predictive device to its use on the grounds that all children must exhibit competence in certain school-related content. This is really a shift to an argument in support of a test of achievement rather than a test of intelligence. The arguments in support of the validation of a particular test as an individual diagnostic device would hardly be expected to be the same as arguments in support of that same test as a program-sorting device. However, the experts commonly merge the two.

There are other dimensions to the discussion that create similar confusion in discourse. For example, each time the audience for information changes, the nature of the information that is needed changes as well; thus, a policymaker might wish to know if IQ tests work, if they are cheap, if they can identify gifted children. On the other hand, a teacher may wish for immediate information on a special strategy to use with Johnny Jones. Prescriptive diagnosis and policy recommendation probably require different information or information at different levels of refinement. Yet the teacher and the policymaker are most likely to get the same information, a raw IQ score or a gross label such as "educably mentally retarded (EMR)."

Lack of Validity for Black Children

Teaching and learning are rooted in and dependent upon language, a common language between teacher and student (Lindfors, 1980). Language is rooted in and an aspect of culture (Hall, 1977). *Culture* is nothing more or less than the shared ways that groups of people have created to use their environment. All people have created and are embedded within a culture. Therefore, they have also created language, which is included in culture (Levi-Strauss, 1966).

Using standardized IQ tests for diagnostic purposes with black children may be challenged as invalid because such tests use an unfamiliar European-American vocabulary (Alleyene, 1969; Smith, 1978; Smitherman, 1977) as a part of the measure of mental capacity. This challenge is met frequently by an argument based on the assumption that "all Americans should, for practical reasons, master the general culture." The challenge concerning the lack of validity of IQ tests raises questions regarding the valid measurement of such things as remembering large numbers of words, using words properly, and understanding subtle differences in meanings. If different children are to be compared, verbal ability should be measured using a vocabulary that all tested children have had an equal opportunity to learn. However, there is documentation that such equal opportunity is not the case in the education of the majority of black and poor children (Clark, 1970; Woodson, 1969). Quite the contrary, the educational system has been utilized to certify the inequalities of the larger social system in America (Blauner, 1972; Carnoy, 1972; Hodge, Struckman, & Trost, 1975; Katz, 1972). The responses of IQ test advocates to the challenge just stated change the focus of the discussion from points about the measurement of mental functions to a focus on the practical utility of a common language. Such a response about utility is true but irrelevant to the issue of measuring the child's dynamic patterns of thought.

We know the measured intelligence of people only by reference to standardized tests. For many educators and psychologists, standardized IQ tests are taken at face value (Hilliard, 1979b). By generally accepted professional standards, the most popular IQ tests have established validity. The validity is established when:

1. An IQ test gives results that are roughly equivalent to other IQ tests (concurrent validity).
2. The ranks of subjects on an IQ test are roughly equivalent to their ranks on school evaluations at some point in the future, usually one year later (predictive validity).

These professional criteria, although necessary, are not sufficient to establish test validity in a more comprehensive sense. For example, with predictive validity, bias may be found in both the tests and the criterion, school success. A given IQ test yields a ranking of scores among test-takers that supposedly reflects the ranking that the test-takers will receive when their achievement is measured later and by other means. However, both the predictor and criterion usually contain the same bias because school success and IQ tests are geared to the normative language and culture of white America. Therefore, the relationship between IQ test scores and school achievement may be due in large part to the fact that the same language and culture are used in the two tests. A person who has limited exposure to the language and culture that together serve as a vehicle for interrogation may fail items on two separate tests for the same reason, a lack of familiarity rather than a lack of capacity.

There are still more fundamental ways of looking at the test bias and test results. For example:

1. We may ask if a given test has the linguistic integrity sufficient to guarantee a common semantic base between test language and the test subject's language. Without this communication, interrogation will be distorted or impossible. Indeed, semantic mismatches between test and school language, and test subject language, may well account for certain high discrepancies between test scores and school success (Cole & Scribner, 1974; Shuy, 1976; Sullivan, 1972).

2. We may seek more empirical descriptive information that will help to tell us how and why a given subject gave a particular response to test questions. This would enable psychometricians to distinguish between subjects who appear to have few resources and those who simply choose to employ the resources they do have in nonstandard ways.

3. We may examine the interaction between test-givers and test-takers to determine what goes on in the testing environment.

Every person accumulates a unique pool of verbal resources, a repertoire, which is the result of exposure to specific experiences (Lee, 1978). These responses have meanings that can be fathomed only by reference to their unique history and context. It is not the presence of a specific repertoire, a cultural norm, that means high or low intelligence but the presence or absence of a repertoire that should interest those who seek to forecast the learning ability of others. To say that a given subject does not possess a specific repertoire is not to say that he or she does not possess an equivalent one to the arbitrary normative repertoire.

The makers of standardized tests assume, given a standardized (uniform) test and a standardized administration of that test, that there is a specific intelligent response or narrow range of responses for all subjects (Jensen, 1980). In other words, the repertoires of all subjects are assumed to be created from a common pool of experiences. The makers of standardized tests appear to be unable or unwilling to visualize the actual variety of intelligent response options of which subjects are capable. In part, this inability to perceive reality is due to the absence of systematically analyzed data on the how or why of choice exercised by subjects in responding to a given set of questions (Hall, 1977; Labov, 1970; Tenhouten, 1971).

When such analyses are performed, the variety of intelligent alternatives to standard test items becomes apparent. It appears obvious that it is the unique information, basic assumptions, and the exercise of options and intentions by a subject that provide the parameters within which intelligent behavior will be exhibited. These, then, are the parameters by which intelligence must be measured. Intelligent behavior, although expressed through information or responses to questions, is not necessarily synonymous with this information. Intelligence—the ability of the mind to size up or to create an environment, to impose order, to apply labels, to structure definitions—is not tied to standard cultural information (Hall, 1977). In other words, intelligence cannot be made synonymous with information drawn from one specific culture.

The study described in this chapter provides us with the unique opportunity to examine the historical and social contexts in which testing takes place, therefore enabling us to retrieve some of the answers to the "how" and the "why" of certain behaviors of the children involved.

SAMPLE PROJECT

Background

The data for this chapter are derived from a longitudinal study of black children called Toddler and Infant Experiences (TIES). The TIES research project presently being conducted in a large western city is a descriptive, developmental study of the home settings and family environments of 25 black children 1–3 years of age. The specific objectives of TIES (Carew, 1980) are as follows:

1. To document and trace longitudinally from age 1 to 3, the daily experiences (behaviors, interactions, activities) of black children, including both the experiences that the children generate for themselves in their independent pursuits and those in which their caregivers and others in their families play some part.

2. To document and trace longitudinally the course of development of major socioemotional, intellectual, language, creative, self-care and physical competencies among black children.

3. To examine the connections between children's daily experiences (both self-generated and environmentally produced) and their development of the competencies referred to, using three types of assessments. The first assessment is based on videotaped observations of children in the home; the second, on caregiver reports; and the third, on performance in a standardized test situation.

4. To document and trace longitudinally the childrearing practices and styles used by black caregivers in socializing their infant–toddlers and to identify the underlying rationales, life experiences, life conditions, and personal characteristics that influence these practices and their associated attitudes and expectations.

5. To document and describe the lives of black families, focusing both on (a) delineating factors that commonly cause stress for black mothers and influence their ability to cope with the problems of parenthood and of living in a society in which racial and social discrimination are pervasive aspects of daily life; and (b) documenting and describing the sources of happiness, satisfaction, self-esteem, hope, and pride that are characteristics of these black families.

Each facet of this study is important, but the current questions raised about IQ makes this project more relevant today than ever before. This chapter focuses on the videotaped performance of 15 study children in the standardized test situation referred to in Objective 3. The data presented have been drawn from the actual videotaped tests of TIES children and represent all the test tapes available on children who were tested at 24 months of age.

The study sample consists of predominately two-parent working-class and middle-class black families, living in a moderately large northern city on the West Coast, who have a child born between September 1977 and December 1977. The children in the study are currently being cared for at home and do not spend over 20 hr a week with a babysitter, at nursery school, or at a daycare center. Although the study families are selected on a voluntary basis, recruited from many sources, and cannot be considered representative of black families in the city, the state, or the nation in which they live, they are nevertheless examples of ordinary, law-abiding, hard-working black families.

The sample spans the socioeconomic spectrum, from families who are on state aid and getting below $500 per month to those earning over $2000 per month. Most of the families are small, and many of them are young parents with only two children.

Procedure

In order to fully explain the richness of the test data, a brief description of the TIES procedures is necessary.

TIES data are gathered via observations and interviews. An observer–interviewer visits each family once a month and spends 2–2½ hr in each home, filming the child on videotape and interviewing the major caregiver involved with the child (usually the mother). The time sequence is divided into a half hr of videotaping the child's behavior, followed by 1–1½ hr of parent interviews. The parent–caregiver interviews fall into four categories: (a) family background–history interviews; (b) video-playback interviews, where the caregiver is shown part of the videotape filmed that day and is asked about the behaviors that occurred on the videotape; (c) open-ended discussion of specific issues developing out of the videotaped segment or issues of interest to the study; and (d) semistructured and forced-choice questions concerning specific study issues.

When the study children reached the age of approximately 23 months, the interviewer–observer discussed testing of the child with the major caregiver. The caregiver was told that the researchers had many criticisms about the validity of such tests and that, although some children might test well, many children would not necessarily do their best because they might be functioning within an entirely different frame of reference from that of the tester. For example:

1. The child might not be used to being tested.
2. The child might not be familiar with the test materials.
3. The child might be shy with the examiner.
4. The tasks the child would be asked to carry out might not interest him or her.
5. The child might be feeling ill, cranky, or unsociable that day.

The TIES staff asked the caregivers for permission to arrange and videotape a test of the child in the home. It was emphasized that the purpose was not merely to obtain a test score but to observe the child's behavior in a testing situation.

At 24 months the children were given one of the Bayley Scales of Infant Development that concentrates on the child's language and reasoning skills and is referred to as the *mental scale*. The tester was a black female who had met most of the study children and parents at least once prior to the testing. The tester was not informed of our objective for testing. She was instructed to try to get each child to perform at their highest ability level in the testing situation in order to obtain an "accurate" standard assessment of the child's performance on the Bayley.

The testing was done in the homes of 13 of the 15 children tested. The other two children were tested in the office at the request of the parents. All of the tests were videotaped by a member of the TIES staff who was acquainted with the family. After the test was administered, the major caregiver, who was present during the testing, was interviewed about the child's behavior and performance during the test.

The test tapes were then reviewed. All of the child's actual behavior was recorded, including all verbal and nonverbal behavior that occurred throughout the testing session. Following this behavior analysis, the test tapes were scored by a trained tester.

Test-Taking Styles

The results to be presented are centered on the observed behavior of the children in the testing situation. The role of the situational–interactional factors in the testing session has received less scrutiny than it deserves, and it is this theme that we choose to address (Boykin, 1977). Although the issue of cultural bias in the actual test items and test content is an important one, and has received a great deal of attention, it has not been formally or adequately resolved. It should be made clear, however, that the authors concur with past findings that show the test items and content to be biased. Observations of children seemed to show clearly that there were many intelligent though nonstandard ways that children might respond to test items. In other words, there were no unique intelligent solutions to the problems that were presented by the test.

To avoid the issue of race (tester versus child), all children were tested by the same black female. Great efforts were made by the tester to make the child feel comfortable and at ease. The home environment also helped to insure the feeling of comfort in the children.

Each child's testing videotape was reviewed by members of the research team, independently and subsequently in groups for discussion. There was no a priori categorization scheme developed. The initial task was to transcribe the behaviors from the tape as they occurred so that a thorough description of the test situation was obtained. The second step was to cluster the behavior around test items so that one could more readily compare behaviors across children given the same test item. Some behaviors appeared fairly easy to identify, and interpretation posed little, if any problem (i.e., the child gave the tester the item as requested). However, other behaviors were less clear, for example, when a child was given an instruction and then did something altogether different (i.e., the tester requested the cup from the child, the child pretended to drink from it and then put it back down on the table) or when the child did not respond at all to an instruction or request. The researcher who visited the family regularly to do the monthly taping and interviewing was called in to give her assessment of the child's testing behavior and to note whether this was typical behavior given her knowledge of the child. In addition, we obtained the caregiver's assessment of the child's test-taking behavior immediately after the test.

Using these sources, we found four dominant styles of test-taking behaviors emerging among the sample children. The styles incorporate the children's interaction with both the tester and the test items. The styles are (a) the traditional–habitual; (b) the initiative–creative; (c) the reticent–observant; and (d) mixed styles that represent any combination of the first three.

The Traditional–Habitual Style

Children who exemplified this style of behavior fit into the mode of the stereotypic image of what a child should do in a testing situation. The child responded traditionally to the questions posed and requests made by the tester. The child was generally obedient and tried hard to show the tester what he or she perceived the tester as wanting. The child proceeded to label, stack, speak, etc., upon request and followed the rules the tester imposed. Since the tester posed the habitual question, *Do you know what I know?* children using this style were generally doing what they thought was most acceptable to the traditional tester and to the testing situation.

The Initiative–Creative Style

Children in this category appeared very precocious and stimulated by the situation and, at times, by some of the test items. These children might or might not respond to the *"Do you know what I know?"* line of questioning and were more interested in doing what interested and–or challenged them, personally. The child viewed the tester as just another adult to help facilitate or stimulate the creative use of the test items and testing situation. This type of child almost conveyed the message, *I'll show you what I can–want to do,* and is frequently thought of as the problem, hyperactive child by the traditional tester. The following brief descriptions of behavior engaged in by the initiative–creative children give one a more visual image of this style. These descriptions are taken from a variety of children to give the reader a composite picture of this type of behavior:

1. Instead of putting pegs in their holes, the child dropped each peg, one by one, and watched them carefully as they rolled across the table.
2. When the tester gave the child a piece of paper to fold and asked the child to imitate her, the child pushed back the paper and said, *You make one.*
3. The child picked up the cup that was being used to test knowledge of prepositions and pretended to drink from it.

4. The child got up from the table to pick up something the tester had put away.
5. The child, instead of stacking the blocks, pretended the blocks were soap and proceeded to wash her hands with them.
6. The child stacked test items that were not supposed to be stacked instead of labeling and giving them to the tester upon request.
7. The child screwed in each peg instead of just putting them into their holes.
8. The child drew a picture with the crayon and paper instead of following the tester's instructions to imitate the tester's horizontal and vertical lines.
9. Instead of labeling an item, the child played with it, included her mother in the game, and then gave the item back to the tester.
10. Instead of lifting the right cup (the one hiding a ball), the child lifted the wrong cup each of three times and then threw it at the tester.

As one can deduce from these few examples, the child utilizing this style often made up his or her own games and did not always respond to the questions or tasks posed by the tester.

The Reticent–Observant

Children possessing this style did not appear to be actively participating with the tester in the testing session but instead, were carefully observing the tester and the items. The child was generally quiet throughout the session, and if one could assume what the child's agenda was, it might have been to sit back and see what the tester had to offer–show. This style was most difficult to score since the child was not really performing, and one could not make assumptions about what the child chose not to show in such a situation.

Mixed Styles

Children frequently could not be placed in any of the first three categories because they mixed the styles and one style did not predominate. This happened most frequently with children mixing the reticent–observant style with either the traditional–habitual style or the initiative–creative style.

Test Scores

The mean developmental index score on the Bayley Mental Scale for our sample children was 96.8, with a range from 79 to 112. This is well within the normal functioning range for all children and is only slightly below the 100 national mean. Black children usually score somewhat lower than our sample; perhaps our higher scores could be attributed to the conducive testing environment we attempted to create.

Table 8.1 lists the test scores of our sample by the descriptive category into which the child was placed according to our clinical analysis of the videotaped behavior. Clearly, children who exhibited the traditional–habitual style were rewarded for their behavior. The mean score of traditional–habitual children was significantly higher than that of children exhibiting any of the other styles of behavior. As we would have hypothesized, the children with the lowest scores were those who behaved in our child initiative–creative style, with the reticent–observant and mixed styles falling in the middle.

Examples of Individual Test-Taking Behavior

Based on these data we can conclude that testing was indeed a highly interactive process. The interaction and behavior of the children being tested can go in many directions often not understood or expected by the tester. Unfortunately with young children, creative and self-initiating behavior is not rewarded. Quite the contrary, it is more often mislabeled as *problem* or *noncooperative* behavior, and the children are penalized.

Standardized testing can be conducted so as to insure a reliable

TABLE 8.1
Bayley Test Scores of Children with Different Test-Taking Styles

Style	Test score
1. Traditional–habitual	112
	96
	98
	106
	112
	94 $\bar{X} = 103^a$
2. Initiative–creative	87
	91
	87 $\bar{X} = 88.3$
3. Reticent–observant	98
	89 $\bar{X} = 93.5$
4. Mixed Styles	94
	102
	102
	79 $\bar{X} = 94.3$

[a] The mean developmental index score ($\bar{X}$) for the entire sample = 96.8.

presentation of uniform items. A reliable interpretation of results can also be insured. What cannot be assured is a uniform body of information and a uniform effort for test subjects. It could well be expected, and did indeed appear in our data, that some test subjects have their own agenda. Faced with a standard task, some of these children performed in highly creative or idiosyncratic ways. Some saw possibilities other than those that were anticipated by examiners. When historical and contextual information was taken into account, the responses of the children could be seen as intelligent and natural though unanticipated by examiners.

For example, one child, when requested to put the yellow pegs into the peg board, took each peg and carefully screwed it into the hole. On this particular item a child gets credit for both putting the pegs in the holes and the speed with which he or she does it. This child took much longer because he carefully screwed in each peg rather than just dropping it into the hole. The videotaper of the test, who knew the family well, believed that the child screwed in the pegs because he had helped his father add two rooms to their house during the course of the study. The child was very familiar with a screwdriver. After the test, the research assistant asked the mother why the child screwed in the pegs. The mother responded that she believed the child thought the pegs were like his yellow screwdriver.

How and why children respond as they do are both related to the child's unique history and context (Feuerstein, 1979). These things become clear as we observe the videotaped protocols. Clearly, the standardized setting did not carry the same or standardized meanings for all children.

IMPLICATIONS

There are major implications for these findings:

1. A systematic means for collecting historical and contextual data must be required in conjunction with testing, so that test performance can be evaluated in its program context. There are few if any studies of the how and why of children's test performance. When empirical investigations are conducted, the results corroborate our findings. For example, William Labov's work (Labov, 1970) resulted in the revelation that the language of African-American children was logical and equivalent to common or standard English. Systematic empirical studies of the behavior of subjects in testing situations is a prerequisite to the scientific study of behavior through standardized testing.

2. Standardized test-developers have demonstrated an extremely

limited conception of the range of possible variations in testing settings. Item analyses reveal only superficial evidence of variations as "errors." Such views can be held only when one ignores individual historical and contextual antecedents of behavior for test subjects. This has the effect of ascribing to all subjects identical antecedents.

3. We have seen in the test scores, but even more clearly in the videotapes, that the child who takes a fresh, unique, and creative approach to the standardized testing situation will be penalized with low scores. On the other hand, the traditional–habitual child seems to do very well. It seems to us unlikely that anyone who views the videotaped protocols would find in them evidence of greater intelligence or development for the traditional–habitual child over the creative child. Yet test results suggest just that relationship. The Bayley may well be as much a measure of conformity or style as it is a measure of intelligence or development. These ambiguities cannot be seen or challenged in the absence of empirical studies of the responses of subjects—studies that go beyond such elementary things as statistical analyses of responses to test questions. Existing test validation procedures are quite inadequate.

4. The videotape shows itself to be a data gathering tool that is perhaps superior to the individually administered standardized test given in a one-to-one testing setting, without observers. The rich data are preserved on videotape, and results may actually be scored again by as many independent observers as desired.

SUMMARY

In sum, it is not simply the misuse of currently used standardized IQ tests but the inherent scientific inadequacy of such tests that is being questioned. Furthermore, the argument is not simply for the correction of cultural bias in currently used standardized tests. The cultural bias only shows us that standardized, mass-produced measurement is impossible when variable cultural material is being aggregated in cross-cultural settings. The culture and measurement issue is a matter of science first and equity second. Clearly, Pandora's box will be opened in the mental measurement laboratory on the very day that cultural anthropologists and sociolinguists are invited to look at what we do. No existing standardized IQ test can survive that kind of scientific scrutiny. The whole IQ testing movement reflects either a lack of awareness or an unwillingness to deal with relevant academic data, especially sociolinguistic data (Hout, 1977; Jensen, 1980).

Clearly, data such as that presented in this chapter strongly challenge the current use of the phenomenon intelligence particularly as it relates to culture in IQ testing and assessment. If young children being tested are categorized based on their style of interaction in the testing situation, as our data indicates, one must question the purpose of such tests. Are such tests being used to justify an intellectual and cultural superiority of white America and to perpetuate the inadequacies of those not of that culture? It is critical that the deficits of intelligence testing be confronted and dealt with if we are to serve all the cultural varieties in America.

REFERENCES

Alleyne, M. The linguistic continuity of Africa in the Caribbean. In H. J. Richard (Ed.), *Topics in African-American studies*. New York: Black Academic Press, 1969.

Blauner, R. *Racial oppression in America*. New York: Harper & Row, 1972.

Boykin, A. W. On the role of context in the standardized test performance of minority group children. *Cornell Journal of Social Relations*, 1977, *12*, 109–124.

Block, N. J., & Dworkin, G. *The IQ Controversy*. New York: Pantheon, 1976.

Carew, J. V. *TIES: Toddler & Infant Experiences*. Unpublished manuscript, 1980. (Available from TIES Project, 1322 Webster St., Oakland, California 94612).

Carnoy, M. (Ed.). *Schooling in a corporate society, the political economy of education in America*. New York: McKay, 1972.

Clark, K. B. (Ed.). *Racism and American education: A dialogue and agenda for action*. New York: Harper & Row, 1970.

Cole, M., & Scribner, S. *Culture and thought*. New York: Wiley, 1974.

Donaldson, M. *Children's minds*. New York: Norton, 1978.

Feuerstein, R. *The dynamic assessment of retarded performers: The learning potential assessment device*. Baltimore: University Park Press, 1979.

Gallagher, B. C. *NAACP report on minority testing*. New York: NAACP Special Contribution Fund, 1976.

Hall, E. T. *Beyond culture*. New York: Anchor, 1977.

Hilliard, A. G. Standardization and cultural bias as impediments to the scientific study and validation of intelligence. *Journal of Research and Development in Education*, 1979, *12*, 47–58. (a)

Hilliard, A. G. *The ideology of intelligence and IQ magic in education*. Paper presented at the annual meeting of the American Psychological Association, New York, 1979. (b)

Hodge, J. L., Struckman, D. K., & Trost, L. D. *Cultural bases for racism and group oppression: An examination of traditional "western" concepts, values, and institutional structures which support racism, sexism, and group oppression*. Berkeley, California: Two Riders Press, 1975.

Houts, P. (Ed.). *The myth of measurability*. New York: Hart, 1977.

Jensen, A. *Bias in mental testing*. New York: Grove, 1980.

Kamin, L. *The science and politics of IQ*. New York: Wiley, 1974.

Katz, M. B. *Class bureaucracy and schools: The illusion of educational change*. New York: Praeger, 1972.

Labov, W. The logic of non-standard English. In F. Williams (Ed.), *Language and poverty*. Chicago: Markham, 1970.

Lee, L. *The repertoire model for the assessment of social competence.* Technical Report, Hartford, Connecticut, 1978.

Levi-Strauss, C. *The savage mind.* Chicago: University of Chicago Press, 1966.

Levine, M. The academic achievement test. *American Psychologist,* 1976, *31,* 228–238.

Lindfors, J. W. *Children's language and learning.* Englewood Cliffs, New Jersey: Prentice-Hall, 1980.

Mercer, J. Institutionalized anglocentrism: Labeling mental retardation in the public schools. In P. Orleans & Wm. Russell, Jr. (Eds.), *Urban affairs review* (Vol. 5). Los Angeles: Sage Publications, 1971.

Roupp, R., Travers, J., Glantz, F., & Collen, C. *Children at the center, final report of the National Daycare Study* (Vol. 2). Cambridge, Massachusetts: Abt Associates, 1979.

Shuy, R. *Quantitative language data: A case for and some warnings against.* Unpublished manuscript. Arlington, Virginia: Center for Applied Linguistics, 1976.

Smith, E. A. *The retention of the phonological, phonemic, and morpho-phonemic features of Africa in Afro-American ebonics.* Seminar Series Paper. Fullerton, California: Department of Linguistics, California State University, 1978.

Smitherman, G. *Talkin and testifyin: The language of Black America.* Boston: Houghton-Mifflin, 1977.

Tenhouten, W. *Cognitive styles and the social order.* Unpublished manuscript, 1971. (Available from National Technical Information Service, U.S. Department of Commerce, 5285 Port Royal Road, Springfield, Va. 22151).

Sullivan, A. R. Afro-anglo communication in America: Some educational implications. *Pan-African Journal,* 1972, *5,* 231–237.

Woodson, C. G. *The miseducation of the Negro.* Washington, D.C.: Associated Publishers, 1969. (Originally published, 1933.)

9

Assessing Oral Language Ability in Children
ROGER W. SHUY
JANA STATON

PRINCIPLES OF ORAL LANGUAGE ASSESSMENT

One of the surprises emerging from much of the linguistic research on child oral language is that the more we study the way children talk, the better speakers we discover them to be. Early research on Vernacular Black English (VBE), for example, began with the assumption that speakers of a vernacular dialect were unable to do things that other speakers could do.

Thus language researchers set out to discover, systematically, what these differences were. The more data we amassed, the more we learned that there were few linguistic features used by standard English speakers that were not also used by speakers of the vernacular. The differences were quantitative, not categorical. We also learned that the context in which the oral language was elicited had a tremendous effect on the speaker's ability, desire, and strategy of talking. Perhaps most important of all, however, is that we learned that the forms of language—the bits and pieces such as pronunciation and grammar—provided areas for language evaluation inappropriate to their communicative value. That is, people tend to make judgments about the ability, intelligence, knowledge, and even personality of speakers on the basis of language features that have no particular bearing in those areas. It seemed curious to us that children could be judged unintelligent or stupid because they had zero

181

THE LANGUAGE OF CHILDREN
REARED IN POVERTY

past-tense morphemes or deleted final consonants. Certainly something was going on in the mind of the person who made such judgments, but the question was, what? The forms of language were not appropriate to school norms, but the language was still understandable. Once the purpose of the utterance was identified, it was clear that the speakers had managed to say what they wanted to say. That is, the function was clear enough; only the forms were out of place.

If linguistic research was gaining new insights about children's oral language in such matters, the natural question became, how did this research relate to the issues of oral language in the context of education? From the research, we can conclude four principles that undergird any assessment of the oral language of children.

Principle 1. *Oral language cannot be assessed, measured, or diagnosed effectively or accurately outside of the natural contexts in which it occurs.*

If the field of oral language assessment has had a problem in learning to recognize this principle, it is in good company. The field of linguistics also has had its difficulties in learning this lesson. For years, linguists struggled with the need to discover the structure of language by looking only at its component parts. In essence, they were interested primarily in linguistic competence, usually revealed through a speaker's use of grammar or phonology. The idea that context could modify or explain these language forms is a relatively recent development, brought about largely through the efforts of sociolinguists such as John Gumperz and Dell Hymes (Hymes, 1974). There are several models of communicative competence, but the following may serve to provide the basic idea.

The components of sociolinguistic competence make use of the forms of linguistic competence to accomplish an oral language purpose or function. Communicative competence, in this model, is the combination of

TABLE 9.1
Oral Language Communicative Competence

Linguistic competence	Sociolinguistic competence[a]
Phonology	Oral interaction
Vocabulary	Specific functions
Grammar	Narrative abilities
Word semantics	Referencing
	Style shifting
	Sequencing

[a] All viewed in relationship to topic, participants, and setting.

linguistic competence (the forms of language) and sociolinguistic competence (the way a speaker uses language to get things done). It is, in a sense, the combination of form and function.

We use context here to mean several things. First, there is the context of the speech event itself as dictated by social structure (such as parent–child interaction, doctor–patient communication, salesman–customer exchanges). Second, there is the context of the conversational structure (narrating, referencing, sequencing). Third, there is the context in which specific language functions are used (requesting, interrupting, describing, explaining, convincing). Fourth, there is the context of individual participants, topics, and settings and the ability to shift styles for different participants, topics, and settings.

If context is so important and so complex in the everyday events of life in which talking occurs, one wonders why it is not commonly accounted for in oral language assessment or taught in oral language programs for children. Perhaps we decontextualize learning, with the best of intentions, in order to make it simple while ignoring the holistic reality that makes us functional and human. Decontextualization lies at the base of any assessment. Tests are not life; they are, at best, only dim reflections of it. With oral language testing, decontextualization requires children to produce utterances that are not self-generated and are nonfunctional, whereas talking, if it can be characterized, is best described as functional and self-generated.

Perhaps oral language assessment is different from other kinds of testing. Certainly, it cannot be done with a paper–pencil test. More noteworthy is the fact that such assessment cannot be effectively induced externally. The best example of effective language assessment today might be the Foreign Service Institute's approach to measuring the foreign language learning of government employees. The test consists of a conversation between the teacher and the student on the topic of the work that the learner will be expected to perform. Both form and function are measured. This test of communicative competence appears to be something that schools have not yet managed to create (Jones, 1979).

Principle 2. *What matters most in oral language assessment is how language is used to get things done.*

In the previous table, it is clear that linguistic competence focuses on the forms of language, whereas sociolinguistic competence stresses the functions of language. A useful approach to oral language skills does not neglect either kind of competence, and it also sets them in a developmental sequence in which function always precedes form or, stated in the more traditional architectural idiom, *form follows function.*

For example, George Miller's conceptual separation of literacy into coding, meaning, and function can be very useful; such units offer a way of assessing what has been the emphasis in literacy research, learning, teaching, and evaluation in recent years (Miller, 1974). One might also borrow the metaphor of *deep* and *surface structure* from linguistics and suggest that these components have a deep to surface hierarchy (Chomsky, 1966). Elsewhere, the iceberg (see Fig. 9.1) has been used as a symbol of this relationship (Shuy, 1977).

Above the waterline of the iceberg are those features of language and literacy that are visible and, of course, countable. In reading, the visible aspects are primarily decoding issues. In writing, they are primarily mechanical matters. In oral language, they are the features described earlier as linguistic competence. Most assessment measures the surface aspects of language. Much harder to measure and to teach are the "beneath-the-surface" issues related to language concerns; those aspects that deal with meaning relationships (*semantics*), language use (*pragmatics*), and text structure (*cohesion*). And curricula, whether commercial or private, do not address these issues to any great extent.

The basic issue for assessment here, of course, is whether we need to learn to measure better that which is beneath the waterline, that which matters most in the effort to use language to get things done.

How learners acquire this ability to use language to get things done appears to be the major but unrecognized basis of the evaluation of language ability. Some scholars refer to this as *functional language ability,* referring to the way learners use language in life functions such as requesting clarification, denying, requesting, refusing, asserting, and sequencing. These "beneath-the-surface" aspects of language have only recently begun to be recognized and researched, but it is clear that the ability to use language effectively matters a great deal more than the form in which these functions are realized (Shuy, 1978, Shuy & Griffin, 1981).

Principle 3. *Language, oral and written, reveals variability of performance rather than categorical performance.*

Knowing that a child uses a double negative once is not the same as knowing the *extent to which* a child uses a double negative. Research in language variation in the past decade has revealed that the forms of language most commonly studied show relatively consistent patterns of frequency of occurrence across age, race, sex, and socioeconomic status. The assessment issues that grow out of such knowledge are obvious. In 1978, for example, our research team was asked to help assess the language ability of VBE-speaking children in the Los Angeles schools.

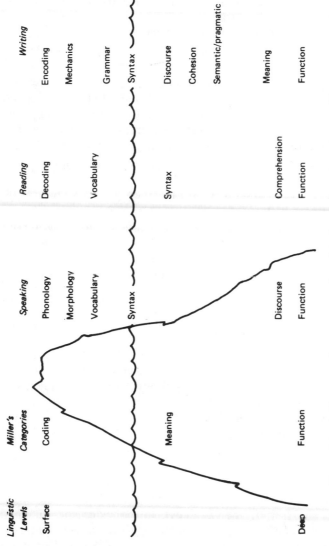

Figure 9.1 A deep to surface representation of the language context aspects of language.

The problem was a real one: *How can we determine such language ability in a way that can be helpful to the schools?* At first, we examined the "above-the-waterline" forms of language used by the children in tape-recorded conversation. The traditional categorical approach has been to note the correctness or incorrectness of the target features such as past-tense markers, plurals, etc.

An understanding of the natural variability of language leads to a different approach: determining the relative frequency of those forms in natural use (such as a tape-recorded conversation). Our goal is to tell the teacher something useful for pedagogy, namely, whether the feature is used *often, sometimes,* or *rarely* by a particular child. Such a record for each child can serve to guide teachers into realizing that it is a different matter to teach children to increase or decrease the school-expected features than to assume that they are teaching children something totally new. An individual assessment of language variability also allows instruction to be tailored to individual needs since, although there is a common inventory of VBE forms, there is not a uniformity in their frequency of occurrence.

The basic issue for assessment here, then, should be obvious. Discrete point testing in language is probably less helpful in language-related matters than in other subjects. If language use is variable, then language assessment must recognize and even take advantage of such variability.

Principle 4. *Oral language goes by so fast and is so multilayered that it is not possible to assess it effectively or accurately without tape recording it and studying it at length.*

Again, language may be somewhat different from other kinds of data in this regard. Perhaps this is because language is purposive (i.e., used by autonomous agents, simultaneously multileveled, and quick to pass us by). We have found no way to assess oral language efficiently without resorting to tape recording. There are only so many things that an analyst can attend to at one time. For instance, if we listen for consonant cluster deletion, we probably will miss past tense forms. Even if it were possible to assess the forms of language at a single spontaneous listening, how do we account for an individual's reduction of consonant clusters 41% of the time or use of multiple negation in 61% of the instances where negation occurs? And when we begin to consider sociolinguistic competence, spontaneous analysis completely breaks down. As listeners, our minds enable us to respond to the message of an oral communication without particularly attending to its forms. Because we are listening for meaning, we may get the sense that some nonstandard speech is being used, which leads to the feeling that the speaker is uneducated, but we can seldom put our finger on exactly why this conclusion is drawn.

To analyze functions on the spot is a clear impossibility. If we are listening at all, we are seldom listening for the units that can be analyzed as functions, sequencers, referencing, etc. We can get the effect of such features but not attend to their structure or use. An additional value of tape-recorded data comes from the usefulness they have to the speaker as well. With taped speech samples, one can let the speakers listen and relisten to their own speech, thus providing an excellent opportunity for self-assessment.

This principle leaves us with a paradox then. We know that function matters more than form, but we cannot assess function analytically without freezing it long enough (on a tape recorder) to come back to it and see how it worked. The features at the top of the iceberg of Figure 9.1 are possible to assess, one at a time, but the further we move down the iceberg, the more impossible becomes our assessment task.

These four principles of oral language assessment are seldom followed in practice either in assessment or instruction today, despite the fact that they are extremely difficult, if not impossible, to refute. Few would deny that communicative competence is the larger issue of which linguistic competence is only a part, that functions matter more than form, that language use is variable rather than categorical, or that oral language is difficult to assess without being frozen on tape. Yet little is done about the situation, largely because the task seems too immense. The remainder of this chapter is an account of our recent efforts to do something about it.

A PROJECT IN ORAL LANGUAGE ASSESSMENT

Initial Measures of Linguistic Competence

In 1978 we were asked to help assess the oral language ability of primary school children in a Los Angeles public elementary school. This particular school was in a lower-class, overwhelmingly VBE-speaking community. Our twofold task was a difficult one: to determine the oral language ability of 500 children in attendance so as to be scientifically adequate and capable of providing the school with the basis for constructing oral language lessons, and to be economical enough to complete the program within the 18 months available to us. At first we fell into the trap of seeing only the linguistic competence because it was most visible to us and was that aspect of language most commonly studied by linguists. Most of the research on VBE in the 1960s and 1970s focused on the forms of language, not on the functions. Consequently, we addressed our early efforts toward improving the traditionally oriented assessment, which attempts to test oral language ability with paper–pencil tests or which tests only a small part of even linguistic competence. We devised a procedure in which certain teachers were taught how to elicit and tape record 10–15 min of continuous oral language discourse from individual children. These tapes were then sent to us for an analysis of the forms of VBE. Instead of taking the usual testing stance that the presence or absence of a feature is worthy of measurement, our position was that it was necessary to determine the relative frequency of these forms (such as past tense markers, plurals, consonant cluster reduction, etc.). This position prevented the teachers from assuming that children who deleted a given feature some of the time should be taught the standard form as though they had never learned it at all. Previous research in VBE clearly pointed out the importance of the relative *frequency* of occurrence of such features instead of categorical presence or absence.

We analyzed some 500 tapes of Los Angeles VBE-speakers in this way, producing a one-page summary sheet for each child, which we encouraged the teachers to include in the children's individual files. It was hoped that such a record would guide the teachers in teaching children to increase or decrease standard features.

Measuring Sociolinguistic Competence

As our work progressed, we began to realize that we were touching only the tip of the iceberg. We were being trapped by the same principle that makes most language tests less than useful as valid mirrors of ability. We further realized that, although our work to this point was an improvement in assessing language forms, we were still a long way from measuring the most important aspects of language: language use.

Our discomfort with this assessment of oral language forms used by VBE-speakers in Los Angeles led us to attempt a further step in our analysis. Would it be possible to examine these same tape-recordings from a different perspective? Could we determine anything helpful about the use of language by these children and employ use of such information for the teachers as a guide to individual or group instruction?

In an effort to accomplish exactly this, we devised a second one-page summary that encapsulates the language functions we felt were most useful for classroom learning. We derived these functions from several sources, including our own experiences in the classroom and intuitions along with workshop evidence from teachers in seven counties in and around San Diego, California. The question for our pilot research was simply this: How do your students need to use language to get things done? This question is not often asked of teachers, and it took time to get at the most useful level of abstraction and generalization. (The response, "to go to the bathroom," for example, become a part of two larger ability categories: to introduce new topics, and to request.) Nobody can deny that it is important to learn how to do these things effectively if one is to survive in school or, actually, in life. A better test of children's language ability then became clear, which was to assess their ability to use language to accomplish the things that must be accomplished in order to do well in life. Following the structure of Figure 9.1, such ability is termed the child's *sociolinguistic competence.*

Categories of Sociolinguistic Competence

The research team finally agreed upon four major categories: (*a*) conversational abilities; (*b*) narrative abilities; (*c*) referencing; and (*d*) style shifting. Lynn McCreedy and Carolyn Adger then modified the instrument as they tried it out on existing tape-recorded interviews done by the Los Angeles teachers. The single-page tally sheet marks the specialist's assessment of the skillfulness of the speakers on an ungraded continuum from "skillful" to "inept." Such an assessment, however, is at the mercy of certain constraints. For example, a child might possess the language functions in our categories yet never exhibit them during the taping (McCreedy & Adger, 1981).

Underlying any analysis of children's oral language is the definition of what kind of oral language will be measured. We chose not to assess oral reading since that is stylized and is heavily determined by reading ability, not oral language ability. Nor did we select prepared oral recitations of songs or memorized poems or stories since the structure of such language is prescribed by its source, eliminating individual structural decision making. Any assessment of such language would be an evaluation of what is elsewhere referred to as *oral interpretation of literature.* What we wanted to assess, instead, is the kind of language likely to be found in classrooms, the kind of conversation that is found in school lessons and is used between teacher and pupil.

Martin Joos (1967) characterized such speech as *consultative,* a transactional give and take that requires standard form, precision, clarity, and economy. It differs from the *casual style,* which can be found in the playground, the home or in recreational, relaxed settings. Consultative speech also differs from what Joos called the *formal style,* which is used more as a monologue by speakers alone before an audience without direct interactional feedback. Although a case could be made for also assessing the casual or peer-to-peer style of oral language, the requirements of the school setting suggested that consultative, or teacher–pupil conversation, is closer to the kind of speech by which the children will be most evaluated. Such a decision justifies the interview of pupil by teacher as the data base rather than, for example, pupils' conversations with each other.

Conversational Abilities

One type of oral language that we wanted to obtain, *conversational abilities,* contains two subcomponents: competence in oral language interaction and the use of specific language functions. Our original thought was that cooperation at turn-taking during conversations would be an appropriate element to measure. As it turns out, this was in error since the children in our sample have already learned this principle. Two other aspects are critical, however: appropriate interrupting and the effective recycling and repair of misunderstandings. Children are taught from the time they begin to speak (by teachers, parents, older siblings, and numerous others) not to interrupt. That such advice is patently inappropriate is recognized by those who study the oral language of natural conversation. Problems do not stem from interrupting. They stem, instead, from inappropriate interrupting. Interrupting can be helpful, charitable, and necessary. Adults who are effective speakers and listeners learn how to interrupt in ways that do not offend or interfere. Great risks are taken by those who do not learn this skill—risks in school, on the job, and in marriage. The ability to recycle and repair misunderstandings and errors in one's own speech and the interpretation of that speech by others is equally important. Until a person learns to do this, there is a risk of being unduly or unnecessarily misunderstood. When one does it badly or ineffectively, one runs the risk of being thought stupid.

The category of conversational abilities includes the actual use of language functions. For the purpose of the classroom, and based on what we were told in our San Diego field testing, the following language functions were considered worth observing if they had the potential of occurring and were then actually used: (*a*) asking clarifying questions; (*b*) introducing new topics; (*c*) answering (providing requested information); (*d*) responding (volunteering new relevant information); and (*e*) requesting. We also noted any other functions that occurred, such as denying or promising, but we recognized their general infrequency of occurrence and unlikelihood in our tape samples.

Narrative Abilities

Our second desired type of oral language, *narrative abilities,* is also subdivided into two subcomponents: competence in oral language interaction and use of specific functions. As forms of interaction, we looked for the ability to produce clear beginnings, transitions, and termination. The functions specifically sought included explaining, describing, giving specific examples, and introducing new topics.

Referencing

The third type of oral language, *referencing,* includes all kinds of anaphoric reference. Some are grammatical, as in the appropriate use of pronouns to reference their antecedents. Others are discourse-oriented, serving to tie pieces of the conversation together.

Style Shifting

The last kind of oral language we wished to obtain, *style shifting,* is one that evidences strong oral language competence. By *style* we mean the levels of formal style, consultative, and casual. Just as it is difficult to imagine a formal speech being presented in the casual style, it is hard to conceive of football being played in the formal style. Speakers in any language learn rather early that one talks to adult strangers in one style, to parents in another, and to small children in still a different style. When children come to school, they are forced to learn the characteristics of the classroom consultative style. Standard English is required, for example, which contains asymetrical rules about interrupting (the teacher can interrupt the pupil but not vice versa). The two aspects of style switching that we assessed are children's ability to suit the style to the situation and their competence in shifting the style appropriately with the topic. Underlying any analysis of style shifting is the ability to sense the appropriateness of switching. An analogy might be a guitarist's ability to switch the chords to suit the melody. As the melody shifts, so do the appropriate chords. An effective speaker learns how to do this.

Model Lessons for Teaching Sociolinguistic Competence

After assessing these children's oral language ability in this manner, it was only natural to try to translate these principles into actual classroom lessons that would help children learn to be more effective speakers. We realized that a functional approach to assessment should be accompanied by contextualized functional language lessons rather than decontextualized pattern drills on standard English forms.

Our model lessons (not a complete curriculum) were designed to develop the level of sociolinguistic competence needed by students at a particular age level in order to negotiate with peers and adults at school and in the community (Staton, 1980). The lessons are thus problems focused on situations the students were currently experiencing or would experience soon and were intrinsically motivated to solve. We made particular use of the fact that children from poor backgrounds are often expected to negotiate directly with a nonparental adult world—buying food, paying bills, interpreting for non-English-speaking parents, looking for work as baby-sitters, etc. In workshops, teachers identified over 30 different combinations of situations plus language functions that even first-grade children typically encounter. Examples included requesting help from the school nurse and giving directions to the bus driver.

One particularly important consideration that we overlooked at first was that classroom lessons should be focused on child–adult interactions in meaningful and psychologically motivating situations rather than on peer interaction, in which nonverbal or informal styles of communicating are entirely appropriate. Our goal in these lessons was to develop the child's competence in the consultative style, which stresses informational content and specificity—adding new information to the listener's (assumed) knowledge. Thus we had to create situations in which the context of place, speakers, and topic would require the consultative rather than informal style.

Referring to our model of communicative competence, which includes both sociolinguistic and linguistic competence, we chose to fashion lessons that began with sociolinguistic practices, or what might be called a *holistic approach,* rather than a *reductionist linguistic approach* which stresses practicing each of the parts in isolation first, then assembling them like building blocks. Research by Corsetti (1979) demonstrated that focusing students' efforts in mastering specific language functions in identified social contexts through structured role playing led to significant improvement in the use of language forms—syntax, pronunciation, vocabulary variation—as well as functions. We believe that by focusing on sociolinguistic competence such as how to get attention from a teacher, which is meaningful to a child, we would also develop the child's linguistic competence in the surface forms.

Two reasons for improvement in linguistic competence resulting from our beginning at the sociolinguistic level can be postulated: First, anxiety is markedly reduced, and language begins to flow naturally and comfortably, without interference; and second, children who do not know the appropriate forms or strategy for carrying out a function they want can self-assess the performance using a tape recording (with the teacher's assistance as needed) and practice only the patterns or forms that are difficult or unfamiliar. Later, we incorporated pattern drills into a sequence of lessons after the child had practiced and mastered the sociolinguistic demands. Our assessment of the students in the school, as we have pointed out, showed great variability within and across each student on all aspects of linguistic competence. The need for an individualized approach was obvious, or we would waste students' time teaching them forms of language they already knew.

An example of a 5-day lesson sequence, focused on a particular language function, is shown in Table 9.2. The use of style switching on Day 2 ensured that students understood that there was a functional equivalent to the statements, *Hey, gimme a hand* and *Could you help me;* or *I wanna see those* and *Could I please look at those green shoes.* The speaker's intention is the same, but the language style and form (including dialect) change because of different contexts and speakers.

One of the important innovations in these lessons was the embedding of assessment in the classroom context and involving both students and teacher as evaluators. Our belief is that learning of language in the classroom could occur much the way it does in real life if teachers would provide modeling of the appropriate language strategies (via tape-recorded dialogues on Day 1), have students practice the entire sequence of language behavior as a whole (first, in pairs and small groups and then, in structured dialogues), and use tape recordings to provide concentrated feedback directly to the students about their performance.

By allowing students to evaluate themselves (which involves a set of introductory lessons to establish what is a good performance in terms they can understand), we have found that students begin to use the natural skills they have for language learning in the classroom. The lessons stress the students' ability to evaluate their own language, free of external correction but using mutually agreed on criteria. The teacher is also involved in the ongoing assessment by listening to the tapes and helping children who are having difficulty.

At the end of a lesson sequence, there are real-life assignments to be done. One teacher currently field-testing the lessons has her students observe instances of complaints and interruptions in their own life, which they report to the class for discussion about how to complain and interrupt effectively. For these students, the language they are learning to use has become the powerful instrument for getting things done in the world that it was meant to be, thus enabling them to be competent, successful adults.

Conclusion

Our purpose here is to provide some insights into the issue of assessing the oral language ability of children. As in many other areas of assessment, practice has too long been focused on the superficial aspects of forms rather than functions. Recent theory and research has begun

TABLE 9.2

Overview of Lesson Sequence for Individual Language Functions Unit III: Requesting Help from Someone—Five Lessons

Day 1	Day 2	Day 3	Day 4	Day 5
Introducing the function	Switching styles and dialects	Communicative competence practice	Evaluation	Extension—written and oral
Problem situations	Structured dialogues using formal and informal "hats" Whole class Small groups	Structured role playing in pairs or small groups	Discussion of criteria	Written extension
Model dialogue (audio tape)	Presentation to whole class—each group	Presentation to whole class—each group	Evaluation of appropriate style and dialect Model tape Students' tapes from Day 3	Real-life assessment (oral) Review and additional practice for students needing more help

to open our understanding of ways to conceptualize what matters most in the use of language, that which we have called language functions. We have also argued that any effort to assess oral language ability will need to take into account the fact that assessment that wrenches language from the natural context in which it occurs will distort the results. Such reductionism also disguises the variability that natural language contains, again overlooking structural aspects of great importance for assessment purposes. Finally, we assert that oral language is so fleeting and temporal that instantaneous analysis can assess little more than affect.

We then outlined our beginning efforts to construct a process (*not* an instrument) that accounts for sociolinguistic competence and the initial attempt to produce classroom lessons that address such competence; although we regard this effort as exploratory, we are convinced that the process addresses the principles noted at the outset of this chapter. Linguistic competence is not enough. Communicative competence, the combination of linguistic and sociolinguistic competence, is much more complex and difficult to measure. But it brings us a great deal closer to our goal of actually measuring children's oral language ability.

REFERENCES

Chomsky, N. *Aspects of the theory of syntax.* Cambridge, Massachusetts: MIT Press, 1966.

Corsetti, S. *The teaching and performance of speech acts in the language classroom.* Unpublished doctoral dissertation, Georgetown University, 1979.

Hymes, D. *Foundations in sociolinguistics.* Philadelphia, Pennsylvania: University of Pennsylvania Press, 1974.

Jones, R. L. The oral interview of the Foreign Service Institute. In B. Spolsky (Ed.), *Advances in language testing* (Vol. I). Washington, D.C.: Center for Applied Linguistics, 1979.

Joos, M. *The five clocks.* New York: Harcourt, 1967.

McCreedy, L., & Adger, C. *Assessing oral language skills.* Mimeographed paper, Georgetown University, Washington, D.C., 1981.

Miller, G. Introduction. In G. A. Miller (Ed.), *Linguistic communication: Perspectives for research.* Newark, Delaware: International Reading Association, 1974.

Shuy, R. Quantitative language data: A case for and some warnings against. *Anthropology & Education Quarterly*, 1977, *1*(2), 78–82.

Shuy, R. What children's functional language can tell us about reading or how Joanna got herself invited to dinner. In R. Beach (Ed.), *Perspectives on literacy: Proceedings of the 1977 perspectives on literacy conference.* Minneapolis: University of Minnesota, 1978.

Shuy, R., & Griffin, P. What do they do at school *any* day. In W. P. Dixon (Ed.), *Children's oral communication skills.* New York: Academic Press, 1981.

Staton, J. Getting things done with words. In B. Christenson (Ed.), *Teacher's guide and model lessons.* Los Angeles: Los Angeles Unified School District, 1980.

IV

Language Interventions

Intervention programs for poverty children began with great hopes for increasing children's skills and, in turn, their subsequent school performance. The first examination of such programs indicated that the initial gains produced by the preschool programs dissipated after a few years in public school. Recent evidence on the long-term effects of these preschool programs has given renewed energy to those involved in intervention for poverty children. The following two chapters renew some of the previous intervention attempts, with an emphasis on language, and they each describe a present ongoing preschool program for poverty children. Betty Hart describes a series of experimental manipulations within her language intervention program, designed to determine factors that affect language output. Gael McGinness presents a digest of implications from previous language intervention programs and then describes an evolving language program, in which she is involved, based on teacher training.

10

Process in the Teaching of Pragmatics[1]
BETTY HART

The goal of intervention is to have an effect. Intervention on the language of children reared in poverty is directed toward having an effect on the language displayed by those children, and research is designed to show that effect. Research on language intervention thus concerns itself with showing changes in language and associating those changes with processes occurring within the intervention program.

Intervention research thus has two, interrelated goals (Cazden, 1972; see McGinness, Chapter 11). One is to show the relationship between process (what children and adults do within an intervention program) and product (what children do in extra-program settings such as tests or public schools). The second goal of intervention research is to establish the relevance of the product (outcome) of intervention to success or failure in later life. The importance of the second goal becomes apparent when one considers the implications for public policy of Bronfenbrenner's (1976) finding that intervention had no lasting effects with children reared in poverty in contrast to the findings of Lazar, Hubbell, Murray,

[1] This work was supported by a grant (HD 03144) from the National Institute of Child Health and Human Development to the Bureau of Child Research and the Department of Human Development at the University of Kansas. The contribution of Dr. Todd R. Risley (Principal Investigator) to the research reported here was essential and is gratefully acknowledged.

199

Rosche, and Royce (1977), who did see lasting effects. Bronfenbrenner (1976) used primarily IQ test scores as outcome measures, whereas Lazar *et al.* (1977) used social measures such as assignment to special education classes, nonpromotion, and feelings of competence in school. As Cazden (1972) and Raizen and Bobrow (1974) have pointed out, such social outcomes may be as important to success in later life as are cognitive outcomes.

The issue of the relevance of the outcome is of particular importance when the target of intervention is language. Through language children display both cognitive capacities and social learnings. Up to now, language studies have tended to focus on language competence, on children's knowledge of language. Outcome measures have thus focused on cognitive variables, of which IQ is, for instance, representative. But the results of this focus often indicated that intervention had no lasting effects (Bronfenbrenner, 1976).

The distinction between language competence and language performance may, however, no longer be a fruitful one (Givon, 1979). What an individual knows about language can be assessed only on the basis of that individual's performance. All tests are performance measures. That the behavior of children reared in poverty is different in testing conditions than it is in non-adult-structured situations is well attested in the literature (cf., Labov, 1970; Williams, 1970; Williams & Naremore, 1969; see also Moore, Chapter 15). The problems of children reared in poverty, this suggests, may not be so much cognitive, as performance, ones.

Recent work in pragmatics (Halliday, 1978; Hart, 1980) stresses not only that all language data are in fact performance data but that language performance is primarily determined by the context of performance. Language use is controlled by the context, which includes both the physical setting (testing room, home, classroom, playground) and the social setting. Social variables affecting language performance include such things as the sex and race of the participants (Labov, 1970), the formality of the interaction (Ochs, 1979), and the communicative purposes of those present (Brown & Levinson, 1978; Psathas, 1979).

Language tests, then, measure not just children's knowledge of language but their knowledge of communicative contexts and how language "fits" in those contexts. Although we know quite a bit about language, particularly in terms of its structure, we do not yet know very much about its use, about the pragmatics of language. There is an urgent need for data concerning the language demands placed on poverty children by their homes and community, by tests, and by public school classrooms.

For instance, if there is no demand for the kinds of language performance measured by tests, improved test scores are unlikely to be related to lasting changes in performance. Also, if the demand for certain kinds of language performance—the kinds of performance characteristic of advantaged children—occurs in the school but not in the community where the majority of the children's language use is occurring, any effects of intervention are likely to be eroded. Particularly this is the case when children take their community with them, into noncommunity settings.

However, intervention is likely to have an effect on the community as well as the child, chiefly through lateral and horizontal diffusion (Klaus & Gray, 1968). Over time, a whole community may change. For instance, for the past several years the teachers at Turner House Preschool in Kansas City, Kansas, have remarked upon the differences between the behavior of the children currently enrolled in the preschool and the behavior of the children enrolled at the inception of the program in the mid-1960s. In the ghetto community from which the Turner House Preschool children are randomly selected each year, preschool enrichment programs such as Head Start have enrolled nearly every child for the past 10 years. Not only is the behavior of the current population of children different from that of the population of 10 years ago, but there seems to be a general improvement in IQ scores (chiefly attributable, perhaps, to the decrease in IQ scores below 60).

Data analysis is currently under way at Turner House Preschool in order to document such long-term changes in language use within the community served by the preschool. We are comparing 10-year-old records of children's spontaneous speech in the preschool setting to identically recorded current records. Ten years ago we found important differences (to be discussed later) between the spontaneous language used by poverty children and that used by advantaged children in terms of the size of the lexicon and the numbers of different words introduced. Preliminary results of the current data analysis suggest that, although differences in language use across poverty and advantaged populations will still be evident, they will not be as large as they were 10 years ago. The spontaneous speech of the poverty children has, it appears, gradually become more similar to that of advantaged children.

The processes that have contributed to this difference can only be conjectured. We can suggest the relevance of preschool attendance and the importance of diffusion, but information on causes—information on processes that can become part of intervention programs—can be derived only from research that focuses on isolating such processes. This, however, requires creation of a data base because processes involved in performance in school settings can be isolated only on the basis of data collected in those settings. Relating performance in one setting to performance in another setting is *product* (outcome) *research* (Cazden, 1972). Both types of research are, of course, necessary to intervention, but the majority of intervention research so far has been product, rather than process, research (McGinness, Chapter 11).

The research conducted at Turner House Preschool is process research. The goal is the isolation of effective processes in language learning. However, a great deal of the research effort has been devoted to establishing the necessary data base. In order to isolate processes for changing how children use language in everyday preschool interactions, we have had to develop measures of that use; thus, a lot of the research conducted at Turner House Preschool has been descriptive.

In the remainder of the chapter, I will first summarize some of the results of the descriptive research conducted at Turner House Preschool and discuss what this research shows about the everyday language used by preschool-age children reared in poverty. Second, I will present the results of some process research and discuss what this research indicates concerning factors influencing the ways in which poverty children use language in their everyday interactions.

THE DATABASE: DESCRIPTIVE RESEARCH

As a basis for research on processes contributing to language learning, we needed data on the everyday language used by preschool children reared in poverty. Therefore, a technology was developed for recording the spontaneous speech of preschool children while they were engaged in free play activities. Observers were assigned to write down in longhand everything said by each child in the preschool, for a standard 15-min period during free play, every day across a 9-month preschool year.

The records of language use were coded and entered for computer analysis. Details of the coding and definitions of categories coded, as well as reliability coefficients, are given in Hart and Risley (1980). To summarize, two separate computer analyses were performed; one counted words (by part of speech, new, used, and different per 15-min sample), and one counted sentences within several structural categories (simple active affirmative declaratives, questions, imperatives, sentences containing subordinate clauses). The categories for analysis were chosen to permit comparison of the results of the present data analysis to the results of prior analyses of the speech of preschool children (McCarthy, 1954; Menyuk, 1969).

The results of the data analysis would also show us, we hoped, which aspects of poverty children's everyday language were most important to target in intervention. The question of whether children reared in poverty had a "language deficit" had been largely resolved, with general acceptance that a language difference does not constitute a language deficit. Data concerning language differences between advantaged and poverty children were, however, largely derived from children's behavior during brief, adult-structured interactions (Bernstein, 1973). The influence of immediate context on language use, as the growing pragmatic literature makes clear, is so important that mandatory corroborative data on spontaneous speech in unstructured situations was needed.

Data were needed that would show the extent to which the language differences found in adult-structured situations were characteristic of the poverty child's habitual use of language. Especially, in order to know what to target in intervention, data were needed that would show the nature of the differences between the ways advantaged and poverty children used language in their everyday spontaneous interactions. Therefore, a program of research was undertaken at Turner House Preschool in which identically recorded samples of spontaneous speech were collected in three separate preschool settings. Over a 9-month preschool year 15-min samples of children's spontaneous speech during free play were observer-recorded in the three settings. Then the samples from each setting were computer-processed in terms of language categories.

The three settings in which spontaneous speech during free play was recorded were as follows. The first setting was the Turner House Preschool, an experimental preschool program enrolling children from a black, economically impoverished community in Kansas City, Kansas. Language data were recorded during free play 4 days each week for 9 months from 11 children [average age 5:0; average IQ as measured by the Peabody Picture Vocabulary Inventory (PPVI), 75]. A rounded total of 178,000 words (31,000 sentences) was recorded for the group in 1245 15-min samples. The second setting was a nearby Head Start class serving children from the same community as the Turner House Preschool. Spontaneous speech data were recorded 1 day per week for 9 months from 8 children (average age 5:0; average IQ as measured by the PPVI, 71) who were randomly chosen from a preschool class of 27. A rounded total of 13,000 words (3000 sentences) was recorded for the group in 182 15-min samples. The third setting was the Edna A. Hill Child Development Laboratory Preschool at the University of Kansas, a setting that enrolled chiefly children of University staff and professors. Language data were recorded during free play 4 days each week for 9 months from 12 children (average age, 5:2; average IQ as measured by the PPVI, 117) who were randomly chosen from two preschool classes of 16 and 17 children each. A rounded total of 115,000 words (21,000 sentences) was recorded for the group in 824 15-min samples.

The results of the computer analysis of the spontaneous speech data recorded in the three settings essentially confirmed the findings of Tough (1977). The children, in all three settings, displayed well-developed and context-appropriate language. They produced well-formed, complete sentences of varied length and structural complexity. The children showed an ability to adapt language structure, context, and style to a variety of persons and to the expression of needs, concepts, and feelings. Moreover, the poverty children regularly used both Black English and Standard English structures; for instance, the only auxiliary–modal form that was recorded in use among the advantaged children, but never among the Turner House Preschool children, was *shall*.

In these data on spontaneous speech, as in Tough's (1977) data, the differences between the advantaged and the poverty children were in frequencies not instances. The poverty children displayed as great a variety and complexity of language as did the advantaged children, but specific instances were less frequent. For example, comparative and superlative forms of adjectives appeared within the Turner House Preschool children's group lexicon, but only 9% of the lexical items were so inflected. In contrast, 21% of adjectives appeared in inflected form within the lexicon of the advantaged children. Similarly, 27% of the recorded sentences of the poverty children at Turner House Preschool, and 26% at Head Start, were more complex than simple imperative or declarative. In contrast, 40% of all sentences recorded were complex among the advantaged children. Furthermore, although all parts of speech were adequately represented in the group lexicon in each of the three settings, the lexicon among the poverty children at Turner House Preschool consisted of 1975 different entries, whereas the lexicon among the group of advantaged children consisted of 2721 different entries.

The essential difference between the language used by the advantaged and the poverty children, then, could be characterized as a difference not of quality but of quantity: The advantaged children simply appeared to have more of everything. In comparison to the advantaged children, the poverty children had smaller lexicons, used fewer different words, and fewer complex sentence structures per 15-min sample. Also, the poverty children used language less often. Across the 9-month preschool year, the average number of words used per 15-min sample among the poverty children at the Head Start setting was 59, whereas the average among the advantaged children was 150.

The language performance of the poverty children at the Head Start setting was characterized by generally low rates of talking and using complex syntactic structures and different words per sample. In contrast, the language performance of the advantaged children at the University preschool setting was characterized by high rates of talking and using complex syntactic structures and different words per 15-min sample. These significant differences between the overall language performance of the poverty children at Head Start and that of the advantaged children did not change over 9 months of preschool attendance. Even after 9 months of preschool, there were significant differences between the two groups in terms of the quantity of language produced per recorded sample.

Among the Turner House Preschool children, however, a marked change was seen. At the beginning of the preschool year, the language performance of the poverty children at Turner House Preschool was not significantly different from that of their peers at the Head Start setting. However, at the end of the preschool year, the language performance of the poverty children at Turner House Preschool was not significantly different from that of the advantaged children at the University setting. Apparently, as a result of generalization from the intervention program conducted at the Turner House Preschool (Hart & Risley, 1980), the language performance of the poverty children at Turner House Preschool became in certain ways indistinguishable from that of economically and educationally advantaged children.

The descriptive data collected over the preschool year showed, first, a steady increase in the amount of talk among the Turner House Preschool children. At the beginning of the preschool year, the average number of words used per 15-min sample among the Turner House preschool children was 89, comparable to the year-long average among the poverty children at the Head Start setting. At the end of the preschool year, the average number of words used per 15-min sample among the Turner House Preschool children was 185, comparable to the year-long average among the advantaged children at the University setting.

Second, the descriptive data showed that as the frequency of using language to interact increased, the frequency of using different words and complex sentence structures increased correspondingly. By the end of the preschool year, certain of the initially significant differences between the language used by the poverty children at the Turner House Preschool and that used by the advantaged children at the University setting had disappeared. Not only were there no significant differences at the end of the preschool year between the poverty children at Turner

House Preschool and their advantaged age-mates in terms of the average frequency of using language, there were no significant differences between their language performance in terms of numbers of complex syntactic constructions and numbers of different words appearing per 15-min sample. The marked improvements in language use among the poverty children at Turner House Preschool were general across individual children and were evident in the language used both to teachers and to other children (Hart & Risley, 1980).

The reason why the frequency of different words and complex syntactic structures increased when talking increased among the poverty children lies in the nature of language use. Since language use is controlled by the context of use, and the context of use changes in subtle ways with every utterance (Halliday, 1978), language performance, if it is to remain appropriately matched to the speech-act context, must vary from moment to moment. The more a child talks during free play, thus, the more different aspects of the situation become topics for comment, and the more often others' responses serve to influence the content of further comments. When a child uses language relative to more different objects, actions, and relationships, this shows up in language data as increases in numbers of different words used and in numbers of different relations syntactically expressed.

Thus our data, like Tough's (1977), indicate that the differences between the language performance of poverty and advantaged children are not syntactic–semantic differences, but pragmatic ones. The observation that poverty children simply do not talk very much may be found explicitly (Bereiter & Engelmann, 1966; Williams, 1970) or implicitly (Hertzig, Birch, Thomas, & Mendez, 1968) in the literature. But our data indicate that when poverty children do talk as much as advantaged children, many of the differences in language performance disappear. This finding has important implications for intervention.

The fact that the complexity of the language in use improves with increases in the frequency of language use implies that a primary target in intervention should be rate of language use. There was a highly significant correlation—both within and across the Turner House Preschool, Head Start, and University groups of children—between the frequency of using language and each aspect of language complexity (size of lexicon in use, numbers of different words, and complex syntactic structures in use). At each setting the children who talked most frequently had the largest lexicons in use and used more different words and complex sentences. Actually, this is what might be expected if, at age 2, as Nelson (1973) reports, talking a lot is a strategy positively related to all aspects of language acquisition.

INTERVENTION: PROCESS RESEARCH

The descriptive research conducted at Turner House Preschool indicated that the more often children talk, the more elaborated the language they use becomes. The process research conducted concurrently in the preschool was directed at isolating processes for producing increased rates of using language. A series of experiments was conducted using a multiple baseline design (Baer, Wolf, & Risley, 1968) to demonstrate that particular forms of language increased in use during free play when, and only when, the process of incidental teaching was applied to that particular form (Hart & Risley, 1968, 1974, 1975). The effects of the process on general language use (i.e., on aspects of language not targeted in the experimental intervention) were assessed within the descriptive data base; these effects have been reported in this chapter. Not only was incidental teaching shown to be an effective process for increasing specific aspects of language use, but it appeared to have beneficial effects on general language use (Hart & Risley, 1980).

The process of incidental teaching is one apparently used naturally by mothers of children who progress particularly well in language acquisition (White, 1978). Incidental teaching describes that brief, positive, one-to-one interaction in which an adult focuses on a child-chosen topic as an occasion for teaching. The adult waits for the child to initiate the interaction. This waiting seems particularly important, for it allows the child to determine both when a conversation is to begin and what it is to be about; the literature suggests that a child's early experiences with ability to control the responses of others can facilitate later learning (Finkelstein & Ramey, 1977; White, 1978). Furthermore, when a child chooses a topic for conversation, the topic is one about which the child wants to talk, one that is momentarily of enough importance that the child will pause or interrupt whatever he or she is currently doing to talk about that topic. The child's high level of interest makes the child particularly receptive to teaching.

In the process of incidental teaching, the adult focuses clearly and exclusively on whatever topic the child uses to initiate conversation. The adult confirms to the child, often by repeating the child's topic word, the adult's understanding of, and interest in, whatever the child wants to discuss. Then the adult asks the child to elaborate, through language, on that interesting topic. The familiarity of the interaction may be seen in the following example.

CHILD: *Hey, teacher, look at the house I made.*
TEACHER: *A house, yes. Who's gonna live in it?*

This is the sort of interaction in which a teacher can continue to elicit further description and elaboration from the child for as long as the teacher can think of challenging and appropriate questions.

Incidental teaching thus centers on occasions when children bring up topics to talk about and teachers are especially responsive to the child's use of language through successive turns at talk. Such occasions tend to be brief, positive moments of focused one-to-one attention between teacher and child. On such occasions, children seem to be particularly receptive to teaching incidental to the conversational topic. Another familiar example is:

> CHILD: *No, I said that orange paint.*
> TEACHER: *I know you said orange, but this is orange paint. That's red paint.*
> CHILD: *I want red paint.*

or:

> CHILD: *My mama has one of those.*
> TEACHER: *She does? What's that called?*
> CHILD: *It makes letters.*
> TEACHER: *That's right, it's a typewriter.*
> CHILD: *Typewriter.*
> TEACHER: *Right, a typewriter. What does your mama typewrite?*

The antithesis of incidental teaching may be illustrated through McNeill's (1966) frequently cited example of the relative impenetrability of early child grammar to adult models:

> CHILD: *Nobody don't like me.*
> MOTHER: *No, say, "nobody likes me."*

Identical turns are repeated eight times until the child finally says, *Oh! Nobody don't likes me.* The child finally shifts to the adult's topic (grammar). The child may not have learned better grammar from the interaction but may well have learned something about who controls the topic in interaction and the relative importance to that person of the child's interpersonal problems.

The fact that an adult focuses with attentive interest on the topic the child has chosen, and asks for elaboration on that topic, appears to encourage children to talk more often about more different topics (Hart & Risley, 1980). As children talk about more different topics, they use more different words and describe more different relationships in more complex syntactic structures. Incidental teaching is thus pragmatic language teaching, teaching focused on language use in ways that entail benefits for both the knowledge of language and the knowledge of how, why, and where language is used.

The process research conducted at Turner House Preschool thus showed, that, using incidental teaching, it was easy to increase the frequency with which poverty children used language and so bring aspects of their everyday language use into comparability to that of advantaged children. When looked at locally, within limited samples of language use during free play (for instance, during the first and last weeks of the preschool year), the changes in language use were highly significant. The initially significant differences between the language used by poverty and advantaged children had, in the last weeks of the preschool year, almost completely disappeared.

The process research, however, had as its base longitudinal descriptive data, and those data revealed unchanged aspects of language use. Data collected over 9 months' time showed that the pronounced and beneficial changes so easily made in language use, and so readily apparent within small, local measures of language use, had not affected long-term patterns of lexical growth.

The descriptive data showed that over the long term, the advantaged children were regularly adding new words to their recorded lexicons in use more often than were the children reared in poverty. Even when the poverty children used language more often—relative to more different objects, actions, and relations—they continued to add new words to their lexicons in use less often that did the advantaged children. And the rate of adding new words to the lexicon in use did not noticeably change either with time or intervention. Over time—a month versus a day, for example—the poverty children were apparently introducing fewer new topics into conversation, focusing on those topics in fewer novel ways, and/or commenting on fewer novel aspects of those topics. The poverty children's lexicons in use were growing (i.e., receiving new entries) more slowly than those of the advantaged children. The long-term effect of this difference is to create a cumulative, ever-widening gap between the size of the lexicon in use by poverty versus advantaged children.

The processes contributing to lexical acquisition are as yet unexplicated: Currently, "We have no methods to follow the total process of lexical acquisition in which the child is engaged [Miller, 1978, p. 1003]." What we have are tests, such as tests of verbal IQ, that assess at particular points in time the results of long-term lexical acquisition. We know that lexical acquisition is correlated with school achievement

(Carroll, 1971), but we do not know why some children come to school with larger lexicons than others.

Nelson's (1973) investigation of early vocabulary acquisition suggests that parent–child interactions may help to establish both different rates of talking and different patterns of introducing into talk new lexical items being acquired. In any case, the longitudinal Turner House Preschool data show that by age 4, when syntax has been largely acquired (Menyuk, 1969), patterns of acquiring new lexical items in use are firmly in place and not readily changed.

The Turner House Preschool data showed, for both the advantaged and poverty children, that the total size of the lexicon in use, within the first 20 15-min language samples, was significantly correlated with mental age as measured by the PPVI: The larger the lexicon in use, the higher the mental age tended to be. But when the effects of frequency of language use were parcelled out, by comparing size of lexicon in use across children within a fixed number (5000) of words said, there was no longer any marked correlation between mental age and size of lexicon in use for the advantaged children. Apparently, for advantaged children it is not how much they talk, but other factors such as lexical content or test-performance skills that influence measures of mental age. But for the children reared in poverty, the highly significant correlation (.8) between measured mental age and size of lexicon in use remained. The fact that mental age and size of lexicon in use remain correlated even when children are equated for frequency of language use suggests that for children reared in poverty, those factors that contribute to rate of using language in interaction may also contribute to lexical acquisition.

Current work in discourse analysis suggests how lexical acquisition and language use may interact. New information (potentially, new lexical items) tends to cooccur with introduction of a new topic or with a new focus on an old topic (Creider, 1979). Foregrounded utterances tend to maintain identity of subject and to summarize indispensible event-related information, whereas backgrounded utterances are used for elaboration, describing details of setting, mood, and motive (Hooper, 1979). Individuals who talk a lot tend to introduce many new topics and focus on them in many new ways, examining and elaborating them through backgrounded utterances. Each new topic is potentially an occasion for the individual to learn from a listener a corrected pronunciation, a new word, or a new meaning for an old word. But children who do not often talk tend to talk about a limited number of topics (things they really need or want) and to focus on those topics in limited, primarily foregrounded, ways. Such children have ordinarily mastered syntax, semantics, and the functions of language by age 4, just as have children who talk a lot.

But what language does for them—and thus what language is (Halliday, 1977)—may be different from what language is for a child who talks a lot. And it may be this difference that is reflected in the long-term rate of lexical growth.

For the past several years, the process research at Turner House Preschool has been concerned with attempts to isolate factors contributing to a long-term rate of lexical growth. The 15-min language samples recorded during free play every day across a 9-month preschool year on each of the children enrolled in the preschool are used to construct a cumulative curve displaying for each child the relative rate of introducing new lexical items into use (Hart & Risley, in press). The effects of factors contributing to rates of lexical growth are assessed by dividing the preschool population into experimental and control groups, with individual children matched in terms of rates of introducing new lexical items into use. Intervention is then introduced into the experimental group, and the data are examined for any changes in rates of introducing new lexical items into spontaneous speech.

We have so far assessed the contribution of three factors to long-term patterns of lexical acquisition: context, experience, and instructional mediation. The first intervention examined the role of context. It is virtually certain that poverty children, like all children, know more words than they use in everyday spontaneous speech. Simply, the context does not call for them to introduce (as new words) all the words they know. However, poverty children are presented, in enrichment programs, with a preschool context that was originally designed for advantaged populations. It may be, as Labov (1970) has suggested, that a context designed by and for advantaged populations is not the context most conducive to the display, or use, by poverty children of the full extent of the lexical resources they actually have.

To test the hypothesis that in a more culturally similar context poverty children would display accelerated rates of introducing new lexical items into spontaneous speech, we arranged within the preschool a free play context very similar to that which we saw in the children's homes. The context had the overall appearance of a large living room, with a couch, coffee table, TV, radio, and magazines such as *Ebony* and *Jet*. Play materials were those often provided by parents (two of the children helped teachers choose them at the store); battery-operated vehicles, Barbie-type dolls, mechanical-set toys, coloring books, plus the sorts of miscellaneous, multiple-use materials that tend to collect in a home.

An effect of the experimental context was seen, but it was not the effect predicted. The number of new words appearing in the language samples of the experimental group was not larger than the numbers appearing in the data of the control group that remained in the standard preschool setting. Rather, the rate of using language decreased in the experimental context, and contextual observations (Cataldo & Risley, 1974) indicated that the experimental group children tended to play more often alone. Teachers and observers commented that the experimental environment "really did look like a home," where children often occupy themselves alone, interact with other children (siblings) chiefly when competing for materials, and talk relatively little—perhaps because the TV and radio maintain a background ambiance of noise and/or because adults, occupied elsewhere, must be interrupted in order to initiate conversation. The findings of this experiment suggest strongly, then, that a standard preschool context is much more appropriate as a setting for language intervention than is the home. Particularly, the standard preschool setting seems to cue more frequent use of language and more social interaction through its materials and nonhomelike environmental arrangements.

The second intervention was designed to examine the role of experience. The first intervention had indicated that the lexical resources of poverty children and advantaged children are sampled to an equal extent within a standard preschool setting; perhaps, then, the differences in rates of lexical growth could be attributed to differences in the kinds of experiences available to poverty and advantaged children. Children reared in poverty may, because of their poverty, have fewer and less varied experiences than do advantaged children, and this restricted experience shows up as restricted lexicon in use. To test this hypothesis, the Turner House Preschool children were taken on a series of field-trip experiences. The control group children were taken to local parks where they engaged in large-motor activities very similar to those available during outdoor free play at the preschool. The experimental group, though, was taken to a series of "enrichment" settings such as a library, fire department, music store, and train yard. The results of the intervention showed no differences between groups in rates of lexical growth. When the children returned to preschool free play (where all the language data were collected), they tended to talk about ongoing play activities and very rarely mentioned what they had seen or done on a field trip. Enriched experience alone, apparently, does not lead to an enriched lexicon in use.

Potentially, all experiences are rich in language; however, it may be necessary that individuals interact relative to an experience in order for this potential to be realized in language use. Thus it may be that poverty children, although they have sufficiently varied experience and are drawing upon the full extent of the lexicons they have, need the kinds of interaction concerning their experiences that can help them understand, organize, and generalize those experiences. They may need the sort of adult mediation (Haywood, in press) that seems to characterize many of the language interactions between well-developing advantaged children and their parents (White, 1978).

To examine processes of adult mediation, a third intervention was designed. The particular process examined, as a first stage, was the contribution to lexical growth of preparatory and follow-up teaching sessions related to specific enrichment experiences. Eight pairs of preschool children matched on rates of lexical growth were randomly assigned to control and experimental groups. All 16 children were taken on "enrichment" field trips to, for instance, a bank, grocery store, and gas station. All 16 children were also provided, on the day after each field trip, access to a newly arranged free play context containing materials conducive to role play of the previous day's field trip experience. Language data, as usual, were collected only in the free play setting.

To the experimental group alone were presented preparatory and follow-up small-group sessions designed to help the children understand, organize, and generalize the field-trip experiences. Preparatory sessions were conducted for one-half hour immediately before each field trip and involved discussion of what the children already knew about the planned experience, role play of the experience at the children's level, and teacher-directed attention to the specific activities and concepts the children were to note on the field trip. Follow-up small-group sessions, lasting about one-half hour, took place immediately prior to free play on the day following the field trip. The children and a teacher discussed the field trip, with the teacher prompting narration, recall, questions, and elaboration calling for specific, field-trip-related vocabulary items.

Within the language data collected during free play, no significant differences in rates of lexical growth were seen. Patterns of introducing new lexical items into ongoing talk during free play remained essentially the same for both experimental and control group children. All the children acquired in use many new lexical items related to role play of the enrichment experiences, but no children introduced new lexical items into conversation more frequently than they had prior to intervention. The new intervention-related words apparently replaced, rather than added to, the number of new lexical items that would normally be expected to appear in the data as a result of interaction with the regular preschool materials and activities. The different (experimental) context called for different new words than did the regular preschool context—but not for more new words.

The results of the intervention did show clearly, though, the relevance of diffusion and demand. Experimental group children nearly always initially modeled the role behaviors and vocabulary appropriate to a novel role-play setting (thus indicating that they had indeed gained in understanding and word knowledge from the preparatory and follow-up sessions). But the control group children quickly acquired the new vocabulary needed in order to participate in the role play. The rapidity and extent of lateral diffusion that took place (such that new intervention-related words appeared in all the children's lexicons) suggests that it may not be necessary to teach all children directly, especially if conditions can be arranged that promote interaction between children with sophisticated language and children whose language needs improvement. (Arranging such interaction is, of course, quite different from merely arranging for the potential for interaction, as is done through incorporating children of varied skill levels within the same school or the same classroom.)

Also salient during the intervention was the relevance of demand. The new words children introduced into role play were primarily those words they needed in order to successfully maintain the role play, and, especially, those they needed in order to interact with the materials involved. A brief follow-up experiment addressed this issue: The results showed that merely introducing new role-play materials (e.g., a doctor's kit) into free play was sufficient to generate child use of numbers of new lexical items. Interaction with the new materials seemed to demand from children the use of new forms of language; recognition of such demand is of course the basis for the enriched curricula of all intervention programs.

The relevance of demand, though, was also apparent when children did not introduce new words. For example, two Turner House Preschool children role-playing gas station attendant and customer during intervention were observed in the following exchange:

CHILD 1: *Give me some gas.*
CHILD 2.: *What kind do you want?*
CHILD 1.: *That kind.* (Pointing to one of the facsimile pumps.)
CHILD 2: *How much do you want?*
CHILD 1: *A lot.*

If the teacher had intervened and prompted use of more specific terms, the children would almost certainly have produced one or more of the lexical items (i.e., *regular, gallons*) introduced during preparatory and follow-up small-group sessions and perhaps added them as new words to their lexicons in use. But the design of the experiment expressly prohibited teaching new intervention-related vocabulary during free play, in order to assess generalization from the small-group sessions. It was apparent, though, that the demands of the listeners in free play (children and teachers who would accept, *That kind*) were markedly different from the demands of the teacher during the small-group sessions.

In ordinary conversation, it appears, listeners such as other children may demand only as much specificity and elaboration as is required for effective communication. Listeners may enjoy, or prefer, lexical elaboration (for instance, the contextual data collected at Turner House Preschool showed that both teachers and children responded most frequently to the utterances of the children with the most elaborated lexicons in use), but they seem to require only appropriateness and communicative effectiveness. It is teachers (and sometimes parents) who tend to differentiate between a child's use, for instance, of *under* versus *underneath;* for the ordinary listener, the two words are likely to be functionally synonymous. Thus, once poverty children have developed functional language use, they are likely to have, as Shuy (1970) pointed out some time ago, all the language they need in order to meet the demands of their community. Even in schools and other contexts where poverty children do need the patterns of vocabulary use and lexical growth characteristic of advantaged children, there may be little demand for them. Teachers are very likely to respond appropriately to the language used by the poverty child (to understand it, and act on it, even when they do not approve its form) and thus assure that the poverty child's language is functional—and maintained.

CONCLUSION

Research on processes contributing to language learning has been based at Turner House Preschool on daily 15-minute samples of children's spontaneous language use collected over 9-month periods of time. From such long-term data we have been able to assess differences in the language used in everyday interactions among poverty children as compared to advantaged children and to examine changes (or their absence) in patterns of language use across time and intervention. The results of this research have convinced us of the need for, and the usefulness of, collecting long-term data and recording language as it is used in spontaneous, unstructured interactions within classrooms and free-activity settings.

These long-term data have shown, first, that children reared in pov-

erty appear to command as full a range of syntactic structures and semantic relations as do advantaged children. The differences between the
language used by poverty and by advantaged children seem to be differences not in quality but in quantity: Poverty children often tend to
talk less than advantaged children and so to use complex or elaborated
language forms less frequently.

Frequency of using language seems to be an important diagnostic
because language use and language elaboration are highly correlated.
Given that children's language use is under appropriate contextual control, the more often children talk, the more different aspects (objects,
actions, relations) of an ever-changing context they tend to comment on.
The more different aspects of the context that children comment on, the
more different words and syntactic relations are called into use, and the
more feedback the children receive relative to the forms, structures, and
meanings of language.

Frequency of language use has been shown in process research to
be easily increased through teacher use of incidental teaching—the process of brief, positive teacher-focus on elaborating with a child whatever
topic the child chooses to discuss. And when the rate of language use
increases, correlated aspects of language elaboration—different words
and complex syntactic structures—also increase in use, without having
to be directly targeted in intervention.

The long-term data collected at Turner House Preschool have shown,
however, that children reared in poverty appear to be acquiring fewer
new lexical entries per utterance than are advantaged children. The differences in rates of lexical growth that appear in the long-term records
of language use across poverty and advantaged populations—differences
that seem to be captured in measures of IQ and reflected in reading
comprehension scores (Becker, 1977)—seem not only to be well established by 4 years of age, but, given the differing patterns of lexical
acquisition, the gap between advantaged and poverty children is increasing over time.

Process research has shown that these long-term patterns of lexical
growth are, unlike general rate of talking, not readily changed. Stable
patterns of lexical acquisition in use do not seem to be affected simply
by changes in context, new experiences, or brief periods of instruction.
Moreover, once poverty children have acquired functional and appropriate language use, there seems to be little demand, at least on the part
of the listeners the children encounter in preschool (and, perhaps beyond
as well), for the kinds of lexical elaboration that characterize the speech
of advantaged children. Further research is needed in order to delineate
the nature and source of the demand for lexical elaboration, that to which

the language use of advantaged children may be assumed to be responding, and to establish that demand within the everyday interactions of children reared in poverty.

REFERENCES

Baer, D. M., Wolf, M. M., & Risley, T. R. Some current dimensions of applied behavior analysis. *Journal of Applied Behavior Analysis*, 1968, *1*, 91–97.

Becker, W. C. Teaching reading and language to the disadvantaged—what we have learned from field research. *Harvard Educational Review*, 1977, *47*, 518–543.

Bereiter, C., & Engelmann, S. *Teaching disadvantaged children in the preschool.* Englewood Cliffs, New Jersey: Prentice-Hall, 1966.

Bernstein, B. (Ed.). *Class, codes and control.* London: Routledge & Kegan Paul, 1973.

Bronfenbrenner, U. *A report on longitudinal evaluations of preschool programs. Is early intervention effective?* (Vol. 2). Washington, D.C.: DHEW Publication No. (OHD) 76-30025, 1976.

Brown, P., & Levinson, S. Universals in language usage: Politeness phenomena. In E. N. Goody (Ed.), *Questions and politeness.* New York: Cambridge University Press, 1978.

Carroll, J. B. *Learning from verbal discourse in educational media: A review of the literature* (ETS RM 71-61). Princeton, New Jersey: Educational Testing Service, 1971.

Cataldo, M. F., & Risley, T. R. Evaluation of living environments: The MANIFEST description of ward activities. In P. O. Davidson, F. W. Clark, & L. A. Hamerlynck (Eds.), *Evaluation of social programs in community, residential and school settings.* Champaign, Illinois: Research Press, 1974.

Cazden, C. B. Some questions for research in early childhood education. In J. C. Stanley (Ed.), *Preschool programs for the disadvantaged.* Baltimore, Maryland: Johns Hopkins University Press, 1972.

Creider, C. A. On the explanation of transformations. In T. Givon (Ed.), *Syntax and semantics. Discourse and syntax* (Vol. 12). New York: Academic Press, 1979.

Finkelstein, N. W., & Ramey, C. T. Learning to control the environment in infancy. *Child Development*, 1977, *48*, 806–819.

Givon, T. Preface. In T. Givon (Ed.), *Syntax and semantics. Discourse and syntax* (Vol. 12). New York: Academic Press, 1979.

Halliday, M. A. K. *Explorations in the functions of language.* New York: Elsevier North-Holland, 1977.

Halliday, M. A. K. *Language as social semiotic.* Baltimore, Maryland: University Park Press, 1978.

Hart, B. Pragmatics and language development. In B. B. Lahey & A. E. Kazdin (Eds.), *Advances in clinical child psychology* (Vol. 3). New York: Plenum Press, 1980.

Hart, B., & Risley, T. R. Establishing use of descriptive adjectives in the spontaneous speech of disadvantaged preschool children. *Journal of Applied Behavior Analysis*, 1968, *1*, 109–120.

Hart, B., & Risley, T. R. Using preschool materials to modify the language of disadvantaged children. *Journal of Applied Behavior Analysis*, 1974, *7*, 243–256.

Hart, B., & Risley, T. R. Incidental teaching of language in the preschool. *Journal of Applied Behavior Analysis*, 1975, *8*, 411–420.

Hart, B., & Risley, T. R. In vivo language interaction: Unanticipated general effects. *Journal of Applied Behavior Analysis,* 1980, *13,* 407–432.

Hart, B., & Risley, T. R. Grammatical and conceptual growth in the language of psychosocially disadvantaged children: Assessment and intervention. In M. J. Begab, H. Garber, & H. C. Haywood (Eds.), *Prevention of retarded development in psychosocially disadvantaged children.* Baltimore, Maryland: University Park Press, in press.

Haywood, H. C. Intelligence, cognition, and individual differences. In M. J. Begab, H. Garber, & H. C. Haywood (Eds.), *Prevention of retarded development in psychosocially disadvantaged children.* Baltimore, Maryland: University Park Press, in press.

Hertzig, M. E., Birch, H. G., Thomas, A., & Mendez, O. A. Class and ethnic differences in the responsiveness of preschool children to cognitive demands. *Monographs of the Society for Research in Child Development,* 1968, *33*(1, Serial No. 117).

Hopper, P. J. Aspect and foregrounding in discourse. In T. Givon (Ed.), *Syntax and semantics. Discourse and syntax* (Vol. 12). New York: Academic Press, 1979.

Klaus, R. A., & Gray, S. W. The Early Training Project for disadvantaged children: A report after five years. *Monographs of the Society for Research in Child Development,* 1968, *33*(4, Serial No. 120).

Labov, W. The logic of nonstandard English. In F. Williams (Ed.), *Language and poverty.* Chicago: Markham, 1970.

Lazar, I., Hubbell, V. R., Murray, H., Rosche, M., & Royce, J. *The persistence of preschool effects.* Final Report: Grant No. 18-76-07843. Washington, D.C.: U.S. Government Printing Office, 1977. (No. 017-000-0202-3).

McCarthy, D. Language development in children. In L. Carmichael (Ed.), *Manual of child psychology.* New York: Wiley, 1954.

McNeill, D. Developmental psycholinguistics. In F. Smith & G. A. Miller (Eds.), *The genesis of language.* Cambridge, Massachusetts: MIT Press, 1966.

Menyuk, P. *Sentences children use.* Cambridge, Massachusetts: MIT Press, 1969.

Miller, G. A. The acquisition of word meaning. *Child Development,* 1978, *49,* 999–1004.

Nelson, K. Structure and strategy in learning to talk. *Monographs of the Society for Research in Child Development,* 1973, *38*(1–2, Serial No. 149).

Ochs, E. Planned and unplanned discourse. In T. Givon (Ed.), *Syntax and semantics. Discourse and syntax* (Vol. 12). New York: Academic Press, 1979.

Psathas, G. *Everyday language: Studies in ethnomethodology.* New York: Irvington, 1979.

Raizen, S., & Bobrow, S. B. *Design for a national evaluation of social competence in Head Start children.* Santa Monica, California: The Rand Corporation, 1974.

Shuy, R. W. The sociolinguists and urban language problems. In F. Williams (Ed.), *Language and poverty.* Chicago: Markham, 1970.

Tough, J. *The development of meaning: A study of children's use of language.* New York: Wiley, 1977.

White, B. L. *Experience and environment* (Vol. 2). Englewood Cliffs, New Jersey: Prentice-Hall, 1978.

Williams, F. Language, attitude, and social change. In F. Williams (Ed.), *Language and poverty.* Chicago: Markham, 1970.

Williams, F., & Naremore, R. C. On the functional analysis of social class differences in modes of speech. *Speech Monographs,* 1969, *36,* 77–102.

11

The Language of the Poverty Child: Implications from Center-Based Intervention and Evaluation Programs

GAEL D. McGINNESS

In 1961 J. McVicker Hunt published a book called *Intelligence and Experience* that, along with Bloom's *Stability and Change in Human Characteristics* (1964), helped to foster the movement toward compensatory preschool programs for the disadvantaged child. Reviewing the 10–30-point gains in IQ made by nursery school pupils in a program run by Samuel Kirk and his colleagues in the late 1950s, Hunt remarked: "Such findings suggest that society would not be wasting its time to provide a nursery-school experience to disadvantaged children prior to school entry [1961, p. 334]." Such a nursery-school experience it was thought, would give children a kind of inoculation against school failure. Kirk's result, as popularized by Hunt helped to formulate the expectation that preschool experience might do for school failure what vaccinations had done for smallpox.

The history of compensatory preschool language intervention and evaluation over the past two decades has much to teach. This chapter will (*a*) review the success of early intervention and the problems encountered in its evaluation; (*b*) offer a digest of related research implications for future intervention and evaluation; and (*c*) briefly summarize the recent development of the Carolina Abecedarian Project's language program for disadvantaged children at the Frank Porter Graham Child Development Center.

219

THE LANGUAGE OF CHILDREN
REARED IN POVERTY

SHORT-TERM INTERVENTION GAINS

Because of the optimism generated in the early 1960s about the initial results from preschool intervention programs, few protested the grandiosity of the inoculation model of preschool education. In a variety of intervention projects, children from disadvantaged families had shown dramatic IQ gains. But within a few years, it began to seem that both the brief traditional, and the cognitively intense, early education intervention programs could not give lifetime protection from the disease of school failure. Instead, the early optimism gave way to clear disillusionment. Beilin (1972) stated in a review of many of the follow-up studies of the early intervention projects: "The most disappointing fact to face about preschool compensatory education is its inability to live up to the high expectations set for it. Even the best among the innovative programs, although they demonstrate short-term gains in intellective performance, inevitably show the gains to be short-lived. Gains do not survive, even with continued educational enrichment [pp. 165–167]." Bronfenbrenner (1975) reiterated this disillusionment:

> But the experimental groups do not continue to make gains when intervention continues beyond one year, and, what is more critical, the effects tend to "wash out" after intervention is terminated. The longer the follow-up, the more obvious the latter trend becomes [p. 335].

LONG-TERM INTERVENTION GAINS

Not only did the early intervention evaluations engender pessimism about the enduring effects of a short-term intervention, they ultimately led to a second hope and a second disappointment about longer-term intervention. The hope invested in longer intervention arose in reaction to the inoculation model's failure. A different approach seemed necessary: Perhaps the school failure syndrome could be properly likened to a nutritional deficiency requiring ongoing therapy, rather than a disease requiring some sort of vaccination.

The proposals for longer intervention grew out of such reasoning and made somewhat better sense to those who approached the problem of compensatory education from a language background. If the language of the poverty child really could be viewed as different or (depending on one's theoretical orientation) deficient, it makes little sense to think it could be fundamentally changed in a few weeks of summer education, anymore than it would make sense to teach English-speaking children

German and then place them in an environment where German was rarely required while expecting their German fluency to remain at post-instructional levels. Obviously a continuous instruction in and practice of the new "language" taught during intervention would be needed to keep pace with middle-class peers. The argument in favor of what was called the Follow Through Program[1] was that the higher-level cognitive–abstract language supplement needed by the poverty children was not provided by conventional public school instruction. At least, it was not provided at a sufficient level of intensity to allow the disadvantaged pupils to compete with their middle-class counterparts, whose home environments were so much richer in stimulation. A variant of public school instruction was, therefore, required in elementary grades in order to maintain the gains realized in Head Start. Yet even those programs did not maintain IQ gains as the children entered public school. "What is not reinforced is not maintained" became so basic a dictum in psychology following the renaissance of behaviorism that the logic of a need to "Follow Through" seemed compelling indeed. But then the third wave of disillusionment set in. Follow Through, it appeared, did not produce lasting gains in IQ, either (Travers & Rupp, 1978).

The most hopeful findings to date about the long-term effects of early intervention programs have been reported by Lazar, Hubbell, Murray, Rosche, and Royce (1977) in a follow-up of pupils who received preschool intervention prior to 1969. These programs ranged greatly in intensity, the preschool age of intervention, and the philosophy behind the intervention. Participants in 14 such projects[2] were followed up by a collaborative effort of the original 12 investigators in 1976–1977. Secondary analyses were done of the original Stanford-Binet IQ data and compared with WISC-R follow-up data on the more than 1100 children who were located from the original sample of over 2000.

---

[1] For a review of the evolution of Follow Through, see Haney, W., *A technical history of the Follow-Through program.* Washington, D.C.: USOE, 1976.

[2] Projects included in the Lazar *et al.* study were those involving matched controls whose programs collected initial IQ data and were completed prior to 1969 and whose investigators cooperated to follow up and test subjects who could be located in 1976–1977: *The Philadelphia Project:* Dr. Kuno Beller; *Institute for Developmental Studies:* Drs. Martin and Cynthia Deutsch; *The Parent Educator Program:* Dr. Ira Gordon; *Early Training Project:* Dr. Susan Gray; *Family-Oriented Home Visitor Program,* Dr. Susan Gray; *Curriculum Comparison Study:* Dr. Merle Karnes; *Mother–Child Home Program:* Dr. Phyllis Levenstein; *Experimental Variation of Head Start Curricula:* Dr. Louise Miller; *Harlem Training Project:* Dr. Francis Palmer; *Perry Preschool Project:* Dr. David Weikart; *Curriculum Demonstration Project:* Dr. David Weikart; *Carnegie Infant Program:* Dr. David Weikart; *Micro-Social Learning System:* Dr. Myron Woolman; *Head Start and Follow Through New Haven Study:* Dr. Edward Zigler.

The evidence seems to indicate that, on the average, well-run early education programs can increase a child's ability to perform well on IQ tests, and that this increase in skills lasts for several years but eventually fades. The effect of early education then, in terms of skills which are measurable by IQ tests, is certainly of far more value than a temporary fluctuation in skill levels, but does not constitute a permanent increase in intellectual skills [Lazar *et al.*, 1977, p. 61].

Indeed, it seemed clear that there were no lasting IQ gains, but, they argued, this one test should not be used as the only criterion of a successful program. Thus, Lazar *et al.* also did analyses on other outcome measures—retention in grade and placement in special education—on the grounds that whereas IQ tests merely predict achievement, these two measures are direct (negative) indices of acceptable school adjustment. They found that children who had received early intervention, in comparison to comparable groups who had not, were retained in grade less and were less often referred for special education. Therefore, the authors argue that children who received early preschool intervention did display lasting positive effects beneficial to them and to the public.

Though pessimism about the effectiveness of center-based preschool intervention has been widely tempered by the Lazar *et al.* findings, they must be accepted provisionally until more replications of programs and evaluations begun in the 1970s can be done. It seems premature to assume that absence of grade retention and referral to special education reflect actual achievement of school skills, especially when IQ data do not differentiate experimental and control groups. Children's achievement may have been influenced by continuous promotion policies or differential availability of special education programs; and, until actual achievement data are available for year-by-year comparisons on experimentals and controls, it is impossible to rule out alternative explanations of school promotions (for example, parents' tactics for influencing placement–promotion decisions, perhaps through social contact with early intervention programs). Some recent evidence from one project (Schweinhart & Weikart, 1980) has indicated that a follow-up through age 15 of the children in the High/Scope project actually produced a 1 year advantage in achievement for the preschool intervention group over the nonintervention group. Further evidence of this kind would certainly argue for long-term gains in achievement.

We have learned from results of early intervention programs, therefore, that effecting lasting gains in IQ for disadvantaged children, in the context of such programs, has been difficult to demonstrate, at least with research and evaluation designs employed to do so; but there is some evidence that beneficial results are discernible in other areas of school adaptation.

EARLY OUTCOME EVALUATIONS

Many research design and methodological problems complicated evaluations of early intervention programs; these are particularly exemplified in the large-scale evaluation of Follow Through (Travers & Rupp, 1978). Comparisons across Follow Through intervention models were frustrated because, in studying programs as they were implemented, evaluators found much more within-model than between-model variation. There was inadequate matching of experimental and control groups on variables such as socioeconomic status, which may have confounded results, and analysis of covariance techniques to correct for initial differences have been questioned (Cronbach, Rogosa, Floden, & Price, 1977). Finally, the achievement tests[3] used may have been insensitive measures:

> It may be that gains were severely masked by the narrowness of the traditional tests used to measure outcomes of the early childhood models. As a whole, though, the data did not show dramatic results. In the *Abt* Associates evaluation, the Follow Through models as a whole did no better than the public school classes to which they were compared [Hutchins & House, 1977, p. 6].

When the dust had settled from the controversies surrounding evaluation of early intervention programs, an evaluator assessing the available technology was moved to this conclusion:

> We are not in a position from a research and evaluation stance to demonstrate the long term effectiveness of any early childhood program. The presumed demands of the policymakers outstripped the state of our art in methods, instruments, and resources [Takanishi, 1979, p. 154].

Also contributing to the inadequacy of most outcome evaluation studies of group programs is the fact that they assume the environments and the programs therein to be static, unchanging entities, whereas practitioners know these to be "dynamically evolving [Guttentag, 1977, p. 19]."

PROCESS EVALUATIONS

Even if early intervention programs had been applied to well-matched groups, even if outcome measures had shown the experimental

---

[3] Metropolitan Wide-Ranging Achievement Test and the Stanford-Binet IQ were the two measures largely employed by the Follow Through evaluation. A further source of evaluation error is that the programs to be evaluated were "often aware of the tests to be used" and "openly advocated 'teaching to the test' [Hutchins & House, 1977, p. 7]."

treatments to be highly effective, and even if we had comfort in the appropriateness of the instruments used to measure effectiveness—evaluation thus far leaves much to be desired. Most early programs were described in molar, rather than molecular, terms. For example, in the Lazar *et al.* report, language program emphases were categorized as "low, moderate, or heavy [1977, p. 107]." In describing programs along 15 such dimensions, the Lazar *et al.* study was unable to correlate any program characteristics with children's gains. Unless finer-focus program descriptions are provided, evaluators are in the position of reporting summative data on participating children "without knowing with any degree of certainty or detail, what the nature of the program *was* whose impact is being documented [Zimilies, 1973, p. 7]." Shipman (1977) saw a similar problem.

> Early evaluation studies of Head Start which concluded the program had no effect provided an extreme example of [evaluation] error. Head Start was not a single-type program serving similar children in similar settings. Moreover, even today, within particular sponsor model programs, we must still ask, "What did the children actually experience?" The question becomes: What program aspects had what effects for what children? Most of us in evaluation research today are still asking that question [p. 58].

Not only is it necessary to describe these programs in detail, but it is even more important to describe the strategies or ways in which the programs were trying to effect change.[4] Only such process information can generate data that "will be of practical use to those presently attempting to generate new preschool intervention programs [Dunkin & Biddle, 1974, p. 428]."

Because the language intervention history of the past decade and a half is so much the history of preschool and early elementary compensatory education, and because the evaluation of these programs has been so much the story of the programs themselves (especially in the public media), this discussion has so far been heavily weighted in the direction of intervention–evaluation.

If this is an instance of reversing the order of the alpha (what was done?) and omega (how effective was it?), there is some basis for doing

---

[4] In this context, it is sobering to realize that our May 1980 Study Conference will be one in a considerable series of conferences on a similar theme—the Hyman Blumberg Symposium at Johns Hopkins University in 1971, the North Carolina conference in 1971, the Indiana International Conference in 1977, to name only three—and that the questions posed therein are very much with us even today. "Child development research experiences a major gap in conceptual integration and, specifically, in theory development. . . . At present we have a knowledge base which has perhaps too many major gaps to be truly fertile ground for the development of theory . . . [Sparling & Gallagher, 1971, p. 11]."

so. In the minds of the public commentators,[5] effectiveness is the first question. If intervention cannot be shown to effect gains, then the nature of the interventions is of reduced interest. The fact that interventionists are unable to point to success in reaching the aim implied in the early 1960s Head Start proposals has produced considerable "bad press" and encourages future modesty in raising public expectations.

In terms of professional concerns, the evaluation difficulties of the last 15 years have limited the kinds of statements that can be made—or the levels of confidence in statements made—about what has worked. At present, designers of programs for language development of poverty children cannot build on a solid foundation of methods or models that have been demonstrated to effect substantial long-term gains. In a flippant mood, one might survey the intervention history of the past 15–20 years and conclude that what we can primarily learn from earlier attempts is a renewed respect for the first two parts of Murphy's Law:

Nothing is as easy as it looks; and
Everything takes longer than you think.

We are a far cry indeed from those sanguine days of planning summer preschool programs that would make poverty children the intellectual equals of middle-class children by the first day of school.

IMPLICATIONS FOR FUTURE PROGRAMS: A DIGEST

While acknowledging this fact, however, it seems nevertheless necessary to avoid despair or nihilistic retreat. Evaluation and intervention problems are complex, but in Marion Blank's words: "Complexity implies difficulty, not impossibility [1972a, p. 159]." It is also true that the literature of the last decade is rich with implications derived from interventions that have effected short-term gains. These are so numerous that they will be summarized in digest form below. With the advent of improved evaluation strategies, future interventions may benefit from formative guidance while in progress and from more sensitive assessments of their multiple cause–effect interactions.

Methodologies to address some evaluation needs, such as analyzing large bodies of interactive factors, may be emerging—methods like those suggested by Gallagher (1979):

---

[5] See, for example, James Kilpatrick's lurid media coverage quoted in Hutchins and House (1979, p. 8).

Glass and Smith's meta-analysis technique for synthesizing information from multiple studies on a similar subject; and path analysis, a variation on multiple regression analysis that allows statements of a causal nature to be qualified by the conditions under which they hold: e.g., If p, then q, when r, s, and t are true; but not if w, y, and z are true [pp. 26–27].

The following pages of this chapter present a summary of research implications that have been drawn[6] from both the intervention literature and a wider body of related studies, together with references to their sources, and selected comments. Included are suggestions concerning five groups or factors that future programs might explore:

AN INTERVENTION DIGEST

Staff

Implications	Selected References	Discussion
1. Select teachers for verbal ability and for a high rate of spontaneous verbalization to children.	1. Blank & Solomon, 1968, 1969; Bernstein, 1970; Scarr & Weinberg, 1976.	1. "Children can rarely speak better than the models around them" (Gallagher, 1979).
2. Keep the functional (i.e., engaged) staff ratio high during instructional times, and provide at least 20 minutes per day of 1:1 instructional interaction with an adult for each child.	2. Risley, 1972; Blank, Kolhuv, & Wood, 1972; Bronfenbrenner, 1975.	2. Extended dialogue skills can probably develop best in 1:1 or very small group interactions where each speaker can discourse at length.
3. Provide for frequent staff planning meetings and close supervision, to insure teacher participation in setting objectives and developing activities, and to provide adequate teacher support for implementing the stated objectives.	3. Weikart, Roger, Adcock, & McClelland, 1971; Hutchins & House, 1979.	3. Weikart et al., in particular, remark on the need for a high intensity of cooperative planning and supervision to prevent "program drift."
4. Study the relationships between work loads, responsibilities, and various perquisites for staff -- and the amount of high quality engaged time staff are able	4. Weikart et al., 1971; Tizard, Cooperman, Joseph, & Tizard, 1972; Bronfenbrenner, 1975; Katz, 1973a, 1973b, 1977.	4. Staff as well as children are influenced by the total system's ecology and may also

[6] The intervention implications drawn from the sources cited involve my own reasoning in some cases and should not be attributed entirely to the authors of the studies referenced.

to provide for children; use this situation-specific information to guide administrative policymaking.

go through developmental stages presenting special needs.

5. Select staff for their use of linguistically mediated, cognitively-oriented social-control strategies; in practice, this may require selecting middle-class or transitional-class staff rather than those from the child's own SES stratum.

5. Cook-Gumperz, 1973; Hess & Shipman, 1966; Bernstein, 1961; Kohn, 1975.

5. Even the best training programs may find long-established non-verbal, positional or authoritarian strategies hard to modify.

6. Evaluate staffing pattern (e.g., single adult working autonomously vs. team approach) since pattern as well as staff ratios predicted children's receptive language scores better than teacher's educational levels; adults often function better as communicative/instructional models when no other adult is around to serve as a conversational partner, and a hierarchical teacher/aide pattern may reduce productive activity in the subordinate.

6. Tizard et al., 1972; Travers & Rupp, 1978.

6. There might be reductions in staff morale or creativity to be studied in conjunction with moves to a non-team staffing pattern, where one adult works alone with children.

Program Content

Implications	Selected References	Discussion
1. Program objectives and activities need to be specified in behavioral/ecological and frequency terms so that results (outcomes) can be related to program components and so replications are possible.	1. Zimilies, 1973; Dunkin & Biddle, 1974; Risley, 1972.	1. We need to know more than that a drug is potent; we need to know what is an effective dose, for what problems, in what organisms—similarly for language interventions.
2. At the very least, effective minimums can be specified-especially for time-on-task or engaged time, which is so predictive of achievement.	2. Blank et al., 1972; Far West Research Labs BTES Study, 1979.	2. The amount of engaged time spent by individual children during the same program conditions is widely variable; in 2, 10-minute observations at Frank Porter Graham, where a teacher provided identical materials and the identical language elicitations for two children, one child produced 33 utterances in replying, the other child 4.
3. Positive and frequent verbal interaction with an adult around a joint activity of cognitive significance is a component of all programs that have produced gains of any duration in disadvantaged children: Blank recommends a minimum of 15-20 tutorial minutes, three to five times a week.	3. Lazar et al., 1977; Weikart et al., 1971; Bronfenbrenner, 1975; Blank & Solomon, 1968, 1969.	3. Scheduling 20 minutes daily of 1:1 time for each child may be difficult in the context of most day-care programs.

4. Acceptable social behavior accounts for substantial amounts of variance in adequate school adjustment; social behavior ratings through second grade can be positively affected by training in personal problem-solving skills at age 4.	4. Bryan, 1979; Haring & Phillips, 1962; Spivack & Shure, 1974.	4. The Spivack and Shure strategies were effective even when taught only to children, but were more effective when taught to parents as well.
5. Task orientation or task persistence distinguishes successful students from unsuccessful ones at elementary school levels; verbal rehearsal strategies for problem-solving can be taught to children as young as 5 years, with reductions in impulsive responding and errors.	5. Meichenbaum, 1977; Bryan, 1979; Emmerich, 1971; Sigel, Secrist, & Forman, 1972.	5. Non-attending or impulsive responding effectively reduces the total engaged time or time on task that a child spends; learning cognitive distancing strategies (developed by Sigel et al.) increases task orientation in preschool children 2-5 years old.
6. Quantity of linguistic stimulation alone promotes better receptive language, but quality of stimulation is also critically important; quality language involves such informative, abstract uses as reasoning, predicting empathizing, and imagining, and reduces the proportion of imperative, administrative talk.	6. Tough, 1973, 1976; Halliday, 1970, 1977; Hess & Shipman, 1966; Streissguth & Bee, 1972; Tizard et al., 1972.	6. See Ramey, McGinness, Cross, Collier & Barrie-Blackley, in press, for further discussion.
7. Concrete learning via manipulative materials has been touted as the optimum means for learning by the neo-Piagetians, but other research has shown that didactic verbal instruction can teach the same concepts; moreover, most existing curricula teaching specific concepts (e.g., conservation) are narrow and do not accord with Piagetian accounts of how thought develops.	7. Beilin, 1972.	7. Vygotsky's 1962 research showing that learning can proceed "from the top downward as well as from the bottom up" (Harms & McGinness, 1977) suggests that more investigation of conditions appropriate for verbal mediation would be helpful.
8. Linguistic interactions requiring a child to verify his/her conclusions, to justify what s/he knows are essential for developing the abstract attitude and high-level reasoning/linguistic ability needed for success in school.	8. Blank et al., 1972; Blank, Rose, & Berlin, 1978; Tough, 1973, 1977.	8. Extended discourse is required for these interactions; to avoid losing a group's attention and promoting behavior problems, this implies a need for tutorial or small group interactions.
9. Verbally reporting and recalling details of a story or procedure are critical skills for school success, and are often deficient in disadvantaged children; even where they show ability to act out a story or can report a procedure, they often forget information or add irrelevant details in verbalizing their	9. Tough, 1973; Harms & McGinness, 1977; Cook-Gumperz, 1973; Bruck & Tucker, 1974; Feagans & Farran, in press.	9. Intervention to improve verbal reporting may occasionally require a naive listener or distant partner in communication, who realistically needs a more complete, explicit communication.

recollection, and use
vague references
in discussion ("it", "that").

10. Playing referential communication games such as Reporter
or Walkie Talkie can increase
a child's sensitivity to the
information needs of a distant
partner and improve the explicit-
ness of his/her communication.

10. Gahagan & Gahagan, 1972.

10. Writing is the end-
game in referential
communication; as
children reach
kindergarten age and
older, language
experience approaches
to reading/writing
can help extend their
referential skills
(at first through
dictation to the
teacher).

11. Teachers can improve children's
verbal ability to represent the
non-present or abstract through
"distancing" or increasingly
abstract questioning strategies;
they can also help children
improve reasoning by requiring
them to justify their conclusions.

11. Sigel & Saunders, 1979;
Beilin, 1972; Weikart
et al., 1971; Blank et al.,
1978; Blank, 1972a, 1972b, 1973;
Blank & Solomon, 1968, 1969.

11. Question-asking is
important; asking a
question creates an
opportunity to re-
spond; like all
tactics, this needs
to be individualized
so that it does not
put pressure on a
low-verbal child who
needs more modeling
and more acceptance
of his/her nonverbal
interactions,
especially early
in a relationship.

12. Children's ability to use
language for such functions
as self-maintaining and
imagining can be increased
through fantasy play and
pretend games.

12. Bronfenbrenner, 1975;
Vygotsky, 1962, 1978;
Leontiev, 1964/1974.

12. Bronfenbrenner, in
pilot studies testing
his activity code,
observed the most
complex cognitive
operations in the
realm of fantasy
play and decries
American invest-
igators' virtual
neglect of this area
in developmental
research.

13. Role playing both in fantasy/
pretend and social curriculum
problem-solving has high
potential for improving
cognitive/communicative
skills, social behavior,
and motivational attributes
such as task persistence and
flexibility in examining
alternatives.

13. Nichols & Williams, 1960;
Shaftel & Shaftel, 1967;
Golden, 1973; Spivack &
Shure, 1974; Moreno, 1946;
Satir, 1967; Gowen, 1978;
Maccoby, 1959.

13. Psychodrama and role-
switching are
familiar counseling/
therapeutic tools
that have been little
used in classroom
situations; they
show good promise for
such applications.

14. Learning needs to be made
relevant and meaningful to
the learner (whether adult
or child); e.g., preschool
children retained color names
when these were made relevant
by requiring a child to name
play materials s/he requested
by color; likewise, requiring
cooperation by limiting
materials or placing them
out of a child's reach constitute
contrived relevance for these
skills.

14. Risley, 1972; Sigel &
Saunders, 1979;
Brophy, Good, & Nedler,
1975.

14. Making learning of
adult-valued skills
relevant to pre-
schoolers requires
sophisticated
engineering of the
total environment.

15. Content of intervention programs
has been studied overwhelmingly,

15. Barker & Wright, 1954;
Barker & Gump, 1964;

15. Bronfenbrenner (1976)
cites the painstaking

to the neglect of social-inter-
active processes involved,
though these may be prepotent
causes of achievement.

Barker & Schoggen, 1973.

research on the psy-
chological ecology of
childhood undertaken
by social research-
ers; variables such
as dominance, nur-
turance, compliance
and avoidance
in interactions need
more exploration.

Environment

Implications

1. Ecological variables such as
   irrelevant noise level
   (noise irrelevant to the
   ongoing activity of the child)
   have correlated -.7 with child
   achievement; effects of lighting,
   acoustics, random interruptions
   by visitors or center personnel
   during instructional time--all
   these merit study as potential
   factors in instructional outcomes. In industrial studies
   of productivity, interruptions
   and unplanned intrusions in
   general were most destructive
   to high output levels.

2. All events in the school day
   should be evaluated for their
   impact on total system effectiveness: teacher, administrative, parent, and child effectiveness.

Selected References

1. Hunt, 1980;
   Galbraith & McCormick,
   1939.

2. Risley, 1972; Bronfenbrenner,
   1975; Katz, 1973a, 1973b.

Discussion

1. Causes of behavior
   that may reside in
   physical character-
   istics of settings
   (e.g., Prescott-
   Jones' "softness"
   dimension) are almost
   unexplored; sources
   like these become
   potent as they assume
   the dimensions of a
   building renovation
   during instructional
   times.

2. Lilian Katz speaks
   of the cook's time
   schedule and jan-
   itors' cleanliness
   demands that influ-
   ence programming;
   total engaged time
   in language inter-
   action can also be
   influenced by
   curriculum events
   such as films, field
   trips, or parties;
   whether their influ-
   ence is positive or
   negative is an open
   question to be asked
   continually, not
   limiting effect-
   iveness to effects
   on children.

Evaluation

Implications

1. Program evaluation requires
   process as well as outcome
   data: what exactly was done,
   how often, with what staff
   (specifying demographic and other
   data for staff as well as for
   children who received the
   program), requiring what setting
   characteristics, costs, etc.

Selected References

1. Hutchins & House, 1979;
   Takanishi, 1979; Bron-
   fenbrenner, 1975; Cazden,
   1972; Beilin, 1972; Zimilies,
   1973; Dunkin & Biddle, 1974.

Discussion

1. Unless what was done
   is clear, replication
   is bound to fail, and
   reporting outcome
   data alone is mere
   advertising. How-
   ever, the costs (and
   in Caldwell's 1977
   phrase, "the sheer
   tedium") of such
   accounting may prove
   quite high.

2. Using multiple logistic risk analysis, evaluation should attempt to specify variables that predict which children are best able to profit from a preschool intervention program; to the extent that parents and other members of the total system are involved, their involvement also should be specified.

2. Paffenbarger & Wing, 1969; Bronfenbrenner, 1975.

2. A triage system could emerge from such a "who benefits?" analysis: A method of identifying children who need only low cost custodial/enrichment care; those who can profit from educational intervention; and those too involved to profit from present group intervention, and who need alternate services.

3. Process evaluations must include studies of the functional relationships between particular teacher/parent behaviors and child outcomes, as well as those between other system components and child outcomes.

3. Bronfenbrenner, 1976; Cazden, 1972; Beilin, 1972; Gallagher, 1979.

3. Bronfenbrenner and others say we have paid mere lip service to the idea that teacher-child dyads are reciprocal relationships, and have collected data on only one member of the pair, usually the child; we have even less information about the system components beyond teacher behavior.

4. Evaluation of the relative effectiveness of group approaches must involve adequately matched groups from the outset; further, models to be compared must be implemented consistently if comparisons are to be valid.

4. Hutchins & House, 1979; Takanishi, 1979.

4. The Follow Through evaluation showed that analysis of covariance techniques are unable to correct for poor group research design flaws such as inadequate initial sample matching.

5. Future outcome evaluations might explore designs where the child is the unit of analysis, pooling comparable data for large-scale compilations of results.

5. Gallagher, 1979; Caldwell, 1977.

5. Focus on the individual accords well with current social mores, and may become more practical as technology develops.

Child/Family

Implications	Selected References	Discussion

1. Pupil characteristics that are likely to influence achievement need to be documented and later related to achievement; some of these are: number of days present; number of well versus sick days while present; and health conditions that influence language (e.g., recurrent ear infections).

1. Herzog, Newcomb, & Cisin, 1972; Gray & Klaus, 1970; Deutsch, 1960; Shipman, 1977.

1. What the child brings to the instructional situation has been somewhat ignored; if we are to specify what child characteristics predispose him/her to better gain from treatment, these predictor variables must be documented.

2. Family variables are likely to impact on cognitive/linguistic

2. Bronfenbrenner, 1975; Hetherington, Cox, & Cox,

2. Teachers' anecdotes place much importance

achievement also; these have
been noted as particularly
influential: number of caregivers in family (especially
father present/absent); family
SES status (noting whenever
changes occur); behavior
problems or strengths; times
of particular stress (arrival
of siblings, moving, death or
illness in family and other
negative stressors indicated
in Holmes' & Rahe's life
stress scale).

1977, 1978; Holmes & Rahe,
1967.

on the influence of
family situation; it
would be useful to
have some precise
indications as to
what amount of
achievement
variation these
aspects can account
for. Stratifying a
sample, and working
out multiple
interactive effects
of such second-order
system components
may be difficult
now but if the
documentation were
collected,
retrospective
analyses pooled from
large numbers of
projects could
provide information
later on.

BRIEF REVIEW OF CAROLINA ABECEDARIAN APPROACH TO LANGUAGE DEVELOPMENT

The following is a summary of the sociolinguistic program that the Carolina Abecedarian Project is developing for poverty preschool children.[7] The program has benefited not only from the short-term successes and occasional failures of the past but from recent focused programs targeted to increasing the use of language for abstract purposes in disadvantaged children (Blanks, *et al.* 1978, Tough, 1976), already alluded to in the digest. Thus the program to be described here has evolved from our own and other's experiences in an effort to enrich the language skills of the poverty children such as those at the Frank Porter Graham Child Development Center.

The aim of the Carolina Abecedarian Project has been to develop and demonstrate methods for preventing mild mental retardation and consequent school failure in children at risk for such failure who are enrolled in a demonstration day-care center from infancy until kindergarten entry. Our staff has had quite a practical interest, therefore, in the compensatory education program design and evaluation issues raised thus far in this chapter. The children admitted to our center are drawn from a disadvantaged population with a high risk of developing social and linguistic deficits that would create problems for successful school adaptation (Bernstein, 1961; Hess & Shipman, 1966). Potential families

[7] See Ramey, McGinness, Cross, Collier, and Barrie-Blackley (1979) for a discussion of the program's status a year ago.

were identified by a High Risk Index of 11 predictor variables such as maternal I.Q., family income, parent education, and intactness of family. The children were randomly assigned at birth to the full-day 50-week-per-year daycare treatment group (experimental) or an untreated group (control) and followed into public school until they were 8 years of age. From the outset, the project has had an emphasis on developing linguistic competence since failure to develop such competence contributes so heavily to adult socioeconomic dysfunction and especially to children's failure in school. However, the direction and intensity of emphasis on language and social behavior, and on the interactions between them, have altered within the past 2 years. Some alterations occurred in response to insights into the children's development during the course of the preschool program. Others emerged as the first cohorts of children to leave the project have been followed into public school; follow-up data have indicated that language and social abilities needed more intensive development during the preschool years if the high-risk children were to adapt successfully to school.

The intensified emphasis on sociolinguistic competence has also involved a shift away from traditional syntax and vocabulary development and toward more pragmatic aspects of communicative interaction; that is, on the child's competence in using language for various purposes rather than simply on the form and content of the language. We elected this pragmatic emphasis because language development programs in years past have seemed to us to focus much more on form than on substance—on whether a child used correct grammar rather than on how well he or she used language as a tool for reasoning or problem solving. Halliday, McIntosh, and Strevens (1964) have labeled this traditional focus on form as being akin to teaching a starving man how to use a knife and fork.[8] Labov (1970) has shown that children are capable of complex discourse processes, such as reasoning, quite well in a nonstandard dialect. As we see it, the problem in preparing a child to succeed in acquiring "school-talk" skills is to raise more abstract social and

---

[8] A possible explanation for traditional emphasis on modifying the child's syntax and vocabulary may be that such measures as *mean length of utterance* or *type-token ratio* distinguished children with language disorders from normal children so well that applying intervention to impact on these aspects of language seemed attractive to early workers in compensatory education. However, it appears that the disabilities common to children with serious delays and disorders are not necessarily the disabilities displayed by children who simply use some linguistic functions with more frequency and facility than others. The strategies for impacting on a child's ability to use middle-class functions versus exclusively lower-class ones would seem to be to provide contexts and experiences that elicit those functions and models who exhibit good use of them.

cognitive uses of language in the child's response hierarchy to such a high level that he or she tends to employ them readily. To do this, we are providing the longitudinal population of high-risk children with a daycare experience structured to develop sociocommunicative competence.

Joan Tough's work (1976, 1977), the delineation of a language framework with the child's characteristic uses of language categorized into seven different functions, was extremely useful to us in developing a program with a more pragmatic focus. Tough's seven categories, although not necessarily ordered in a developmental sequence, do begin with basic functions and progress to more abstract functions of language that are "disembedded," as Marion Blank says (see Chapter 4) from the situation. They are (a) self-maintaining (referring to one's own physical and psychological needs); (b) directing (monitoring one's own needs as well as directing others); (c) reporting (labeling and referring to objects and events); (d) logical reasoning (explaining the relationship between objects and events); (e) predicting (anticipating the sequence of events or solutions to problems); (f) projecting (projecting into the feelings and experiences of others); and (g) imagining (developing an original story or situation based on fantasy or real life). Unlike many systems for categorizing uses of language, which focus primarily on cognitive levels of abstraction, Tough's system seemed to us to provide an essential emphasis on *social* uses of communication—particularly with its two categories of self-maintaining language (talk designed to meet the physical or psychological needs of the speaker—e.g., stating one's wishes or threatening others) and the projecting category (imagining the feelings, expectancies of others) that we have re-named *empathizing–projecting* in our adaptation of Tough's framework.

We have further adapted the Tough framework by adding an eighth social category of language use: the interpersonal one, with strategies such as offering approval, praise, encouragement, reassurance, or some other positive evaluation to another; using politeness forms that serve mainly to "oil the gears" of social interaction (e.g., *please, thank you*); comforting or consoling another; suggesting, advising, persuading another to some course of action with a primary view to meeting his or her needs rather than one's own; and apologizing for injuries to another. In our high-risk sample, a focus on such interpersonal categories seemed likely to promote better social adjustment to the middle-class world of school.

Through workshops and demonstration sessions these eight categories of language use were explained to the teachers at our daycare center. Once teachers' consciousness of these uses of language was developed, they were helped to arrange classroom experiences and their own questioning strategies to elicit specific categories of language. Working as language consultants to the daycare staff, we have developed sample eliciting questions and language extensions keyed to classroom storybooks, activities, and lessons in the *My Friends and Me* social curriculum (Davis, 1977) used in the preschool 3-year-old and 4-year-old groups. Such sample elicitations, keyed to ongoing activities or stories in the classroom, function as models for the teachers, who gradually take over some of the writing themselves. In doing this, they learn elicitation and questioning strategies applicable to less structured situations. Our data-based observations showed, however, that it was much easier for teachers to use high-level information-sharing or information-eliciting language in structured rather than in unstructured situations (i.e., in skills—development sessions as opposed to free play or mealtimes). As teachers have practiced more and more of these responses, transfer and generalization to new situations has begun to occur.

Combining Tough's teacher strategies in dialogue with components of the insights about managing nonadequate responses developed by Marion Blank and her colleagues (1978) has taken us, we feel, a step further down the road to effective intervention. After mastering the adapted Tough framework, teachers were able to elicit different language functions, but, when faced with a response that seemed inadequate, they needed more sophisticated skills for "diagnosing" the error and responding to it so that the child's language functioning was facilitated.

Key elements in Blank's tutorial approach are (a) dealing with wrong answers or error responses by diagnosing children's difficulties and (b) simplifying the problem for them so that they are able to experience success at some level. To date we have applied these strategies primarily in an adapted small-group (versus tutorial one-to-one) mode. We have tried to provide a certain amount of one-to-one teacher–child interaction every day; we feel that Marion Blank is quite accurate in observing that there is no substitute for tutorial intensity dialogue with an adult who provides a good language model and who presses a child to stretch his or her cognitive functioning. We have pilot data to support Blank's notion that some children can make dramatic gains if provided 20-min tutorial sessions at least three times a week. However, in the context of a group daycare program, we have not yet managed 20 min *daily* of one-to-one adult–child interaction. Teachers initially set a goal of 3 minutes a day with each child and were able to increase this by the end of the year to 5–10 min.

The third major element in the approach has been an emphasis on direct measurement of both teacher and child responses. We have built on the work of Ogden Lindsley and other behaviorists, particularly at the Child Development and Mental Retardation Center in Seattle where Rieke, Lynch, and Soltman (1977) have applied direct daily measurement to communication problems. We have developed methods of taking observational data on the audiotaped verbal interactions of teachers and children. So far, observations show that the rate of teachers' verbalizations to children can be increased to a desirable level, that the amount of directive–imperative or administrative language can be reduced to 25% or less of their verbal interactions with children, and that children's verbal responses following such interventions increase in quality, as measured by an experimental rating scale (McGinness, 1979).

What we have not yet done is to take simultaneous data on both teacher and child members of the dyad. We hope in the near future to develop videotape sampling of communicative interactions to improve inservice training of teachers and to facilitate maintenance observations as well as to capture the very important nonverbal elements of communication.

These remarks reflect the dynamic, evolving quality of intervention that Guttentag (1977) refers to; certainly the Carolina Abecedarian approach is different now from what it was a year ago (Ramey, McGinness, Cross, Collier, & Barrie-Blackley, in press). In order to accommodate a research emphasis in the context of such *euphenics,* or modifying of the environment,[9] there is a special need for process–descriptive documentation that can capture the changing picture. We thus are brought back again to the evaluation issues with which we began this discussion. As is true of so much in the social sciences, our Abecedarian process evaluations are developmentally young and provide few answers as yet, but we feel we are beginning to ask of them good questions. In particular, when the Abecedarian Project reaches completion in the next two years, we hope to ask: "What precisely did the intervention consist of?" "To what extent was the prescribed program implemented?" "What were the characteristics of the children who benefited?" and "What implications do the intervention results have for further work?"

REFERENCES

Barker, R. G., & Gump, P. V. *Big school, small school: School size and student behavior.* Stanford, California: Stanford University Press, 1964.
Barker, R. G., & Schoggen, M. *Qualities of community life.* San Francisco: Jossey-Bass, 1973.

---

[9] *Euphenics* is Joshua Lederberg's neologism; he is a professor at Rockefeller University in New York.

Barker, R., & Wright, R. *Midwest and its children: Psychological ecology of an American town*. New York: Harper & Row, 1954.

Beilin, H. The status and future of preschool compensatory education. In J. C. Stanley (Ed.), *Preschool programs for the disadvantaged*. Baltimore, Maryland: Johns Hopkins University Press, 1972.

Bernstein, B. Social class and linguistic development: A theory of social learning. In A. H. Halsey, J. Flond, & C. A. Anderson (Eds.), *Education, economy, and society*. New York: Free Préss of Glencoe, 1961.

Bernstein, B. A sociolinguistic approach to socialization: With some reference to educability. In F. Williams (Ed.), *Language and poverty: Perspectives on a theme*. Chicago: Markham, 1970.

Blank, M. The treatment of personality variables in a preschool cognitive program. In J. C. Stanley (Ed.), *Preschool programs for the disadvantaged: Five experimental approaches to early childhood education*. Baltimore, Maryland: The Johns Hopkins University Press, 1972. (a)

Blank, M. The wrong response: Is it to be ignored, prevented, or treated? In R. K. Parker (Ed.), *The preschool in action: Exploring early childhood programs*. Boston: Allyn & Bacon, 1972. (b)

Blank, M. *Teaching learning in the preschool: A dialogue approach*. Columbus, Ohio: Merrill, 1973.

Blank, M., Kolhuv, M , & Wood, M. Individual teaching for disadvantaged kindergarten children: A comparison of two methods. *Journal of Special Education*, 1972, *6*, 207–219.

Blank, M., Rose, S. A., & Berlin, L. J. *The language of learning: The preschool years*. New York: Grune & Stratton, 1978.

Blank, M., & Solomon, F. A tutorial language program to develop abstract thinking in socially disadvantaged pre-school children. *Child Development*, 1968, *39*, 379–389.

Blank, M., & Solomon, F. How shall the disadvantaged child be taught? *Child Development*, 1969, *40*, 47–61.

Bloom, B. *Stability and change in human characteristics*. New York: Wiley, 1964.

Bronfenbrenner, U. Is early intervention effective? In U. Bronfenbrenner & M. A. Mahoney (Eds.), *Influences on human development* (2nd ed.). Hinsdale, Illinois: The Dryden Press, 1975.

Bronfenbrenner, U. *The ecology of human development*. Cambridge, Massachusetts: Harvard University Press, 1976.

Brophy, J. E., Good, T. L., & Nedler, S. E. *Teaching in the preschool*. New York: Harper & Row, 1975.

Bruck, M., & Tucker, G. R. Social class differences in the acquisition of school language. *Merrill Palmer Quarterly*, 1974, *20*, 205–220.

Bryan, T. *Current issues in learning disabilities*. Keynote presentation to the Third Annual Learning Disabilities Conference, University of North Carolina at Chapel Hill, April 1979.

Caldwell, B. M. Child development and social policy. In M. Scott & S. Grimmett (Eds.), *Current issues in child development*. Washington, D.C.: National Association for the Education of Young Children, 1977.

Cazden, C. *Child language and education*. New York: Holt, Rinehart, and Winston, 1972.

Cook-Gumperz, J. *Social control and socialization: A study of class differences in the language of maternal control*. London: Routledge & Kegan Paul, 1973.

Cronbach, L. J., Rogosa, D. R., Floden, R. E., & Price, G. C. *An analysis of covariance in nonrandomized experiments: Parameters affecting bias*. Occasional paper of the Stanford Evaluation Consortium, Stanford University, 1977.

Davis, E. E. *My friends and me*. Circle Pines, Minnesota: American Guidance Service, 1977.

Deutsch, M. Minority group and class status as related to social and personality factors in achievement. *Society for Applied Anthropology Monograph No. 2*. Ithaca, New York: Cornell University, 1960.

Dunkin, M. J., & Biddle, B. J. *The study of teaching*. New York: Holt, Rinehart and Winston, 1974.

Emmerich, W. *Disadvantaged children and their first school experiences*. Princeton, New Jersey: Educational Testing Service, 1971.

Far West Research Labs' Beginning Teacher Evaluation Study (BTES). *Educational Research and Development Report*, 1979, 2 (4): 4.

Feagans, L., & Farran, D. C. How demonstrated comprehension can get muddled in production. *Developmental Psychology*, in press.

Gahagan, D. M., & Gahagan, G. A. *Talk reform: Exploratives in language for infant school children*. London: Routledge & Kegan Paul, 1972.

Galbraith, F., & McCormick, E. J. *Human factors in engineering*. New York: McGraw-Hill, 1939.

Gallagher, J. J. *The search for theories in child development: Language*. Harry G. Waisman Memorial lecture, Madison, Wisconsin, 1979.

Golden, L. *Occupational awareness through dramatic play*. (Parts I and II). Chapel Hill, North Carolina: Frank Porter Graham Child Development Center, University of North Carolina at Chapel Hill, 1973.

Gowen, J. *The role of pretend play in the psychosocial development of preschool children*. Paper presented at the American Psychological Association Meeting, Toronto, Canada, 1978.

Gray, S. W., & Klaus, R. W. The early training project: The seventh year report. *Child Development*, 1970, *41*, 909–924.

Guttentag, M. On quantified sachel: A reply to Apsler. *Evaluation*, 1977, *4*, 30–34.

Halliday, M. A. K. Language structure and language function. In J. Lyons (Ed.), *New horizons in linguistics*. Middlesex, England: Penguin, 1970.

Halliday, M. A. K. *Explorations in the development of language*. New York: Elsevier North-Holland, 1977.

Halliday, M. A. K., McIntosh, A., & Strevens, P. *The linguistic sciences and language teaching*. London: Longmans, 1964.

Haring, N. G., & Phillips, A. L. *Educating emotionally disturbed children*. New York: McGraw-Hill, 1962.

Harms, T. O., & McGinness, G. D. *Framework for kindergarten curriculum: Design and evaluation*. Paper presented to the National Association for the Education of Young Children, Chicago, November 1977.

Herzog, E., Newcomb, C., & Cisin, I. H. But some are more poor than others: SES differences in a preschool program. *American Journal of Orthopsychiatry*, 1972, *42*, 4–22.

Hess, R. D., & Shipman, V. C. Maternal influences upon early learning: The cognitive environment of urban preschool children. In R. D. Hess & R. M. Bear (Eds.), *Early education*. Chicago: Aldine, 1966.

Hetherington, E. M., Cox, M., & Cox, R. *The development of children in mother-headed families*. Paper presented at the Conference of Families in Contemporary America, George Washington University, Washington, D.C., 1977.

Hetherington, E. M., Cox, M., & Cox, R. The aftermath of divorce. In J. H. Stevens & M. Mathews (Eds.), *Mother–child, father–child relations*. Washington, D.C.: National Association for the Education of Young Children, 1978.

Holmes, T. H., & Rahe, R. H. Social readjustment rating scale. *Journal of Psychosomatic Research*, 1967, *11*, 213–218.

Hunt, J. McV. *Intelligence and experience*. New York: Ronald Press, 1961.

Hunt, J. McV. *Concepts of and factors in early development important for infant education*. Paper presented at the Distinguished Scholars Colloquium Series, Frank Porter Graham Child Development Center, Chapel Hill, N.C., April 1980.

Hutchins, E., & House, E. Issues raised by the follow-through evaluation. In L. G. Katz (Ed.), *Current topics in early childhood education* (Vol. II). Norwood, New Jersey: Ablex Publishing, 1979.

Katz, L. G. Developmental stages of preschool teachers. *The Elementary School Journal*, 1973, *23*, 50–54. (a)

Katz, L. G. Where is early childhood education going? *Theory into Practice*, 1973, *12*, 137–142. (b)

Katz, L. G. Teachers in preschools: Problems and prospects. *International Journal of Early Childhood*, 1977, *9*, 111–123.

Kohn, M. L. Social class and parent–child relationships: An interpretation. In U. Bronfenbrenner & M. A. Mahoney (Eds.), *Influences on human development* (2nd ed.). Hinsdale, Illinois: The Dryden Press, 1975.

Labov, W. The logic of nonstandard English. In F. Williams (Ed.), *Language and poverty: Perspectives on a theme*. Chicago: Markham, 1970.

Lazar, I., Hubbell, V. R., Murray, H., Rosche, M., & Royce, J. *The persistence of preschool effects*. Ithaca, New York: New York State College of Human Ecology, Cornell University, 1977.

Leontiev, D. B. [*The psychology of preschool children*] (A. V. Zaporozhets & D. B. Elkonin, Trans.). Cambridge, Massachusetts: Harvard University Press, 1974. (Originally published, 1964.)

Maccoby, E. E. Role-taking and its consequences for social learning. *Child Development*, 1959, *30*, 239–252.

McGinness, G. D. *McGinness child language responses rating scale*. Unpublished manuscript, 1979.

Meichenbaum, D. *Cognitive-behavior modification: An integrative approach*. New York: Plenum Press, 1977.

Moreno, J. L. *Psychodrama*. New York: Beacon House, 1946.

Nichols, H., & Williams, L. *Learning about role playing for children and teachers*. Washington, D.C.: Association for Childhood Education International, 1960.

Paffenbarger, R. S., & Wing, A. L. Effects of single and multiple characteristics on risk of fatal coronary heart disease. *American Journal of Epidemiology*, 1969, *90*(6), 527–535.

Ramey, C. T., McGinness, G. D., Cross, L., Collier,. A., & Barrie-Blackley, S. The Abecedarian approach to social competence: Cognitive and linguistic intervention for disadvantaged preschoolers. In K. Borman (Ed.), *Socialization of the child in a changing society*. London: Pergamon Press, in press.

Rieke, J. A., Lynch, L. L., & Soltman, S. F. *Teaching strategies for language development*. New York: Grune & Stratton, 1977.

Risley, T. Spontaneous language and the preschool environment. In J. C. Stanley (Ed.), *Preschool programs for the disadvantaged: Five experimental approaches to early childhood education*. Baltimore, Maryland: Johns Hopkins University Press, 1972.

Satir, V. *Conjoint family therapy* (Rev. ed.). Palo Alto, California: Science and Behavior Books, 1967.

Scarr, S., & Weinberg, R. Intellectual similarities within families of both adopted and biological children. *Intelligence*, 1976, *1*, 170–191.

Schweinhart, L. J., & Weikart, D. P. *Young children grow up: The effects of the Perry Preschool Program on youth through age 15.* Ypsilanti, Michigan: High Scope Press, 1980.

Shaftel, G., & Shaftel, F. *Role playing for social values.* Englewood Cliffs, New Jersey: Prentice-Hall, 1967.

Shipman, V. Research findings as related to educational programming. In M. Scott & S. Grimmett (Eds.), *Current issues in child development.* Washington, D.C.: National Association for the Education of Young Children, 1977.

Sigel, I., & Saunders, R. An inquiry into inquiry: Question-asking as an instructional model. In L. G. Katz (Ed.), *Current topics in early childhood education* (Vol. 2). Norwood, New Jersey: Ablex Publishing, 1979.

Sigel, I. E., Secrist, A., & Forman, G. Psychoeducational intervention beginning at age two: Reflections and outcomes. In J. C. Stanley (Ed.), *Compensatory education for children ages two to eight: Recent studies of educational intervention.* Baltimore, Maryland: Johns Hopkins University Press, 1972.

Sparling, J. & Gallagher, J. *Research directions for the seventies in child development.* Chapel Hill, North Carolina: University of North Carolina, 1971.

Spivack, G., & Shure, M. *Social adjustment of young children: A cognitive approach to solving real-life problems.* Washington, D.C.: Jossey-Bass, 1974.

Streissguth, A. P., & Bee, H. L. Mother–child interactions and cognitive development in children. In W. W. Hartup (Ed.), *The young child: Reviews of research* (Vol. 2). Washington, D.C.: National Association for the Education of Young Children, 1972.

Takanishi, R. Evaluation of early childhood programs. In L. G. Katz (Ed.), *Current topics in early childhood education* (Vol. II). Norwood, New Jersey: Ablex Publishing, 1979.

Tizard, B., Cooperman, O., Joseph, A., & Tizard, J. Environmental effects on language development: A study of young children in longstay residential nurseries. *Child Development,* 1972, *43,* 337–358.

Tough, J. *Focus on meaning: Talking to some purpose with young children.* London: Allen & Unwin, 1973.

Tough, J. *Listening to children talking.* London: Ward Lock Educational, 1976.

Tough, J. *Talking and learning: A guide to fostering communication skills in nursery and infant schools.* London: Ward Lock Educational, 1977.

Travers, A., & Rupp, T. *National day care study.* Cambridge, Massachusetts: Abt Associates, 1978.

Vygotsky, L. S. *Thought and language.* Cambridge, Massachusetts: MIT Press, 1962.

Vygotsky, L. S. An experimental study of concept formation. In M. Cole (Ed.), *Mind in society: The development of higher cognitive processes.* Cambridge, Massachusetts: Harvard University Press, 1978.

Weikart, D. P., Roger, L., Adcock, C., & McClelland, D. *The cognitively oriented curriculum.* Urbana, Illinois: University of Illinois Press, 1971.

Zimilies, H. *A radical and regressive solution to the problem of evaluation.* Paper presented at the Minnesota Round Table in Early Childhood Education, Wayzanta, Minn., June 1973.

V

From Theory to Practice— Some Implications

The chapters in this volume stem from a conference on the language of poverty children that was held at the Frank Porter Graham Child Development Center, May 12–14, 1980. The last session of that conference closed with a summary discussion that focused on four questions. These questions were formulated by the author to elicit the discussants' broadest statements concerning the language development and language education of poverty children. The following short chapters were derived from their comments.

DISCUSSION SUMMARY

The first three questions presented to the discussants concerned theoretical and research issues in the language development of poverty children. Each of these questions will be stated in turn, followed by brief highlights of the resulting discussion.

Question 1: What Are the Differences between the Language of Middle-Income and Poverty Children?

Three subquestions addressed aspects of this overall question as follows: Are there differences in overall rate of development? Are there differences in patterns of language skills? Are there specific areas in which the most important differences lie?

There seemed to be a consensus among the discussants that a consideration of poverty children's language should be more concerned with function than form and that it should be concerned more with relationships among sentences than with isolated words or sentences. Furthermore, as language is controlled by context, the critical difference between the language of middle-income and poverty children lies in the fact that they come from different environments.

There also seemed to be agreement that within-group differences in overall rate of language development do exist, although such individual differences have generally been overlooked by linguists and psycholinguists. Moore cautioned, however, against generalizations concerning between-group differences in individual language development. Snow added that the differences between middle-income and poverty children lie in their knowledge of the world, which is reflected in their language.

Question 2: What Are the Processes by Which Environmental Differences in Language Input Affect Language Acquisition?

Again, there were three subquestions, as follows: Do the important differences lie in caregiver–child and/or teacher–child dialogues? Do the important differences lie in the way the overall environment (home, school) is structured? What theoretical framework should be used to guide future research?

There was a consensus that both the caregiver–child relationship and the teacher–child relationship are important. There seemed to be a difference, though, in the discussants' perceptions of problems children would have in moving from the home to the school. In Moore's view, the language problems of poverty children come from a mismatch between what the school expects and what the home has provided. Snow, in turn, felt that the school matched lower-class children's expectations in some ways, but that it matched middle-class children's expectations in others. Thus the children in the best position to excel in school would be the children who have many strategies for dealing with new situations. Finally, Tough stated that what disadvantaged children encounter in school may reinforce what they have learned at home about taking part in their own learning experiences. The problem for the children is not that they meet a different sort of culture at school, but that the school culture may fail to promote the children's thinking skills and attitudes necessary for learning.

Question 3: Can We Assume That the Language Development of "Normal" or Typical Middle-Income Children Can Be Used as a Basis for Understanding the Language of Poverty Children?

If so, can we use a framework based on psycholinguistic research and theory in syntax, semantics, and pragmatics for the language development of poverty children?

There was some difference of opinion in the answers to this question. Blank felt that we should not use the middle-class or well-functioning child as a prototype, but rather we should try to set up a standard of essential skills necessary to achieve at each level. Moore and Shuy thought that a study of middle-class children could serve as a basis for understanding the language development of poverty children, if proper care were exercised.

Finally, there was a general discussion question posed to summarize the discussants' recommendations concerning the application of research and theory to language intervention.

Question 4: What Are the Implications of Theory and Research for Intervention and Evaluation?

Specifically, what would you recommend we do to facilitate the language development of poverty children?

Much of the discussion period was directed toward answering this last question. There did seem to be a consensus that language is learned in interaction with others, and that any language intervention program should concentrate on extending children's thinking through dialogue. Implications for the classroom would include the provision of considerable time for one-to-one interaction between the teacher and the child and an emphasis on teachers placing language behavior under control of the child, so that children's language is functional for them. Three of the discussants (Blank, Hart, Tough) have developed programs to facilitate language development that can serve as models for language intervention programs.

Moore emphasized that poverty children are not deficient, but rather different. Thus language intervention programs for these children should teach skills that help them adapt to a new context. In addition, Snow cautioned that, since there are so many different ways to learn language, no one intervention program can be sufficient for solving all the problems of language learning.

In summary, there did appear to be an underlying agreement in the general discussion period that we should focus on language in context, that language is learned in social interaction with others, and therefore that dialogue should be the focus of our efforts in work concerning the language of children reared in poverty.

VIDEOTAPE SYNOPSES

Two of the chapters (those of Tough and Shuy) refer to videotaped segments of parent–child interactions that were shown to the group by Joan Tough in the session prior to the discussion period. Synopses of the tapes are provided here to aid the reader's understanding.

Timothy and his father. Timothy is a 3-year-old boy seen playing with a truck, van, and fire engine on the floor while his father sits nearby. Timothy's play is independent but involves continual verbal interaction with his father. During one segment, Timothy puts his van on top of the fire engine and calls his father's attention to it. His father questions Timothy with the comment, *I've never seen a van on top of a fire engine before.* Timothy's response is, *Oh, haven't you? I have.* The interaction between them is in the form of a dialogue with both partners contributing content.

Elizabeth and her mother. Elizabeth is a 3-year-old girl seen playing with a doll on the floor while her mother sits nearby. Elizabeth appears to make more overtures to her mother than Timothy does to his father because her mother adopts a very passive role. Elizabeth's mother allows her to play without much comment but is supportive of Elizabeth's overtures. She does not, however, provide much independent content to the verbal interactions. Elizabeth is the one who takes the initiative.

ALICE M. GORDON

12

Moving Beyond the Difference–Deficit Debate

MARION BLANK

I would like to spend this "summary time" in elaborating on some ideas that may help the reader place into perspective the material that I offered. My analysis derives from two basic ideas: One is that the high rate of school failure among children from lower-class backgrounds cannot be attributed solely to forces outside the children (e.g., inadequate teaching, misdiagnosis by education authorities, etc.). Rather it reflects, at least in part, problems the children have in mastering our written language system. Two is that there are inadequacies in the two major approaches that have up until now been offered to explain and treat this problem. For purposes of exposition, it seems most useful to violate sequence and elaborate first on the second point just cited.

As is well known, the 1960s represented a period of intense interest in the analysis and treatment of language in children at risk for school failure. After a surge of activity, research in this area declined rapidly, and in the last several years, the field has been relatively quiescent. Among other factors, this state of affairs has come about as a result of a controversy that has come to be known as the difference–deficit debate. These terms reflect the two approaches that I just mentioned. An examination of some of the key points in each of these approaches will, I believe, illustrate the reasons why each has been of limited value in helping the children.

The initial interest in language remediation derived from the deficit

245

viewpoint. In turn, this approach was predicated on the following: (a) The children's failure in school was attributed to their lacking the skills necessary for school success (i.e., they had a deficit); (b) since success in school is heavily dependent on language, the key deficit was thought to be in the language sphere. Questions however remained as to which of the vast array of language behaviors were central to the children's problems. In an effort to answer this question, the performance of children who were succeeding in school (i.e., middle-class children) was selected as the standard against which the "failures" were to be judged. In addition, not only did the performance of those children on standardized tests become the criterion for identifying children who were likely to fail, but it also became the standard for determining the content of instruction.

As I tried to indicate earlier numerous difficulties follow from this approach. The approach is so pervasive, however, that it seems worthwhile to devote a bit more time to the problems that it raises. One of the fastest and easiest tests that can be given to young children is that requiring the naming of colors. Furthermore, successful performance on this task correlates well with later success in school. As a result, color naming is a useful tool since it allows early identification of children at risk for school failure. It has however been used not only for identification (i.e., selecting the high-risk children) but also for remediation (i.e., children weak in this area are subjected to training in color labeling). This procedure is highly questionable since there is no evidence to indicate that color naming is a necessary or even useful skill for anything other than being able to meet the questions asked by teachers that demand a color label. Indeed, if color naming were as important as early childhood curricula make it, then color-blind individuals would be severely incapacitated in the cognitive realm. In essence, then, a major weakness of the deficit approach has been the tendency to use the test performance of middle-class children as the criterion for both evaluating and treating lower-class children.

Furthermore, although the intervention programs had as their goal the enhancement of "language," in fact only a relatively small subset of language tended to be emphasized—in particular, the subset of semantics wherein labels are applied to perceptible, concrete stimuli. This movement followed from the influence that the content of psychological tests had on program developers. Since the tests tended to stress particular concepts (e.g., color, size, shape, direction, etc.) and categories (e.g., animals, clothing, vehicles, etc.), these concepts and categories became focal in the curricula. Furthermore, because other components of language were minimized, the verbal exchange in these programs often followed a unique format that could be found in few, if any, other settings. For example, in a lesson on animals, a teacher might repetitively ask one child after another, *And what animal do you remember seeing in the zoo yesterday?* Although that single question might be appropriate in any particular circumstance, it would be rare to find a situation in which it would be reasonable to ask it 10 consecutive times. As a result, the verbal interchange in the school was often so artificial and narrow that it provided the child with little mastery over the broad set of skills that are involved in even simple language use.

Difficulties such as these caused me to feel discomfort in pursuing the deficit point of view as it was elaborated in the 1960s. Others, however, selected different reasons for objecting to this view. The most vocal objections were raised by proponents of the difference approach. This approach relied upon a culturally relative view of cognitive and linguistic functioning. Similar to the arguments previously outlined, objections were raised against comparing lower-class children to a middle-class standard. The difference approach, however, went further. Not only was the middle-class–lower-class comparison deemed invalid, any judgment of deficiency per se was also deemed invalid. All cultural groups in the society were said to possess equivalent cognitive and linguistic skills. Any judgment of deficiency was said to be a result of the low esteem in which the ruling class (i.e., the middle class) held behaviors that varied from their own standard. The variations of behavior were acknowledged, but they were to be considered differences rather than deficiencies.

The difference approach has many advantages. It overcomes the serious conflicts raised when the society takes a group who are already victims and blames them for their problems. Furthermore, the difference approach encourages a rethinking about the ways in which the behaviors of a group ought to be evaluated. For example, in many school systems, cultural dialects that had previously been judged as inferior could now be seen as representing a different language style. Nevertheless, the difference approach, too, is beset by difficulties.

One problem stems from the absence of techniques for assessing the range of skills in a culture. As a result, researchers from this point of view have been forced to rely on isolating discrete narrow behaviors that exemplify their viewpoint. For instance, considerable work has been carried out on the different ways in which the single verb *to be* is used in Black English as contrasted with Standard English. At best, it is hazardous to extrapolate from discrete behaviors such as this to judgments about a subgroup's total language system. Yet such extrapolation has been a common feature of the difference approach.

Interestingly, as the *to be* example indicates, much of the linguistic analysis within the difference approach stressed syntax and morphology. This emphasis followed logically from the seminal influence that Chomsky's theory of transformational grammar had on the thinking of the difference advocates. Nevertheless, it had important consequences; specifically, it indicated that although both used the rubric "language," the difference–deficits groups were referring to quite different content areas. In the main, the deficit group was focused on semantics, whereas the difference group was focused on syntax. This distinction was rarely acknowledged, thus adding confusion to already controversial issues. Ironically, both groups did share a focus: Each was concerned primarily with structural components of language and relatively little with the use to which these components were put. Yet the original cause for concern (i.e., the children's school failure in dealing with tests, in answering questions, etc.) suggested that it was in the *use of language* that major difficulties were to be found.

The difference approach also has important implications for education that have not been sufficiently appreciated. A common accompaniment of this framework is a philosophy that might best be termed *noninterference;* that is, the different skills of any group are to be identified and hopefully used in the educational process, but skills that are not readily fostered by the culture should not be imposed upon the children. Again, there is obvious value in this orientation in that it serves to prevent a type of educational imperialism that has at times occurred in our schools. But neglected in this approach is any consideration of the consequences that one set of skills may hold for the development of other skills.

Imagine, for instance, that Group A has skill X while Group B has skill Y. Then imagine further that skill X is critical to a later developing skill W. This is essentially the position I put forth; namely, that a particular set of oral language skills facilitates the acquisition of literacy. If these oral language skills are not encouraged in certain subgroups, then children from those subgroups will inevitably be at a disadvantage in the academic setting. This situation raises difficult issues. Adherence to a strict culturally relative perspective might lead one to view the limited development of these skills as a manifestation of a cultural difference that ought not be interfered with. But the adoption of such an approach may effectively relegate the children in question to a state of illiteracy. This is clearly a matter in need of greater attention than it has received to date.

Another more important issue that has commonly been ignored by the difference advocates relates to an issue that has long been important in developmental psychology—namely, the issue of rate. Human beings master a common set of skills in a variety of spheres including language, cognition, and perception. The rate of their mastery, however, varies. For example, some children learn to use single words at 1 year, others at 15 months, others at 18 months, and so on. Some degree of this variability is probably not significant, but at a certain point the variability does become critical—specifically, slow rates of development are frequently characteristic of difficulties in functioning. It is for this reason that the concept of rate of development has been critical in psychological evaluation.

Although the concept of rate has been central in the area of psychometrics, it has generally been neglected by the proponents of the difference approach. Their central question has been, "Does a skill exist?" They have rarely asked, "At what age has the skill been observed to appear?" This neglect can be seen in the well-known Labov (1970) paper involving an interview between a black adolescent and an adult. The behavior was interpreted as showing that the judgment of verbal weakness as is commonly made about many youngsters is invalid since when the adolescent becomes more relaxed, he is able to express a number of complex ideas. The discussion basically took the following form: The adult asks if God is black, the adolescent responds that God could not be black because, if he were, he would not be treating black people so badly. Labov cites this behavior as evidence that the adolescent possesses high qualities of reasoning (using "if then" formulation, evaluating complex relationships, etc.) that are commonly masked because in test-like interviews many blacks are wary and resistant, thus appearing "nonverbal."

If one turns to the developmental literature, however, one finds evidence that the reasoning shown by the adolescent is analogous to that shown by children at about 5–6 years. For example, it is not uncommon for kindergarten-age children to confront their parents with the charge, *You adopted me.* This statement is then followed by, *You had to adopt me because if I were your own child you wouldn't treat me this way.* There is nothing amiss in an adolescent using the same reasoning as a kindergartener. Throughout our lifetimes we all continue to use the skills that emerge at each stage of development. However, if the child has only begun to exhibit the reasoning of a 6-year-old when he is an 8- or 10-year-old, then something is likely to be awry. Furthermore, the test results of many lower-class children indicate that delay of development is a significant feature of their functioning. Advocates of the difference viewpoint, however, rarely raise the issue of rate of development. Yet the diagnostic importance of this latter variable indicates that we cannot simply ask if a behavior exists in a particular subgroup, but at what age has the behavior been observed to occur and is the age consonant with development norms?

It is against this background that the approach offered here has been developed. The poor performance of many lower-class children in school was seen as representing genuine difficulties that they experienced with academic demands and, particularly, with demands of the written language system. Rather than interpreting these difficulties by comparing middle- and lower-class children, we carried out an analysis on the skills necessary for mastering the written language. Essentially, the view that was offered represents a type of task analysis, albeit a task analysis on a macrolevel, as contrasted to a microlevel. More implicit in this approach is the idea that with proper diagnosis, effective teaching strategies can be instituted.

Clearly there are difficulties in following this route. There is little solid information about the demands entailed in the reading process. It is almost certain that the ideas that I put forth will be shown to be incomplete and in need of major revision. However, they do have the potential of offering a new approach that will enable us to move beyond the stalemate of the difference–deficit debate and provide a basis for fruitful education efforts. As I tried to indicate, any such effort should include major emphasis on the complexities of dialogue (discourse).

Language in use depends in large measure upon the ability to handle not simply words or sentences but sequences of sentences that convey a coherent set of ideas. Understanding the way in which sentences link, and the method through which the child grasps the messages they contain, is central to our progress in this area. Essentially, I strongly agree with Joan Tough that dialogue is a key factor in the school situation; ultimately our understanding of this component of human interaction is essential if the children are to be helped to overcome the difficulties that they are experiencing. Fortunately, there is a growing interest in this area from the point of view of both oral and written language. I believe that the knowledge accrued as a result of this effort will be of inestimable value in helping children progress in the academic setting. It is on this hopeful note that I would like to conclude my comments.

REFERENCE

Labov, W. The logic of nonstandard English. In F. Williams (Ed.), *Language and poverty*. Chicago: Markham, 1970.

13

Contingencies in Communication
BETTY HART

Appropriate language use is controlled by context. There is an essential match between the language used and the context in which it is used. Children who live in different contexts, such as middle-class and poverty children do, necessarily use different language.

Halliday (1977) has said that children learn what language is through learning what language does. For people in different cultures, language does somewhat different things, and what works in one culture may not work the same way in another. For instance, a 9-year-old child working with language at a 3-year-old level has problems because the language that works when a child is 3 does not work the same way when the child is 9. The world responds not just to the language used but also to the person and to the match between person and language.

The situation of a mother with a Down's syndrome child is similar. The mother responds both to the child's language and to the rest of the child's behavior. If the child tends to be unresponsive or inattentive, the mother necessarily changes her interactional style to suit the child's. And the child tends to adapt to the mother's style, to her expectations.

Language use is not just a matter of syntax and semantics, it is, above all, social interaction. Every person's output influences what he gets back from the environment. Cultures are continually giving members feedback about their behavior, about its match to cultural expectations.

There is a difference between communicative competence and communication. Communicative competence is inside the speaker. If I fall in a river, I'm going to shout, *Help, help!* because my communicative competence tells me that when I want someone to save me from drown-

251

THE LANGUAGE OF CHILDREN
REARED IN POVERTY

ing, calling for help is a good way to start. I've learned that my culture tends to respond in predictable ways to the word *help*. But communication is made by the hearer. If, in spite of my intentions, no one helps me, my language does not function.

Functions, then, are consequences. Often, a child who does not talk at all, or who talks in inappropriate ways according to cultural norms, actually has functional language. If a child is operating on the environment, getting things from it such as food and social interaction, the child has functional communication. He has communicative behaviors (forms of language) that are being supported, maintained, by the environment.

What teachers and parents do is arrange functions: They arrange what happens when children talk. But what you sometimes see is teachers who talk and talk and talk, asking children about what they are doing or commenting on children's play: They are very good models of how language is used and what language can do. What is difficult for these teachers is to arrange for the children to learn by doing and to let the children do the talking while the teachers concentrate on showing them how their language works.

The teachers in our situation feel strongly that the important thing is for the teacher to put her behavior under the control of the child's language, that the teacher's primary role is to be responsive. Research has shown that later learning is facilitated by experience with learning to control the environment. What our teachers try to do is show children, by their responses, how language is used to operate on the environment (i.e., what language can do).

When children can do lots of different things with language, they tend to use lots and lots of language. Once you have lots of talking, then you can begin to work on the topography of language. You can begin to correct children, and ask for *aren't* instead of *ain't,* for instance, because this will not affect what the children know can be done with language. But when you start criticizing what children are saying and correcting them before they are talking a lot, before they know what language is for, then you risk wiping out talk altogether. Having children rote-learn sets of syntactic structures before they have learned solidly that language is for control of the environment and for getting things, such as materials and cooperation and listening, may teach children that if they cannot speak correctly, it is better not to speak at all.

REFERENCE

Halliday, M. A. K. *Explorations in the functions of language.* New York: Elsevier North-Holland, 1977.

14

Group versus Individual Differences: Avoiding the Deficit Model

ELSIE G. J. MOORE

Now, just as the others have pointed out about their backgrounds, I want to make it clear that I, too, am not a linguist. I have picked up a few words of the jargon, but I am not very competent at using them, so bear with me.

First question: What are the differences between the language of middle-income and that of poverty children? You have subquestions I would like to address. First, are there differences in overall rate of development? A shortcoming of research in psycholinguistics is that these investigators, in my opinion, have not yet looked at differences in rates of development or considered these differences in their research strategies and conceptual frameworks. Intuitively, as a developmental psychologist, I would say, "Yes, there probably are differences in overall rates of language development." There are individual differences, just as there are in most areas of human development. However, the issue is are we going to talk in terms of between-group differences in levels of language development and rates of language development? If we are, we are getting caught in the whole deficit model that has surrounded the work in intelligence test performance, which I feel does a terrible disservice to poor children in that it obscures our ability to see how we can really help these children achieve in the public school system. I caution against getting caught in the trap of trying to make statements about between-group differences in rates of language development until

253

THE LANGUAGE OF CHILDREN
REARED IN POVERTY

we are sure that the evidence supports such a view. We have not given serious consideration to the role that subcultural differences in attitudes, motivation, and dialects play in children's performance on standardized language measures and laboratory manipulations aimed at assessing children's linguistic competence. It is not clear whether we are seeing deficits or differences in the children's skills.

That third subquestion is the one I would next like to address. Are there specific areas in which the most important differences lie? I would say, "Yes, indeed." I think the differences between middle-income and poverty children's language lie primarily in the situations that elicit language for the two groups and in vocabulary. Those are the major areas where I see differences between the two groups. I am not talking about vocabulary in terms of one group's vocabulary being more limited than the other; what I am talking about is the actual content of the vocabularies. The contents are very different from one another. The groups use different words, words with which other groups (or many researchers) may not be familiar.

Second question: What are the processes by which individual differences in language input affect language acquisition? I think the caregiver–child relationship is really quite critical in language development. Given that we have a mother who has language and a child who does not have neurological damage, then the essentials of language are learned in the caregiver–child situation. By essentials, I mean what Chomsky calls "the capacity to understand deep structure." However, I see the language problems of the child who grows up in poverty as stemming from a mismatch between what the school values and expects and what the home has provided. And again, I do not view this as a deficit but as a difference, a discontinuity. Unfortunately, when scientists, and in particular social scientists, find differences, they feel compelled to make a value judgment, rather than to treat differences as just that and go on.

Third question: Is the language development of typical children a good basis for understanding the language of poverty children? Yes, I think so. I see language as being a human quality, and, after all, poor children are human. You can look at middle-class children's language development in terms of developmental principles and conceptual frameworks. Then we must see if we recognize similar patterns in poverty children. I think the critical issue in this process is whether or not researchers are capable of identifying markers of language competence—that is, different forms of that competence—when they see it in a natural situation versus how they have operationalized it in the laboratory. What the researchers have to do then, if they're going to make any statements or develop any remediation strategies for poor children, is to learn about the children with whom they are working. The best research strategy now is to go out with the children into their natural settings and find out what occurs in these settings. However, if this is to be an effective strategy, researchers must be able to go beyond their own biases, in terms of what they call linguistic competence in that context, so that they can recognize it and record it when it is evident.

On recommendations to facilitate the language of poverty children, I do not view poverty children as being deficient in language capacity. I view them as being different. I think this is a critical distinction that preschool teachers in intervention programs have to make. I like the strategy Betty Hart outlined (see Hart, Chapter 10). It seems very efficient, and I am sure there are others. I do not claim to have the answer for facilitating language development. However, whatever intervention is actually implemented, the interveners have to keep in mind that there is nothing wrong with poverty children. What the intervention is attempting to do is to help them adapt to the system (i.e., the schools) to which they must adapt. Interveners must recognize that poverty children are well adapted to their home situations and community. What interveners are trying to do is to help them develop skills to accommodate the expectations and demands of a different context, one with which they are not familiar. Researchers must keep that in mind at all times. Intervention is not enriching these children as such; intervention is just providing them with another set of adaptive skills.

15

Knowledge and the Use of Language

CATHERINE E. SNOW

Language acquisition is, in an evolutionary sense, a very robust system. It is hard to create a situation in which a child will fail to learn to talk. Children must have some sort of physical or neurological handicap and a highly disadvantaged social situation before they will actually fail to learn to talk.

Growing up in an economically very disadvantaged situation cannot all by itself create language failure. All children, even those growing up in poverty, do learn to talk. They learn to talk through one of the following situations: (a) Their parents are producing semantic contingencies; (b) their parents are training them in comprehension; (c) some sort of highly predictable set of language stimuli in the environment recur in such a way that the children can start initiating and using them; (d) they have discovered that language can be used for social control. But any of these factors can be absent without causing a failure in the language acquisition process.

Grasping the extent to which language acquisition is a robust and buffered process requires collecting and collating information about the social context of language learning across a much wider range of cultures, classes, languages, and social groupings than has been studied up until now. Even from the small numbers of studies of language acquisition outside middle-class North America or Western Europe, we know that wide variation exists in the nature of the social support for language

257

THE LANGUAGE OF CHILDREN
REARED IN POVERTY

learning. There are, for example, societies in which children are not encouraged to talk to adults and in which children's verbal facility is not valued, admired, or encouraged. Those children learn to talk nevertheless. There are societies in which parents do not carry on extensive conversations with their children and rarely produce utterances that are semantically contingent on the children's utterances. These parents select and initiate almost every topic and train for language purely in a comprehension mode. Children of such parents learn to talk nonetheless. Other children learn to talk despite seeing very little relationship between the language they hear and the surrounding activity. There are children who learn Arabic from hearing the Koran recited to them (i.e., from language with little or no nonverbal context). Such acquisition might not be as efficient, fast, or effortless as that to which we are accustomed, but it can and does occur.

Just as there is no one, exclusive way to learn to talk, no single intervention technique or program is sufficient to solve all the problems of language learning for children growing up in poverty. The fact that there are many different kinds of children and therefore many different ways of learning to talk, as well as enormous cultural variation in what is considered to be the appropriate way to teach children to talk and the appropriate language skills to learn, implies a variety of possible intervention strategies.

If language learning is such a well-buffered and robust process, then why do we find large, significant, and consistent social-class differences in children's ability to perform language related tasks such as learning to read, learning to write, accuracy in referential communication, and oral exchange in the classroom?

It has been suggested that children from low SES, low-income homes are more likely to fail because schools create a mismatch for them, posing tasks and situations that are highly unlike those they have encountered at home. It would be hard to make the case convincingly, I think, that classrooms are much more like middle-class than lower-class homes; surely there are many points of match as well as mismatch for all groups of children. Children who excel at school, and in other challenging situations, are those who have many strategies for solving problems and for dealing with new situations rather than those whose parents have simulated a classroom environment in the home.

Another major factor differentiating middle- from low-income children is that of teacher expectation, as Joan Tough mentioned in her discussion. Some children have been trained by their parents, whether consciously or unconsciously, in the skills that teachers value—skills such as saying *Hello, Goodbye, How do you do,* and *Thank you,* such as answering questions, asking questions, and acknowledging responses. That kind of training creates a potential on the part of the child to function effectively in the world. It has nothing to do with actually training him or her to be a better child in any sense of competence. All it does is give the child a different set of skills for interacting with relevant adults.

I do not think that any of these skills has very much to do with language. Sociolinguistic research has shown us this—that disadvantaged children can use language in all the ways that middle-class children can. It is just that they do not use language in some of these ways as often. I would suggest, though, that there may be a deficit for children who come from disadvantaged homes, a deficit that has nothing to do with language, since language is such a robust system, but with basic knowledge. The problems that these children have are in the area of knowledge about the world; their knowledge deficits are reflected in their smaller vocabularies. Vocabulary knowledge involves knowledge of concepts, ideas, and bits of the world. The child who can talk about butterflies and metamorphosis has access to a little chunk of knowledge about the world that the child who does not have those two vocabulary items just does not possess. That is the kind of knowledge imparted in middle-class, advantaged, enabling homes that may not be imparted in less advantaged homes. Such knowledge appears to feed into language. It is reflected in almost all language tests because they are basically tests of vocabulary and not tests of language at all. This deficit in knowledge shows up strongly in the elementary grades, when children start to learn to read on the basis of material that draws upon their knowledge of the world.

Because reading is internally a complex system, acquiring it requires decreasing the degrees of freedom. If children know five of the six things they must know in a given situation, then they can learn the sixth. If they know four of the things, perhaps they can learn the fifth and the sixth, but if they only know two of them, they cannot learn all the other four. So, if children are trying to read words that they already know in an oral language context, and if they can figure out the sense of the sentence that they are trying to read, and if they are able to make connections between sentences, then those children can figure out how to read on the basis of exposure to those words with the decoding skills that they have and the text that is there. If they do not know anything about butterflies and they are expected to learn to read by mastering a passage about butterflies, they are in trouble. Once again, failing the task has nothing to do with inadequate control of language. Deficient knowledge of the world has caused the problem.

Let me finish with a word of warning, which comes from all of us who have talked to middle-class academic children. Every society produces children with a set of skills valued by that society. Along with those skills comes a set of vices that the society is willing to tolerate. You cannot produce a child who is highly knowledgeable and verbally fluent who does not have some "nasty" little verbal traits that go along with that ability. For instance, a verbal child will almost inevitably interrupt adult conversations, show off, sound arrogant, and ask embarrassing questions.

On the other hand, you cannot produce a child who is very tractable and obedient without producing a child who fails to take initiatives in interactions with adults and who fails to demand attention and interest from adults. Each of these cultural values, and they are very different cultural values, automatically produces some culturally acceptable vices. Middle-class parents are willing to accept the fact that their children are annoying at times because that is part of what goes along with being verbally assertive. Societies that strongly value obedience and tractability are willing to accept, evidently, a certain amount of passivity in interaction with adults because that is what automatically goes along with it. We cannot hope to maximize every single aspect of a child's behavior. We have to accept that some less valued, positive behavior trait will be lost when we maximize the behavior that we value highly.

16

The Importance of Understanding Function from a Sociolinguist's Perspective
ROGER W. SHUY

It seems to me that linguists do not have much to say about the issue of overall rate of development, but I think that sociolinguists do have something to say about understanding some of it. I want to mention one research project that we have done in relation to that issue. We have used a technique with 4-year-olds on videotape in which we elicit their sensitivity to the social status of the person to whom they are talking and then determine if they control the changes in the talk as a result of understanding these social statuses.

In order to do this, we took photographs of individual children in classrooms, and then asked questions about these children on the order of a sociogram. We asked each child to identify status and nonstatus children (with confidence that this request was reasonably made). We thereby obtained high-status children and low-status children in every class. Then we engaged one of the selected children in the following dialogue:

RESEARCHER: *Do you have a favorite toy?*
CHILD: *Yes, my teddy bear.*
RESEARCHER: *Suppose you brought your teddy bear to school and Johnny* (who happens to be a high-status child) *wanted to play with it. And you said, "Okay, play with it." Then you wanted it back. How would you get it back?*

261

THE LANGUAGE OF CHILDREN
REARED IN POVERTY

CHILD: *Well, Johnny, I'd like my teddy bear back.*
RESEARCHER: *Suppose he still didn't give it back.*
CHILD: *Johnny, give me my teddy bear back. Miss Jones wants me
   to have it back now.*

This dialogue excerpt is sequenced in intensity in order to understand language directives aimed at a high-status child versus a low-status child. The child's directives to a low-status child would begin with Step 2 in the sequence of intensity. Step 2 would be something like this: *I'm going to tell Miss Jones if you don't give me my teddy bear back.* Then the directives would get a little stronger. The last directive to the low-status child might be: *I'm going to pour milk on your head if you don't give me my teddy bear* (i.e., into the physical and out of the abstract altogether).

We have found that when 4-year-old children talk, they know to whom they are talking. They are not just talking. In other words, in order to understand children's speech, one must understand the whole context of that speech, including to whom they are talking, and the social status of that person.

Another aspect of the question of differences in rate is concern for the specific areas in which important differences lie. I would like to reiterate what we all seem to be agreeing on, that functions seem to be more critical than forms. Being able to use language to get things done is the most important long-term goal of any kind of language learning, whether it be foreign or native. My own perception is that children move from function to form rather than from form to function. This insight comes from a linguist who has studied mostly form all his life.

The second question has to do with the processes by which environmental differences are felt. I want to use the videotape of Timothy (see the Introduction to Part V) as illustrative. I do not know whether I saw this film the same way everybody else did, but the importance of the interaction, for me, lay in the child's control of topic. His father responded and sometimes directed the interactions, but the topics were introduced by the child. Topic recycling, introduction, maintenance, and switching—all of these were controlled by Timothy. When a child gets to school, the situation can be different. All the classrooms and video-tapes of classroom teaching I have observed convey exactly the opposite of the interaction of Timothy and his father. In the classrooms, control by the teacher seems to be critical. I am wondering what we are doing to children by suddenly putting them into an entirely new culture, where the rules are different. We need to worry about that a lot.

Regarding the third question posed, I am doing some work on normal and middle-class children to serve as a basis for understanding the language of poverty children. I am a comparativist. I like to compare what happens in one group with what happens in another, and I do not know that I am ready to say that we have all the information yet. In terms of discourse and functions, I think eventually there may be something useful generated by group comparisons. We need to find the patterns of acquisition of functions in any one group of children first. My interest in middle-class capabilities with language function was triggered by an experience with a neighbor. Let me tell you that story.

A little 5-year-old girl lived across the street from me. Joanna comes from a language-rich environment. Her parents are with the State Department; they speak German, Polish, and English. She has two older, teenage sisters. When Joanna was 5 years of age, she knocked on my door one evening at 7 o'clock and said, *Mr. Shuy, if you look across the street, you'll see that our car is gone.* I said, *Sure enough, Joanna, your car is gone.* To which Joanna replied, *You know, Mr. Shuy, my mother worries if I miss meals.* And I said, *Joanna, would you like to come in?* She came in, stood in the hallway and said, *You know, Mr. Shuy, I eat almost anything.*

Joanna had managed, with three statements about how the world works, to get herself invited to dinner without specifically requesting to be invited to dinner. Now that was amazing to me. It is also a story that adults find funny. I think it is funny because we do not yet expect Joanna to have the ability she demonstrated. It is funny in the same sense as when my 2-year-old was sitting on the floor with a toy wooden hammer and a toy choo-choo train and took his hammer and began hitting the train. And I said, *Joel, what are you doing?* He said, *I'm aggravating my choo-choo.* I think these two stories are funny in the same way—they exemplify nonstandard baby talk or maybe nonstandard "pragmatics." This suggests that there is an order of acquisition for the functions of language; when a child is precocious in attaining some stages, we smile. All children may not acquire the functions in the way Joanna did. I pictured her as advantaged, from a language-rich environment. Her precocity suggests that we should explore the acquisition strategies of other children.

Now let me turn to the last point, about the implications of theory and research. I recommend obviously looking at language in context. I would suggest a communicative competence theory for looking at language that includes both linguistic competence and social competence, with the larger framework determined by the culture.

I would also like to say something about question-asking strategies. My research in question-asking strategies, both from law and classrooms, seems to suggest a kind of hierarchy for asking questions if you are using questions to try to find out what is inside a child's mind. Questions are asked in classrooms for two totally different and contradictory purposes. One of them is to find out what a child knows, that is, the teacher knows the answer and asks a question. For purposes of understanding what a child knows, the best kind of question is one that allows the child to self-generate or control the topic, namely, an open-ended question: *Tell me all you can about Bolivia,* which is a question in statement form. Then if this strategy does not produce the desired effect, the teacher patterns off into a "WH" question that is more specific. If that does not get what is wanted, a yes–no question is used: *Is la Paz the capital of Bolivia?* Lastly, there is the tag question: *Tin is the leading export of Bolivia, isn't it?* The student cannot really disagree with that.

This kind of sequence, from open to very narrow, which almost predisposes the answer to be right, is just exactly the opposite of mastery-learning theories, in which the hierarchy of questions moves the other way. The hierarchy of question-asking strategies is probably not so important as the sequence. Classes with five straight "WH" questions tend to get boring. The teacher must switch them around. There are a lot of constraints on question-asking to produce learning that we have not begun to understand.

In contrast, about probing and understanding what a child knows, the social uses of certain questions absolutely destroys any effort to probe in most classrooms. By social uses, I mean the fact that everybody has to have an equal chance to participate, so the teacher never finds out what one child knows. The teacher asks a question, gets part of an answer from one child, and then probes another child, not the child with the first answer. That strategy insures that the teacher will never engage in meaningful dialogues with any children. I do not know what education can do about this but we have these contradictory question-asking goals— instructional and social control. Somehow or another, we should be thinking in the future about how to incorporate what we know about one into how we use the other.

17

Teachers Can Create Enabling Environments for Children and Then Children Will Learn

JOAN TOUGH

I do not identify myself as a theoretician at all. The role that I see for myself is as the mediator of other people's theories. I try to see the implications of theories for the education of young children and translate them into a form that makes sense to teachers. I think more of us should try to do this because, on the whole, teachers do not have the time to study theory and work out the relevance for their own teaching. That was my position when I was a classroom teacher. When I was in a position to spend time studying theory, I was impressed by some theories that I had not come across before, particularly those theories that showed how language mediated the culture and those that showed the role that language played in learning. I was already a Piagetian, in that I believed that children must learn through their own direct experiences and activity. Those theories continue to be important to my curriculum endeavor, but so also has been the insight gained from my own research into the language of mothers and their children. I began to see the verbal exchange between mother and child about their shared experiences as a critical factor in promoting learning in the preschool years. Many mothers intuitively used language with their children in a way that helped their children to understand more fully their direct experiences. At the same time they recognized their children's difficulties and sought to help them. Mothers were projecting into the difficulties facing a particular child in a particular situation, and they looked for a means to help the child

265

THE LANGUAGE OF CHILDREN
REARED IN POVERTY

overcome the difficulties. Children who had experiences of this kind were at great advantage when they came to school.

Now it seems to me that language has its effect little by little. Children are exposed to sustained interaction for short but quite frequent periods throughout the day, and that is the way it works. They do not make tremendous leaps. Their understanding grows a little at a time, but the experiences of talk must be frequent and offer satisfaction, or the children will seek to avoid conversation. The more I considered the experiences that children like Timothy had with their parents and compared these experiences with what I saw happening in classrooms, the more I became convinced that teachers should provide similar experiences of dialogue if young children are to benefit socially and intellectually from their time in school. We have our enabling programs for the disadvantaged in early childhood, but those programs are not going to bring the looked-for progress unless dialogue is given a central place. Teachers probably interact with their own children at home in much the same way as mothers in our study did, and they have the skills needed to create enabling environments in the classroom. The problem lies in their view of their role in the classroom and their view of what schools should do. I found myself in the position of asking: How can teachers be helped to change their views? How can they gain insight into the way in which young children learn?

We have had the period of "teacher-proof" packs, and that work has not helped very much. These kits were put together by experts who assumed that they had knowledge of the needs of each child. The kit was then used by the teacher, who supposedly could not judge what each child needed. The assumption was that teachers were not capable of being as effective as many mothers in their work with young children. My view is that teachers must be capable of creating learning environments that provide for the needs of each child in the group. Teachers of young children must be highly intelligent, knowledgeable, and highly professional in the context of children's learning. This view of the teacher's role has, I think, been a major factor in the success of the project that I direct. Teachers are helped to gain insight into the language and learning process, and changes in their own practice are the result of their own decisions. We do not tell teachers what they should do in the classroom. We have constructed workshop materials to help teachers examine what they do with children and consider the effectiveness of their own talk with children. The materials do not insult teachers by saying, "We know best, this is the way to teach." They appeal to their professionalism and invite them to examine some aspects of children's learning, discuss with other teachers, and consider the implications for teaching. Teachers modify their practice because of their new understanding of the learning process.

The whole business of helping children to use language is much more complex than just teaching children words or helping them construct a story or immersing them in narrative. There is something about verbal interaction that we have to understand. The child can learn much more than we think from verbal interaction, provided that the context is one that has interest for him. In the example on videotape, Timothy's father accepted that. You can see it in the level of his interaction with his child. The father may seem to be dominating at times, and yet, if you consider again, you see that there is a great deal of choice for Timothy. Timothy was being led along. His father never said, *It is wrong to put a van on top of a fire engine.* He comments only, *I've never seen a van on top of a fire engine before.* This was a challenge to think again. And it is this kind of element, which signals "think again—there's something more," that draws children into the thinking process and makes them reflect on what they are doing and saying. In the other videotaped example, there were few ideas explored in the exchange. Elizabeth was perfectly competent in the activity, but her thinking was hardly challenged by the talk with her mother. In fact, she may be frustrated with the situation because she is left to initiate her own thinking most of the time. Some teachers also seem to take the view that only thinking that originates in the child can be valuable.

What children are really ready to do is join in the thinking process about interesting aspects of the world around them. It must be a satisfying experience for the children if they are to maintain this readiness. They need the interesting, attention-securing activity. And they need the invitation because they have too little experience of thinking to become the initiators themselves. They need the invitation, "Let's think together: I'm interested in what you're doing and what you're thinking about." In this way Timothy's father provided support, encouragement, interest, and new ideas. From it, Timothy got tremendous satisfaction and the extension of his thinking. The world, as a result, became a more interesting place and more meaningful than before because of his new thinking.

The research area in which I would like to see more work is that of interaction through dialogue, that is, talk between parents and children and teachers and children. I want to know the extent to which children's knowledge of the world and their language are facilitated by dialogue with adults about their own direct experiences. I am interested in the role of talk as the mediator of knowledge, as the facilitator of understanding, and as the experience through which ways of using language and ways of thinking are learned. I am not convinced that disadvantaged children's failure in school is explained by the fact that they come into a culture that is different and makes different demands on them from those of their homes. The problem may be that what disadvantaged children meet in school reinforces what they have learned at home about ways of relating to and talking with adults, about ways of thinking, and about ways of taking part in their own learning. School may reinforce their past learning rather than give them some sort of traumatic cultural shock. After the first few days or weeks, they are probably fairly secure within the school culture, but the culture fails to promote their thinking skills and the attitudes they need for learning, skills some children have already developed through their experiences of talk at home.

18

Intervention for Poverty Children: Alternative Approaches

DALE C. FARRAN

There is not sufficient evidence at this point to suggest that the early acquisition of language proceeds any differently in middle-class than in poverty groups. The rate of early development may be identical as far as we know; certainly no studies suggest that the acquisitions of first words or the move to two-word combinations is different in the two groups. (Although there are certainly *individual* differences on these measures, there are no *group* differences.) However, by the time of school entry, there do appear to be group differences in some language skills. Certain vocabulary words that are specifically informative about content likely to be encountered in school are present to a greater degree in the speech of middle-class children. Moreover, middle-class children appear to be more attentive to formal verbal sequences; by formal, I mean the kind of language used to communicate information to a stranger or a group. (Shuy discusses formal speech characteristics in Chapter 9 in this volume.) Formal verbal chains are present in written stories and in sets of instructions and are also likely to be encountered in schools. There is also some evidence to suggest that middle-class children have more familiarity with verbal abstractions—using language to group and conceptualize more frequently than poor children do.

It is likely that middle-class children have learned these skills from verbal interactions with their parents as well as from interactions with other adults. Work by Haskins and his colleagues at the Frank Porter

269

THE LANGUAGE OF CHILDREN
REARED IN POVERTY

Graham Child Development Center provides evidence that middle-class children are more frequently in contact with nonneighborhood adults who are not kin than poor children are. Poor children are much more frequently in contact with relatives than are middle-class children (25 different relatives per month, compared to 4). The language one needs in talking to strange adults is different from language needed to talk to family. The former language is far more formal and follows rules that more closely resemble written than oral language.

It has been argued that middle-class homes are *like* schools and that the similarity accounts for the better performance of middle-class children in school. No middle-class parent of a school-aged child would agree with that statement, having experienced the frustration of the bureaucracy and rigidity of public schools. Schools are *not* like middle-class homes. Schools are much more didactic, with few verbal exchanges of any length between adults and children, with rigid rules for behavior that pertain only to children in large-group settings (e.g. raising hands; standing in lines; spending a finite, predetermined amount of time on a project, etc.).

Middle-class children may perform better in the school situation for a number of reasons, only one of which initially is related to their language. It is likely that they have more familiarity with the way the school day is organized: blocks of time devoted to specific activities. It is likely that they have had more experience in same-aged peer groups as well as with socialization being centered in one or two adults. Their language may also be a factor of specific capabilities they have developed prior to school, for example, talking to strange adults in a formal manner. In addition, they may be more accustomed to putting what they know into words and communicating that knowledge to others. Using words to mediate knowledge is a learned skill; children who come into school with prior experience in communicating what they know should perform better in school. Preschool experience with formal language may become more important as the school content becomes more and more formal, that is, when written language begins to dominate the curriculum.

Given the discrepancy between the prior experiences of poor children and the organization of the educational environment, what should be done to aid poverty children's school performance? The tactic taken for the past 20 years has been to attempt to alter these children prior to school entrance. The ways in which programs have attempted to alter poverty children have, for the most part, assumed that the programs were filling in deficits. Of late, the assumption has been that the parenting styles of poverty mothers during the preschool years are responsible for the children's school failure; parents have failed to educate or prepare their children properly for doing well in school. The solution has been to remediate the deficiencies in the parent by attempting to make the parent behave like middle-class parents.

In some cases the remediation has indeed been bizarre—given the circumstances of the parents. Lazar and Chapman (1972) described all the parent intervention programs funded by the federal government as of 1972. One project involved 14 mothers who were characterized as young, with an average education of ninth grade. They were poor—only two had telephones—and they lived in substandard housing. The intervention provided was to have the mothers attend a 2-hr-per-week program for 12 weeks to teach them to read stories to their children. Assessment of the project consisted of pre–post measures of maternal language in telling stories to a Children's Apperception Test card. The irrelevancy of that sort of intervention, given the living circumstances of those mothers, is heart rending.

There are alternative approaches. One is to attempt to change the living conditions of the poor. There are examples of other countries: Kerala, India, for example, where resources have been reallocated, money has been funneled into primary education, and many of the negative consequences of poverty have been eliminated. One can argue that this alternative is not an actual one because it involved restructuring society. Perhaps that is true: It is not a likely alternative; however, it may still be the *best* alternative. Another alternative is exemplified by Joan Tough, whose curriculum is aimed at instructing teachers in public schools in the skills required to facilitate the development of children who need assistance. Her approach involves a mind-set change, in that it places the burden of education on the educational system and not on the child or the families. Her approach assumes that all children can be taught; teachers need help developing appropriate skills.

Either of these alternatives would seem preferable to the course we are now following, which seems to lay all the blame for the condition of poverty on the people who endure it.

REFERENCE

Lazar, J. B., & Chapman, J. F. A review of the present status and future research needs of programs to develop parenting skills. Washington, D.C.: George Washington University, 1972. (ERIC Document Reproduction Service No. ED 068 150).

Subject Index

EDUCATIONAL PSYCHOLOGY

continued from page ii

Norman Steinaker and M. Robert Bell. The Experiential Taxonomy: A New Approach to Teaching and Learning

J. P. Das, John R. Kirby, and Ronald F. Jarman. Simultaneous and Successive Cognitive Processes

Herbert J. Klausmeier and Patricia S. Allen. Cognitive Development of Children and Youth: A Longitudinal Study

Victor M. Agruso, Jr. Learning in the Later Years: Principles of Educational Gerontology

Thomas R. Kratochwill (ed.). Single Subject Research: Strategies for Evaluating Change

Kay Pomerance Torshen. The Mastery Approach to Competency-Based Education

Harvey Lesser. Television and the Preschool Child: A Psychological Theory of Instruction and Curriculum Development

Donald J. Treffinger, J. Kent Davis, and Richard E. Ripple (eds.). Handbook on Teaching Educational Psychology

Harry L. Horn, Jr. and Paul A. Robinson (eds.). Psychological Processes in Early Education

J. Nina Lieberman. Playfulness: Its Relationship to Imagination and Creativity

Samuel Ball (ed.). Motivation in Education

Erness Bright Brody and Nathan Brody. Intelligence: Nature, Determinants, and Consequences

António Simões (ed.). The Bilingual Child: Research and Analysis of Existing Educational Themes

Gilbert R. Austin. Early Childhood Education: An International Perspective

Vernon L. Allen (ed.). Children as Teachers: Theory and Research on Tutoring

Joel R. Levin and Vernon L. Allen (eds.). Cognitive Learning in Children: Theories and Strategies

Donald E. P. Smith and others. A Technology of Reading and Writing (in four volumes).
> Vol. 1. *Learning to Read and Write: A Task Analysis (by Donald E. P. Smith)*
> Vol. 2. *Criterion-Referenced Tests for Reading and Writing (by Judith M. Smith, Donald E. P. Smith, and James R. Brink)*
> Vol. 3. *The Adaptive Classroom (by Donald E. P. Smith)*
> Vol. 4. *Designing Instructional Tasks (by Judith M. Smith)*

Phillip S. Strain, Thomas P. Cooke, and Tony Apolloni. Teaching Exceptional Children: Assessing and Modifying Social Behavior